ASIA'S NEW MOTHERS

CRAFTING GENDER ROLES AND CHILDCARE NETWORKS IN EAST AND SOUTHEAST ASIAN SOCIETIES

ASIA'S NEW MOTHERS

CRAFTING GENDER ROLES AND CHILDCARE NETWORKS IN EAST AND SOUTHEAST ASIAN SOCIETIES

Edited by

EMIKO OCHIAI
Kyoto University

and

BARBARA MOLONY
Santa Clara University

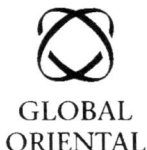

GLOBAL
ORIENTAL

ASIA'S NEW MOTHERS
CRAFTING GENDER ROLES AND CHILDCARE NETWORKS
IN EAST AND SOUTHEAST ASIAN SOCIETIES
edited by Emiko Ochiai and Barbara Molony

First published 2008 by
GLOBAL ORIENTAL LTD
PO Box 219
Folkestone
Kent CT20 2WP
UK

Reprinted 2008

www.globaloriental.co.uk

© Global Oriental Ltd 2008

ISBN 978-1-905246-37-3

British Library Cataloguing in Publication Data
A CIP catalogue entry for this book is available
from the British Library

Set in Stone Serif 9 on 11pt by Servis Filmsetting Ltd, Stockport, Cheshire
Printed and bound in England by Athenaeum Press, Gateshead, Tyne & Wear

Contents

Plate section faces page 112

Preface

Like all collaborative projects, this book could not have been produced without the contributions of many generous people. The editors, a sociologist and a historian, incubated the idea for the book during an exciting presentation of a portion of the research group's work at the 2005 Annual Meeting of the Association for Asian Studies. The papers themselves focused on communities and networks of individuals, but, taken together, they suggested social processes that would have long-term historical significance. Linking gender, globalization, and demographic trajectories, this was a book, we thought, that needed to be published.

The research group, which did not include Barbara Molony, has visited people all over East and Southeast Asia since 2001. Visiting private residences, we asked questions about the residents' daily lives and were able to see every corner of the homes, from kitchen to bedroom. Perhaps we went a bit far in imposing on our hosts, but wherever we went, the great majority of people treated us with the kindness accorded to unusual guests.

We saw much more outside the homes. In the back streets of Chinese cities, where the neighbors all pull chairs outside and enjoy meals while cooling off; in rural villages in Thailand where homes built along a canal are linked only by simple bridges made of bamboo poles; in food courts in Singapore with their array of Malaysian, Indian, and Chinese restaurants, we observed a great variety of lifestyles. Memories of the expressions and mannerisms of the people we met and the scenes we observed are as vivid as if they happened yesterday.

This book was born from experiences such as these in a joint study called "A Comparative Study on Gender in Asian Societies – Japan, South Korea, China, Thailand, and Singapore" (a Grant-in-Aid Scientific Research (A)(1) project funded by the Ministry of Education, Japan). Eleven researchers, all Japanese women, initiated the project. Our starting point was the desire to learn how problems we all face daily, such as balancing housework and childcare with a career and caring for the elderly, were being dealt with in other Asian societies. Our group brought together specialists in Japanese family sociology with researchers specializing in the Asian regions we wished to study. The eleven Japanese researchers were joined by researchers native to Korea, China, Thailand, and other parts of Asia. Most were women; two were men. Thus began a joint project, conducted transnationally and across disciplines, to study the families and ways of life found across the rapidly-changing regions of East and Southeast Asia.

At present, throughout East and Southeast Asia, large numbers of people live in high-rise housing developments, and their societies face the problems of low birth rates and the aging of the population. There may appear, at first, to be little difference between them in this respect. When we observe these areas first-hand, however, we find they are in fact quite different. One is often amazed at the unexpected and different solutions to similar problems. Despite our efforts not to take for granted the standards and practices of Japanese society, this was easier said than done. On our first visit to meet some of the residents in the community we were investigating in China, for instance, we were told that "mostly elderly people and children live here." We asked where the intermediate generation was, and we were surprised to hear that both husbands and wives were living and working elsewhere. It was common, then, for young children to spend a number of years cared for full-time by their grandparents. In Japan, it is widely believed that children not cared for personally by their mother for the first three years will have psychological or behavioral problems in the future – the so-called "three-year myth." By contrast, in China and the other Chinese societies of Singapore and Taiwan (which we visited later), we discovered that people commonly felt that "It doesn't matter who takes care of the children when they are very small. The mother's turn to take care of them comes when they are ready to study at school." Our research group called this Chinese opinion the "seven-year myth" or the "elementary-school student myth," in contrast with the Japanese "three-year myth." Our Chinese interviewees were quite surprised to hear of Japanese mothers' focus on the first three years of a child's life.

This long-term study reminded us once again that we and our neighbors in Asia know too little about each other's daily lives. Beyond this, we were struck by how confined we are by our cultural assumptions. We began this study out of a sense of the heavy burden placed on women by housework and care for children and the elderly. But our research made it clear that identical burdens cannot be assumed for every existing society. We need to learn more about what exactly is considered "taken for granted" or "common sense" in societies other than our own. In this way we may be able to re-think the assumptions of our own culture. Barbara Molony, whose own research is in the history of gender in Japan, became convinced at the Association for Asian Studies meeting in 2005 that there would be great value in making the results of the group's research available in English to researchers and others interested in gender and the family in Europe and North America as well as in the societies of Asia. In addition, she was convinced that the research team had captured a critical historical moment in their studies.

The results of this study have been published in Japanese in two books. *The Asian Family and Gender*, edited by Emiko Ochiai, Yamane Mari and Miyasaka Yasuko (Keisō Shobō, 2007), presents the findings in academic form. *The Twentieth-Century Asian Family* (Akashi Shobō, 2006), edited by Emiko Ochiai and Ueno Kayoko, features essays describing the events that took place during the fieldwork and the impressions of the researchers, and includes photographs. The present volume, published in English, contains the material corresponding to parts of several chapters of *The Asian Family and Gender*, but also includes separate and subsequent research results and conclusions, as well as many additional sections written with the English-speaking reader in mind. It thus should be read as an entirely new book.

Our study is on-going. While continuing on-site investigations in the regions covered in the study, we have added India and Indonesia to the list of areas being researched. The addition of these societies greatly increases the diversity of the study and promises to make our future research more complex and nuanced as well as more appealing.

One study that deserves special mention occurred as this book was going to press. In September 2007, interviews were conducted with a number of full-time housewives in Harbin, China. When the study described in Chapter 8 of this book was conducted, between 2002 and 2004, it was still very difficult to find any housewives in China; in the cases mentioned in Chapter 8, the women who had become housewives were either forced to do so because of unemployment or belonged to the special elite of society. In September 2007, however, in tandem with a project being conducted by Professor Zheng Yang of Harbin Normal University, we were able to conduct a group interview with the members of a "*Hao Taitai Julebu* (Good Wives' Club)" organized by a newspaper company. Out of thirteen women, nine were full-time housewives, two had been, and one was going to be after giving birth. A status change – that is, to become full-time housewives – had taken place almost entirely since the year 2000. The main occasion for becoming a housewife was personnel adjustments accompanying the change in the *danwei* (work unit) system, namely enterprises ceasing to be run by the national government. But there were also women who quit their jobs in order to be involved in their children's education. Women expressed diverse feelings about becoming housewives. While some were bored and wished to return to work, others were glad to be able to pay attention to their husbands' and children's health, or spoke with pride about how their child, who had been at the bottom of his or her class, was now at the top. Housewives are still rare in Harbin, but compared with a few years ago, it is clear that their numbers are increasing among the middle class. More research is needed on this topic.

This research project was made possible by the generous cooperation of many, many people in every region. It is unfortunately impossible to name them all here. However, we would like to give special thanks to the following individuals (unless otherwise mentioned, positions are those held at the time of the study).

In Korea: Kim Kyung-Joon (Korea Institute for Youth Development), Chang Pilwha (Director of Asian Center for Women's Studies, Ewha Womans University), Kong Mee-Hae (Silla University), Kim Soo Young (Kyungsung University), Lee Chang-Kee (Yeungnam University), Eun Ki-Soo (The Academy of Korean Studies; currently at Seoul National University), Suh Ji-Young (The Academy of Korean Studies), Kwon Hee-Jung (Doctoral program, The Academy of Korean Studies).

In China: Wu Yongmei (Beijing Center for Japanese Studies), Lu Jingfeng (Director of Beitang Ward Public Health Bureau, Wuxi City), Zhao Tianlan (Secretary of Beitang Ward All China Women's Federation); staff members of Huishanbang community (in Huishan Jiedao), Xunmin community (in Huilong Jiedao), Jieguantinglong community (in Wuqiao Jiedao), and Qiancun community (in Huangxiang Zhen); Zhou Weiguo (Jiangnan University), Li Min (Graduate student at Ochanomizu Women's University), Dou Xinhao (Graduate Student at Tokyo University); and Wei Ran, Yan Meifang, Zhang Wenfang, and Mang Xia (Graduate students at the Beijing Center for Japanese Studies).

In Taiwan: Ku Yenlin (Director, Taipei City Government Employee Training Center and former advisor for Taipei City); Gao Shu Ling (Director of Jinwen College of Technology Applied Japanese Department) and her colleagues, Ye Bing Ying, Zhao Miao Jing, and Toda Tetsuya, and the fourth and fifth-year students of the college who helped us.

In Thailand: Rungganda and her colleagues (Department of Social Welfare, Bangkok Metropolitan Administration [BMA]), Jinda and Wassana (Chiefs of Local Development Division, Khlong Samwa district [*Khet*] office of BMA) and all the staff members of that office; Boonyarat and Chatchai (Chairpersons of Residents Organization [*Chumchon*] Committees of our research sites) and the other members of the Committees; and Sujinda (Mahidol University, Department of Public Health).

Finally, we would like to give special thanks to Stephen Filler who translated more than half of the manuscript for this volume as well as helping us in formatting the bibliography with his Japanese and Chinese language skills. Thomas Turley of Santa Clara University and Katie Turley-Molony gave indispensible editorial and technical assistance.

We also would like to thank Paul Norbury of Global Oriental for his help with the publication of this book. Putting the results of an international joint study into a single book is no easy task, requiring difficult linguistic and communicative skills; there was no avoiding some tasks taking more than the time scheduled for them. We are deeply grateful to Mr. Norbury for his patient support of the editors as they grappled with the difficult work of preparing this book.

We sincerely hope that this book will serve as a bridge between Western readers and Asian researchers, and as a base for those researchers to engage in ever more fruitful cooperative projects.

Emiko Ochiai and Barbara Molony
May 2008

List of Contributors

FUJITA MICHIYO, a professor of contemporary sociology at Otemae University, is the author of articles on changes in gender and family consciousness as well as inheritence and succession customs in nineteenth-century Japan. She is currently researching changes in gender in East Asia.

HASHIMOTO (SEKI) HIROKO, a professor of comparative sociology at Shikoku Gakuin University, Japan, has joined field research on many academic projects in Thailand since she first studied at Chiang Mai University with the support of a scholarship from the Japanese Ministry of Education (1987–89). Her field of specialization is Thai family studies. Recently, she has been working on the characteristics of the family and women's life course among the Thai urban middle class.

HONG SANG OOK, a professor of family welfare at Yeungnam University, Korea, is a co-author of *Changing Asian Families* (in Japanese, Shōwadō, 2004) and the author of articles on changes in the lives of the Korean elderly, support networks for child-rearing, and child education in cross-border marriage families in Korea. Her current interest is in the development of paternal education programs to encourage fathers to share the burden of family care.

KIWAKI NACHIKO is an associate professor of family sociology and gender studies at Hagoromo University of International Studies. She is currently working on the life/work balance of Japanese businessmen and childcare support systems in Japanese companies.

MIYASAKA YASUKO is an associate professor of family sociology and gender studies at Nara University and a co-editor of *The Family and Gender in Asia* (in Japanese, Keisō Shobō, 2007). Her current subject of study is comparative research on family and gender especially in Asian societies and socio-historical research on the modern family in Japan.

BARBARA MOLONY, a professor of Japanese history at Santa Clara University, is the co-editor of *Gendering Modern Japanese History* (Harvard, 2005) and author of articles on women's political rights, gender and employment, and the politics of maternalism. She is currently working on the intersection of gender, dress, and nationalism in modern Japanese history.

EMIKO OCHIAI is a professor of sociology at Kyoto University, working in the field of family sociology, gender studies, and historical demography. Her publications include *The Japanese Family System in Transition* (LTCB International Library Foundation, 1997), *Modern Family and Feminism* (in Japanese, Keisō Shobō 1989), and *The Family and Gender in Asia* (in Japanese, co-editor, Keisō Shobō, 2007).

ONODE SETSUKO is a professor in the Department of Human Life Studies, Kachō College in Kyoto. She is a co-author of *Families and Partner Relationships: A Comparative Study of Sweden and Japan* (Kyoko Yoshizumi ed., Aoki Shoten, 2004). She is currently working on Japanese men's consciousness about housework and childcare from a gender perspective.

PARK KEONG-SUK is an assistant professor of sociology at Seoul National University and author of *Aging Society: A Future Already Proceeded* (in Korean, Euiam Press, 2003) and editor of *Opportunities of Life: Life and Consciousness of Poor People in Busan, Ulsan, and Kyeongnam Areas of South Korea* (in Korean, Dong-A University, Press, 2006). She is currently working on the moral and political economy of later life and the self.

UENO KAYOKO, a professor of the sociology of social problems at the University of Tokushima, is an author of *Sociology of Child Abuse: Identity, Family, Social Control* (in Japanese, 1996, Sekaishiosha) and co-author of numerous books about child abuse in Japan.

KUA WONGBOONSIN obtained his A.M. and Ph.D. from the University of Pennsylvania. He authored *Population and Development* (in Thai, Chulalongkorn University Press, 2002) and *Business Demography* (in Thai, Chulalongkorn University Press, 2002), and co-edited *The Demographic Dividend: Policy Options for Asia* (Chulalongkorn University, 2005). He is a faculty member of the College of Population Studies, Chulalongkorn University.

PATCHARAWALAI WONGBOONSIN obtained her A.M. from the University of Pennsylvania and Ph.D. from Kyushu University, Japan. Her research areas include population and migration in Asia, human-development based security, and the demographic dividend in ASEAN. She is a faculty member of the Institute of Asian Studies, Chulalongkorn University.

YAMANE MARI, a professor of family studies at Aichi University of Education, Japan, is a co-editor of *The Family and Gender in Asia* (in Japanese, Keisō Shobō, 2007) and *Family as Network* (in Japanese, Minerva Shobō, 2005), and the author of articles on gender and family issues in Japan and Korea. She is currently working on the life course of elderly people in Asian Societies.

ZHOU WEIHONG, a professor of Japanese sociology and history at Beijing Foreign Studies University, is the editor of *Decoding Japanese Society* (in Chinese, Beijing Current Affairs Press, 2002) and a co-author of articles on gender in modern Asia. He is currently working on the changes in rural society and the formation of the aging society in modern Japanese history.

Translators:

STEPHEN FILLER is an assistant professor of Japanese at Oakland University in Michigan. He is currently conducting research on the politics of romantic and naturalistic literature in early twentieth-century Japan. He has published translations of various works of Japanese fiction and film.

FURUKAWA TAKUYO graduated from Santa Clara University in 2004 with a bachelor's degree in political science and minors in Japanese studies and international studies. Following graduation, he worked in Tokyo for two years. He is currently a law student at the University of California, Berkeley.

UTSUGI NAGISA, a native of Tochigi, Japan, studied at Santa Clara University in Santa Clara, California due to her interest in the English language and Psychology. While at Santa Clara, Nagisa used her linguistic abilities as a tutor and director of Japanese conversation courses. She obtained a degree in psychology and currently uses that degree as a Human Resources Generalist at Applied Materials Japan Inc.

List of Plates

CHINA
1. Couple returning home from work
2. New father learning techniques for massaging his newborn baby
3. A grandfather takes his grandson back to his daughter's house
4. A grandchild staying with his grandparents during the day
5. Many Chinese men are good cooks
6. Meal prepared by a Chinese father
7. Child raised within a neighboring network
8. Beds for the kindergarten "full-time" class
9. Youngest kindergarten class
10. Separate households, but living like an extended family
11. Newspaper article about emergence of "full-time mothers"

THAILAND
12. An aunt caring for her niece
13. A family of migrant workers from Myanmar
14. A father and his elementary school-aged son
15. A granddaughter caring for her grandmother
16. Childcare facility in an impoverished district
17. Private elementary cram school
18. Childcare facility that has been closed down
19. Children waiting for their caretakers to pick them up
20. Prepared food packed in plastic bags
21. Cafeteria in a suburban district

TAIWAN
22. A father holding his baby, with his Vietnamese wife
23. Picking up children at a daycare center
24. Mother taking her daughter to school on a motorbike
25. Elementary school students returning from school
26. Daycare facility for schoolchildren attached to a kindergarten
27. State of the art *zuo yuezi* center
28. Nap time at a private infant care center

Researching Gender and Childcare in Contemporary Asia

EMIKO OCHIAI

CONTROVERSIES OVER GENDER ROLE CHANGES IN CONTEMPORARY ASIA

Most Europeans and North Americans today would dispute the notion that motherhood is the main role for women; even those seeing motherhood as fundamental would also stress the importance of other roles. In these parts of the world, participation rates by married women in the labor force have risen sharply since the 1970s, with many women continuing to work even when their children are small. While the role of mother may still be one important part of a woman's life course, it is not obvious that it is the main one. The trends in Asia today, however, are very different.

Figure 1.1 shows the proportions of women who agreed or disagreed with the statement that "men should work outside, and women should take care of the home."[1] A comparison of responses to this statement in surveys in 1982 and 2002 shows that over a span of twenty years, the share of women who agreed with this statement decreased and the number who disagreed increased uniformly across the United States and the three European countries of the United Kingdom, Germany, and Sweden. In Japan, however, the share of women who disagreed or tended to disagree in 2002 was smaller than in Europe and America twenty years earlier. And in the Philippines, the percentage of women who agree is actually increasing. What is the reason for this difference between Asia and the West?

It would be an oversimplification to interpret this as simply a confirmation of the common belief that Asian women are more home-oriented than Western women. South Korean women's attitude is comparable to that in Germany. In the Philippines, the shares of women supporting and opposing the statement are both growing simultaneously, suggesting that

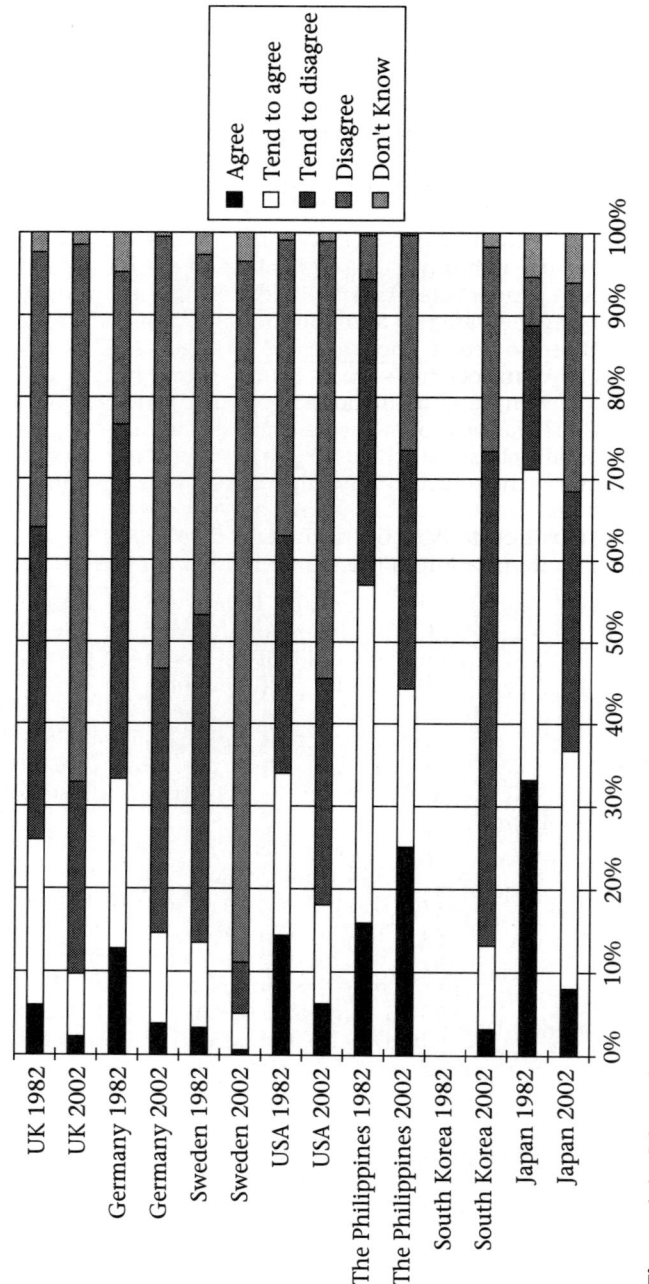

Figure 1.1 Women's attitudes towards the statement that "men should work outside, and women should take care of the home"

Source: *International Comparative Survey on Gender Equality*, conducted by the Gender Equality Bureau, Cabinet Office, Japan

Note: There is no data for South Korea 1982.

gender roles have become a point of controversy with strong opinions on both sides. The actual rates of female employment in many East and Southeast Asian societies, especially among women with small children, are amazingly high. The gap between the reality of life and their attitude suggests that a momentous change is taking place in gender roles in contemporary Asian societies. Economic development from the 1980s onward has engendered rapid social change in East and Southeast Asian societies.

This book presents the outcome of an international joint research project on gender role changes in contemporary East and Southeast Asia. The purpose of this research project is to reveal on an empirical basis the complex changes in gender roles Asian people are currently undergoing and to explore both the varieties and commonalities of trajectories of change among those societies. The project is entitled "A Comparative Study on Gender in Asian Societies – Japan, South Korea, China, Thailand, and Singapore"[2] (Taiwan was also included in our field) and was first conducted in 2001–2003; various follow-up research studies have been done since then. The middle class – which has begun to emerge in each of these societies – is chosen as the subject of investigation because it is comprised of those viewed heralding the establishment of a modern civil society in Asia and serving as the custodians of the modern lifestyle.

The process of modernization in the West and in Japan was marked by a change in gender roles called "housewifization," in which most married women assumed the role of full-time housekeepers. Whether the "housewifization" of women observed in Europe, America, and Japan in the course of modernization will also occur in other areas in Asia is one of the central questions of this project. This study also interrogates whether the Asian societies that have already experienced housewifization will follow the European and American trajectory of "de-housewifization" of women, that is, the disappearance of "housewives" as a dominant category. These questions are examined in the context of the influence of globalization on Asian families, including international migration of domestic workers, and the expansion of modern childcare and education norms.

To investigate the process of gender role changes, we focus on the role of the mother because our hypothesis is that the crucial factor behind a change in gender roles is a change in caretaking practices, especially towards children. The caretaking role was at the center of women's role in modern societies in the West. We would ask, as Asia goes through its own process of modernization, whether the primacy of the mothering role for women is being emphasized in the same way. We also ask if mothers are, in fact, the primary agents of childcare and childrearing in contemporary Asian societies. Our findings actually showed that in most societies, despite their level of economic development, the role of the mother was not as pronounced as might be expected. Nevertheless, there were indications in each of the societies studied of impending change, leading to the birth of "new mothers."

There is no shortage of books on the Asian economy today, and tourism in Asia has never been more popular. Despite this, surprisingly little is known about the way people in Asia lead their daily lives. This is not only true for Westerners, but even for people living in neighboring Asian countries. What is most unfortunate in the academic study of Asia is that researchers in each society compare their own society with Western societies but rarely compare other Asian societies. In this book, by comparatively analyzing six societies in East and Southeast Asia – China, Thailand, Singapore, Taiwan, South Korea, and Japan – we hope to lay the foundation for a common framework for analyzing the phenomenon of gender in Asia.

HOUSEWIFIZATION AND DE-HOUSEWIFIZATION OF WOMEN

Research on modernization and gender underwent major theoretical change in Europe and the United States in the 1970s and in Japan in the 1980s. Modernization and development had been viewed, prior to this theoretical shift, as encouraging women's social advancement and gender equality by offering women access to social and political spaces and economic advantages hitherto held by men. Scholarly approaches since the 1970s have contended, however, that modernization has had the opposite effect; that is, modernity, industrialization, and capitalist development have produced, or at least enhanced, a separation of the domestic and public spheres – the "housewifization" of women – and the specialization of childcare to mothers. While the strengthening of family ties led to an emphasis on family love and established it as an ideal, it also made the family a more exclusive, closed institution, giving rise to the "isolated family" which rejected outsiders and was isolated from the outside. In terms of gender roles, modernization led to the gender division of labor between the "breadwinning" husband who labored in the public sphere and the housewife who specialized in housekeeping and childrearing in the domestic sphere.

Maria Mies developed the concept of "housewifization" to describe this gender division of labor, namely "the creation, under the capitalistic division of labor, of this new couple which is so familiar to us" (Mies 1997: iv). Mies argues that the concept of "housewife" was invented to remove from the concept of "labor" the work involved in the reproduction of life – birth, childrearing, and housework – and make it invisible. A housewife was seen as a woman sustained by the "breadwinning" husband through his wage labor. Through "housewifization," women become the "cheapest producers and consumers in this world market system." (Mies 1986: 4). In effect, "housewifization means the externalization, or ex-territorialization of costs which otherwise would have to be covered by the capitalists. This means women's labour is considered a natural resource, freely available like air and water" (Mies 1986: 110).[3]

From the 1970s onward, the participation rate for women in the workplace increased in America and northwestern Europe. At the same time, the "second wave" feminist criticism of a gender-based division of labor (i.e. men in the workplace, women in the home) has become widely accepted in many countries. This has led to the rapid decline and, in some cases, the disappearance of the category of "housewife" as the assumed, normative, and preferred role for adult women in the United States and northwestern Europe. We can call this phenomenon "de-housewifization" of women.

The economist J. N. Sinha, analyzing data from various areas and social groups in India, has hypothesized that a U-curve relationship exists between economic development and the labor-force participation rate for married women (Sinha 1965). In the early stages of development, a decrease in the farming sector leads to a reduction in employment opportunities for women. Further, an increase in family income reduces the need for the woman to work. Employment opportunities for women only expand following the rise of the post-industrial society, which leads to an increased demand for labor in the tertiary (service) sector of the economy (Ōsawa 1993: 2). The pattern of a decrease in the farming sector in the early stages and an increase in the post-industrial stage has been supported by other research based on census reports from one hundred countries (Durand 1975). Put in terms of "housewifization," we might restate this with the following proposal: Economic development first "housewives" women, then "de-housewives" them.

"De-housewifization" of women belongs to a broader social transformation once known as "postmodernity," or in more recent terminology as "second modernity" (Beck et al. 1994) and "high modernity" (Giddens 1990). In the field of family and private life, the change known as the "second demographic transition" took place, with a decline in legal marriages and an increase in divorces, a dropping of the fertility rate below replacement level, and an increase in children born outside of marriage (Van de Kaa 1987; Lesthaeghe 1991). The traditional "modern family" became a minority group, and the number of people living outside of a family grew considerably. The unit of society is no longer a family but an individual. "De-housewifization" is an inevitable consequence of this process. It has, in turn, encouraged policies supporting the management of both labor and private life and the maintenance of social resources, particularly in northwestern Europe.

THE JAPANESE CASE: AN OUTLIER?

This disappearance of the normative housewife and the resultant need for new policy development to support working parents is not universal, however. In Japan, for instance, it continues to be normative for mothers with young children to devote themselves to childcare. Sociologist Iwai Hachirō, who compared the employment patterns for women in Sweden, Germany, the United States, and Japan, concludes that "Japan as a society has experienced exceptionally little change in the past twenty-five years" (Iwai 2002). He cites the M-curve pattern of female employment as an unchanging distinctive feature of Japan (See Figure 1.2 (1)–(4)).

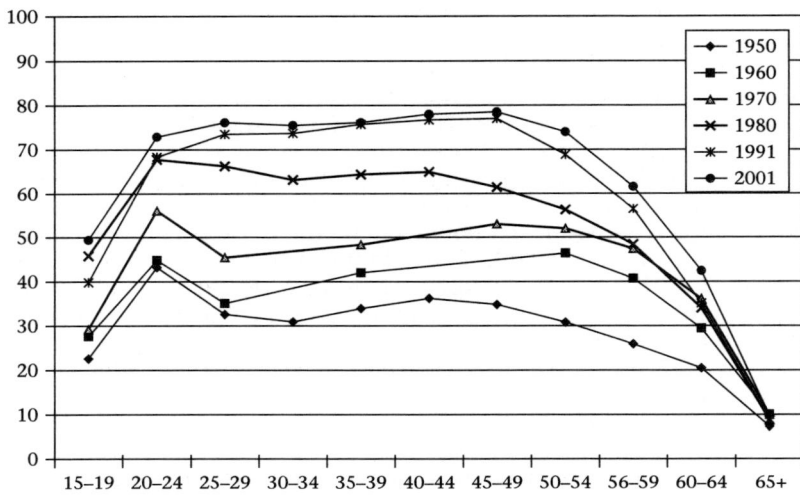

Figure 1.2(1) Female labor force participation rates by age (1) United States
Source: ILO, *Yearbook of Labour Statistics*

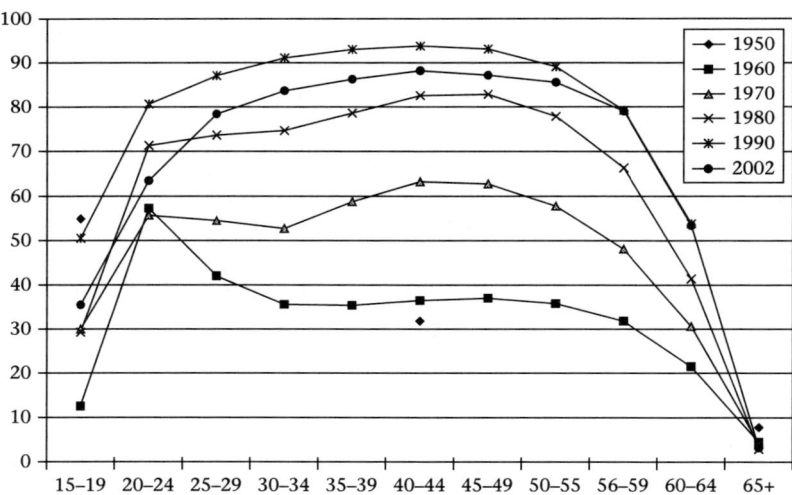

Figure 1.2(2) Female labor force participation rates by age (2) Sweden
Source: ILO, *Yearbook of Lobour Statistics*

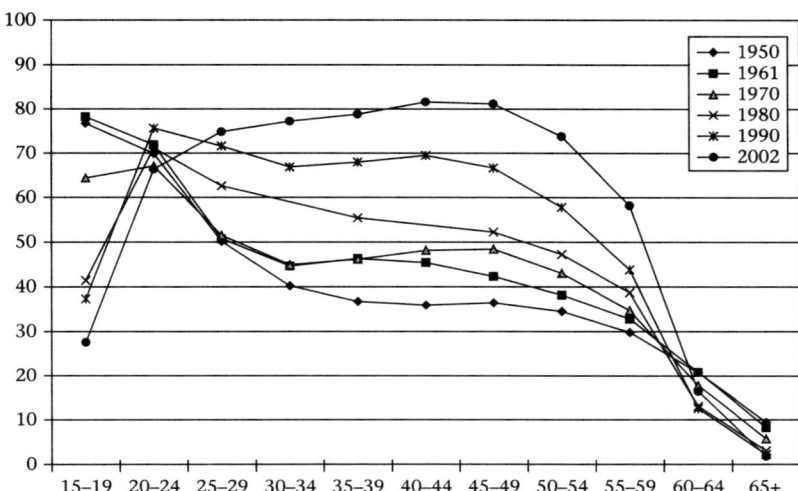

Figure 1.2(3)   Female labor force participation rates by age (3) Germany
Source: ILO, *Yearbook of Labour Statistics*

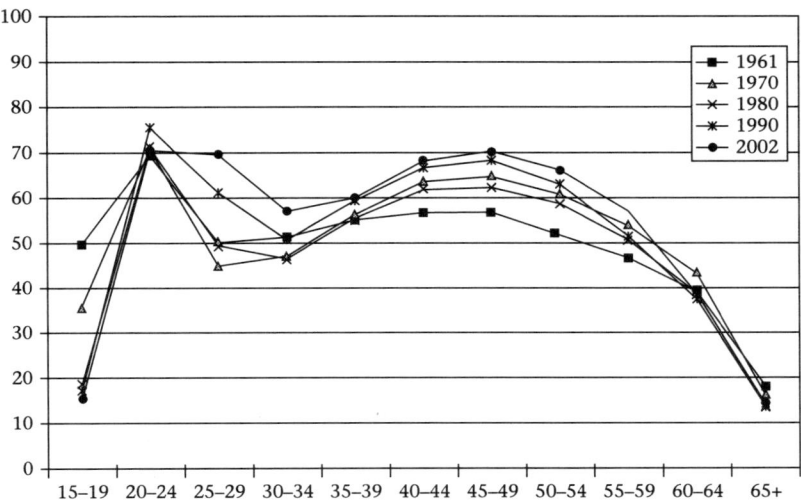

Figure 1.2(4)   Female labor force participation rates by age (4) Japan
Source: National Center for Research on Social Security and Population Issues, *Population Trends*, 2006.

Table 1.1 Criteria of childcare anxiety

Have you been feeling like this recently?

---

1 I become exhausted every day.
2 I wake up refreshed in the morning.
3 I don't like to think about things.
4 I feel as if I keep on the ball every day.
5 I feel I can manage my daily life with ease.
6 I get irritable because my child is such a bother.
7 I think I am raising my child well.
8 I sometimes don't know what to do about my child.
9 I think that, to a certain extent, children grow up by themselves.
10 I am very nervous about leaving my child when I go out.
11 I feel as if the burden of childcare falls totally on me.
12 I can feel myself growing through raising a child.
13 I think I'm just doing the same things over and over, day after day.
14 I think I am always putting up with something or denying myself something
   in order to bring up my child.

Source: Makino (1988)

Only Japanese women maintain the practice of leaving the workplace to perform infant care (See Ochiai 2005b).

On the other hand, Japanese mothers are suffering from a "disease" only rampant in Japan (Makino 1981, 1988; Ochiai 1997, Chapter 8). Social critics have defined as a social problem a phenomenon they call "parenting anxiety" – that is, a vague anxiety felt by mothers whose devotion to childcare has weakened their social networks, leading to their sense of isolation, at the same time as it causes them to sense that they are not performing that care adequately (See Table 1.1). Why has Japanese society, having reached parity with Western societies in economic terms, not followed the same path as these societies? This is an urgent question for a Japan that has yet to fully shake off the legacy of the economic recession of the "lost decade" of the 1990s.

It would be misleading, however, to interpret the departure from the workplace of mothers with infants as an example of Japanese women's home-orientation. Figure 1.3 compares long-term trends in female labor-force participation rates for Europe, America, and Japan. In the first half of the twentieth century, female labor-force participation rates in America and Europe, particularly in countries like England and Sweden, started out at the 20 percent level and then rose gradually. If we correct for the under-reporting of female labor in the agricultural sector, a U-curve pattern appears, for example, in Sweden, with rates declining from the end of the nineteenth century, reaching their lowest levels between the 1920s and 1930s, and then beginning to rise again (Nyberg 1994).

Now for the case of Japan. In Figure 1.3, Japan is distinguished by its maintenance of a high female labor-force participation rate, in the

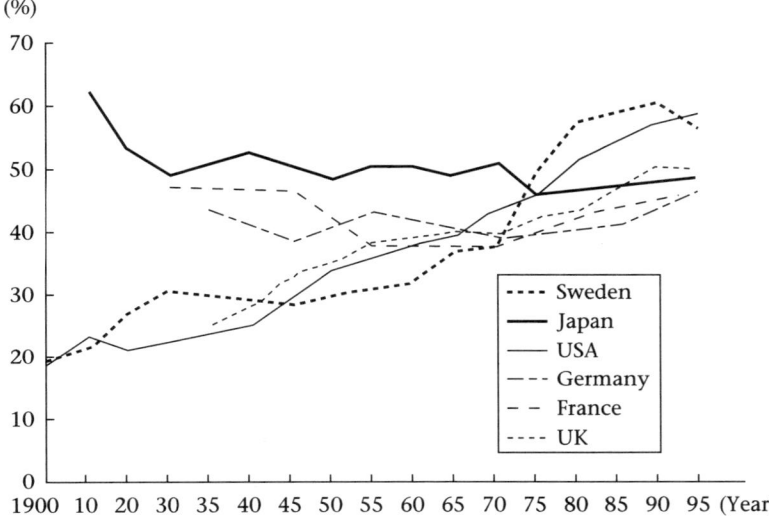

Figure 1.3   Female labor participation rates in the West and Japan (1900-95)
Source: *White Paper on the National Lifestyle*, Economic Planning Agency of Japan, 1997.

upper 40 percent level or above, throughout the twentieth century. This is because the decline represented by the left half of the U-curve (i.e. housewifization) and the increase represented by the right half (i.e. de-housewifization) progressed at nearly the same time, with little gap between them, thus canceling each other out (Ochiai 1997, 2005b).

To more fully examine the historical changes in female labor in Japan, let us look at the changes in the female labor-force participation rate by age. Figure 1.4 puts the estimates by Umemura Mataji (Umemura et al. 1988) for the prewar period in graph form, and combines them with statistics for the postwar period. In 1880, not long after the Meiji Restoration of 1868, levels in the upper half of the 70 percent level were maintained continually for women from their twenties to their forties, with absolutely no indication of women leaving work for marriage or childbirth (Ochiai 2005b). This is the same shape of curve found in present-day northern Europe, Canada, and the United States. Pre-industrial Japan was a society where women worked a great deal, even by international standards.

Therefore, our question is why the M-curve pattern is so persistent. It was created only after World War II. "Housewifization" took place in Japan just as in Europe and America, but de-housewifization has not been fully realized yet. Gender role change in Japan has stagnated for reasons deserving further exploration.

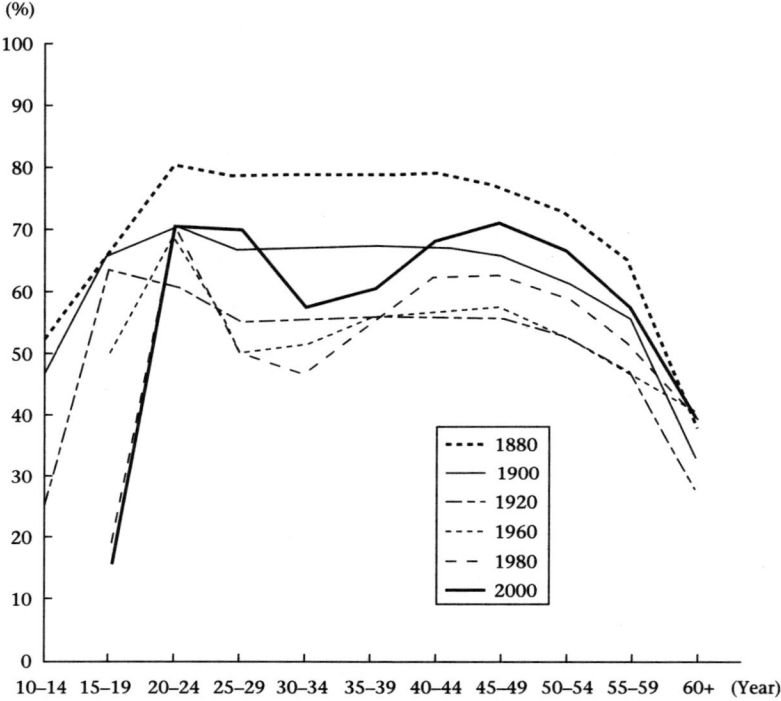

Figure 1.4   Female labor-force participation rates in Japan by age (1880-2000)
Sources: Umemura, Mataji, et al. "Long-Term Economic Statistics 2: The
Workforce," 1998.
National Institute of Population and Social Security Research. "Population
Trends." 2000.

THE AXES OF UNDERSTANDING ASIAN DIVERSITY

How, then, are gender roles changing in Asian societies in the process of
rapid social change following the economic growth, known as the "Asian
miracle," that took place from the 1980s onward? If we restrict our framework to a linear analysis of the birth and demise of the modern family – that
is, housewifization followed by de-housewifization – we run into even
greater difficulties when we consider Asian societies outside of Japan. The
contemporary gender structures among East and Southeast Asian societies
and the paths to the present are, in fact, quite diverse, as demonstrated in
Figure 1.7 (in a later section of this chapter) and in the figures in Chapter 2.

Research on changes in the family and gender is now being carried out
in many parts of contemporary Asia. It would not be practical to try to

describe all of this research. Instead, since our research all deals with the modern family in Asia, it is appropriate to begin with an overview of the work of a Japanese sociologist, Sechiyama Kaku, whose *Patriarchy in East Asia* (1996) is the most immediate predecessor to our research. Although his area is limited to East Asia, he has shown that variations in contemporary gender structures among East Asian societies derive both from differences in traditional gender structures as well as current social regimes such as capitalism and socialism (Sechiyama 1996). In *Patriarchy in East Asia*, Sechiyama emphasizes the diversity of East Asia. While these societies tend to be lumped together as belonging to the "Confucian cultural sphere," all four of the major patterns formed by the nexus of ethnicity and social system can be found in East Asia (South Korea, North Korea, Taiwan, China) (Sechiyama 1996: 199).

The social system axis is, of course, that of capitalism and socialism. Following the collapse of socialism in Eastern Europe, East Asia became distinguished as the home of the residual representative socialist states. Because the theory of the modern family takes capitalist society as its foundation, it cannot be applied without modification to the socialist world, where the entrance of women to the labor force had been strongly promoted from the onset. Sechiyama argues that "the addition of women to the labor force under socialism does not necessarily occur only after de-housewifization. Rather, it is given a distinctive quality by the presence of elements predating housewifization." Modernization in the socialist world does not necessarily follow the two steps observed in the capitalist world. As a result, the end of socialism can potentially bring about housewifization (Sechiyama 1996: 81). With the opening of the Chinese economy in the mid-1980s it was argued that women should return to the home in order to reduce surplus labor (the *funü huijia* debate) (Ochiai 1988). After a period of repression following the Tiananmen Incident (1989), China began its period of fundamental economic reform and growth, and today, as this growth continues, a similar debate is taking place (Yin 2004).

The axis of ethnic culture distinguishes between the Korean and the Han Chinese ethnic groups. The latter can be further divided into the Northern and Southern varieties. In terms of the extent of permeation of Confucian culture in these societies, they may be ranked in descending order as follows: Korean (North and South), Northern Chinese, Southern Chinese. In these societies, the influence of the traditional view of a gender division of space in which the realm of the male is outside and the realm of the female is inside (in the home) can be ranked in the same order. While Northern China was characterized by farm labor using domestic animals, with farming being primarily the task of men, in the Southern rice-cultivating regions, women participated in farm work. The Southern Chinese pattern extends from Taiwan and Hong Kong to ethnic Chinese outside national borders in places such as Singapore. Sechiyama contrasts "the Chinese (especially Southern Chinese) pattern of patriarchy, which is relatively accepting of female participation in labor, with the relatively rigid patriarchy of the Korean peninsula" (Sechiyama 1996: 326). He argues that in contrast to the Korean peninsula, where "ambition to gain promotion to the ranks of the elite civil servant class (*yangban*) led to the permeation of Confucian values to every part of society," in Southern China cultural values and modern-era criticism of Confucianism led to the diminishing of its influence (Sechiyama 1996: 328).

Here the U-curve hypothesis of female employment proposed by Sinha has to be reconstructed. First, there are societies where the gender division of social space was embedded in their traditional culture and the rate of female employment was already low from the beginning. There was no room for decline in the process of modernization. Korea and Northern China belong to this type of society together with the societies from Northern India to the Middle East. Second, the socialist countries took a different path of modernization with no decline in female employment; rather, they promoted it. Now we see the theoretical importance of Asian examples in the study of modern family and gender role changes.

Sechiyama's contribution to the research on the modern Asian family has been to clearly define a theory that takes into account the variables of social system and ethnicity without being reductive. Rather than turning the "Asian type of modern family" into an essentialist concept, he took the diverse conditions of Asia as his starting point. The research that forms this book expands its geographical scope beyond East Asia to include Southeast Asia, bringing still greater diversity into the picture.

COMPRESSED MODERNITY AND GLOBALIZATION

In the decade since Sechiyama's study was published, East and Southeast Asian societies, involved in the vital trends of globalization, have been both enjoying and suffering from the effects of economic growth. Also seen in many Asian societies has been the distinctive phenomenon of "compressed modernity," identified by South Korean sociologist Chang Kyung-Sup, in which the types of changes that took place gradually in the West have occurred along parallel tracks and in a much shorter period of time (Chang 1999). It has been pointed out that since the world had already entered the globalization phase at this point, many Asian societies have experienced modernization and globalization at the same time. The process of modernization as experienced in Asia is considerably more complex than that in the West.

Housewifization is also implicated with globalization. In the 1980s, the housewifization framework was criticized for being a white middle-class feminist perspective that neglected the experiences of lower class women of various ethnicities. The birth of the housewife in nineteenth-century European history was coupled with the emergence of house-maids or domestic workers in middle-class homes. Domestic workers disappeared in early twentieth-century Europe and America but they have been returning since the 1980s – most recently these workers have been of different nationalities from their employers (Fauve-Chamoux 2005). Globalization is manifested in the movement of people and workers as well as ideas, resources, markets, and management. Domestic workers of foreign nationality alter gender roles and dynamics not only in the West but also in East and Southeast Asia.

As a result, gender, childcare, and modernization can most effectively be discussed not by treating each country separately but rather by viewing them as linked through the effects of globalization. In what ways are globalization and gender-role changes linked in Asian society? Do the changes in family and gender that are portrayed by the modern family and the housewifization framework appear in more or less the same form in Asia, or is an entirely different story unfolding there? This question has immediacy, as the reality is unfolding before our eyes today.

There is one more caveat for our analysis of Asia. There is a trend toward focusing on something called "Asian modernity" in comparison with "Western modernity," a trend which really is another instance of the "localization" and "regionalization" that react against globalization and grow alongside it. But Asia is a region made up of societies with a great variety of traditions and social structures. Asia has never been unified under a single empire, nor is there a common religion to the region. Does there really exist a discrete phenomenon that can be called "Asian modernity"? If so, what is the basis for defining it? This question will be kept in mind in the discussion that follows.

LIFE COURSE AND SOCIAL NETWORK

This book focuses on family and gender, taking a comparative approach to investigating their current characteristics and conditions as well as changes in response to modernization and globalization in contemporary Asia.

We begin with an important methodological issue. That is, we cannot use concepts developed on the basis of particular characteristics of specific times and regions to deal with large social changes like "modernization" and "globalization" or to compare conditions among a variety of regions spanning several countries. In particular, the form taken by the "family" differs from society to society. There are strong normative ideals of the family in some societies and not in others. Even the form of the family within a single society varies greatly according to social class, region, and ethnicity, and there are people who do not have families. What kind of analytical framework will give us an appropriate understanding of these changes and diverse conditions?

In this book, instead of beginning with the "family," we will start from the "individual," using an analytical framework that combines the concepts of "life course" and "social network." Both are analytical concepts intended to overcome the limitations of analyzing the "family" as a group. "Life course" refers to the life of an individual and is different from "life cycle," which assumes that each person's life involves the repetition of similar cycles; the expression "course" conveys the idea that each life is unique (see Hareven 2000). Each person, in living an individual, unique life, forms "social networks" with other people, and we treat the "family" as one such social network.

In this framework, the unit of analysis is not a "family" but an "individual." It is an approach needed for the analysis of contemporary society in the period of transformation of intimacy, as Anthony Giddens noted (Giddens 1992), with such phenomena as later marriage, increasing rates of divorce and remarriage, and the experience of remaining unmarried for life. But the theoretical implications go deeper than this. The wide applicability of concepts that can be used even with societies and lives in which "families" and "life cycles" do not exist makes analysis of "life course" and "social networks" very effective for studying change and conducting comparisons.

The social network is, of course, not limited to the family. An individual's social network extends beyond the family to relatives, neighbors, friends, work colleagues, and professionals, who sometimes give support to the individual and his or her family. Elizabeth Bott, a pioneer in social network study, wrote that the immediate social environment of an urban family is best thought of not in terms of the geographical area in which they live, but rather in terms of the complete network of concrete social relationships held by the family (Bott 1957). In other words, both the family itself and the social network that surrounds it can be considered as social networks.

An individual's life course and that individual's social network each influence the other. Consequently, if several individuals make up a "family," the form of the network and the internal structure of the family have a reciprocal relationship (Bott 1957). In this book, focus is directed at those changes in the life course of women defined as "housewifization" and "de-housewifization," hypothesizing that changes in the life course are related to the structure of the social network. Many of the authors have been analyzing the Japanese family since the 1980s using the categories of life course and social network as key concepts.[4] This study tests the applicability of these approaches and the results of research on Japan to the contemporary Asian family.

CAREWORK AND CARE NETWORKS

How should we understand the functions of the family? The standard view is that the premodern family performed a large variety of functions, including production, reproduction, education, welfare, medical care, religion, and even, at times, military matters. With modernization many of these functions were lost, and the functions of the family were reduced to consumption, sex and reproduction, the socialization of children, and emotion (See Parsons and Bales 1956). Recent studies have focused on carework. Carol Gilligan (1982) and others have made a penetrating analysis of the nature of "care." "Carework" is the work of watching over and helping children as well as the elderly and other adults needing care, work that often is delegated to women and performed at home as unpaid work. Much of what is called reproductive labor belongs to the realm of carework. No matter how much the upheavals of modernity "individualize" the family, care is still needed for those persons who are not independent individuals. It is probably for this reason that "care" has been described as the ultimate function of the family or as a remaining function of families that do not fit the classic form of the modern family – for example, single-mother families (Fineman 1995).

However, if we consider the matter more critically, we see that there is no reason that carework *must* be the responsibility of the family, or of women. Men often performed carework in premodern times. For instance, it is known that in the Tokugawa era (1603-1868) in Japan the elderly were often cared for by their sons (Sugano 1999 and elsewhere). In the present day, it is daycare facilities or institutions for the elderly that often perform carework.

Even if, as Giddens (1992) puts it, a society becomes centered not on "family" but just on intimate relationships, it can be argued that along with sexuality, carework forms the core of family relationships (Saitō 2003; Fineman 1995).[5] Focusing on the function of carework, which in the modern era has been seen as ultimately the province of the family, is an excellent way for us to observe how different types of society develop alternative methods to fulfill the same functions.

In this book, by focusing on the social networks that provide carework to children[6] and on gender issues surrounding the individual providers of that carework, we hope to effectively compare and examine the changes in family and gender in contemporary Asian societies. We shall also encounter the phenomenon of globalization of carework, or reproduction, in the course of these analyses. Transformation of intimacy at the micro level is directly connected to the macro transformation of the global world.

DEMOGRAPHIC EFFECTS ON THE STRUCTURE OF SOCIAL NETWORKS

Before turning to the studies of diverse societies in contemporary East and Southeast Asia, a very brief introduction of social network researches of carework in Japan would be helpful. Numerous empirical studies of Japan emphasize the effect of demographic change on social networks, a point that is relevant to contemporary Asian situations.

The period from the late 1950s through the 1960s was a rich time for research on the social networks of urban families in Japan. With the concentration of the population into cities, new urban environments such as large apartment complexes were created, and the conditions of family life in these areas were as interesting to researchers then as the situations emerging today in many Asian societies. Parsons' theory of "the isolated nuclear family" (Parsons and Bales 1956) and the criticisms of that theory by Eugene Litwak (1965), Marvin Sussman (1962), and others were introduced in Japan, leading to attempts to test these theories in the Japanese context.

Masuda Kōkichi's work (1960) represented a relatively early example of research that examined the particularity of Japan. "Recent reports from the U.S. on the residents of suburban housing show that in general, social activity in suburban communities is at a high level". "But in Japan, based on the research up to now on the conditions in suburban apartment communities, *neighboring* by household heads and wives is reported to be at a very low level" (Masuda 1960: 2). Masuda's approach was to determine the "particularly Japanese factors" that govern "neighboring." Masuda demonstrated clearly with statistics that the more often wives visited their parents' homes, the more passive they were about "neighboring" (Table 1.2). According to Masuda, all of these factors had their origin in the strong familism of Japan. Looking back from our current perspective, we can see that the stance of "isolationist familism" regarding neighborhood networks was none other than the privatism of the modern family in the process of development at that time.

From the studies on this topic conducted in the 1960s and 1970s, we can conclude that the distinctive structural features of the social network system of the Japanese urban family in the 1960s, the period of rapid economic growth, included: (1) the large role played by the kin network; and (2) for families sustained by that kin network (especially when very small children were being raised), a corresponding passive attitude towards the neighborhood network (Morioka et al. 1968; Ochiai 1993). Behind all the talk about "privacy" with respect to one's neighbors, families were quietly building up a system of informal support from their relatives.

However, what we found in the study of social networks from the 1980s onward was very different from the 1960s and 1970s (Ochiai 1989a, 1989b Chapter 5, 1993; Yazawa, Kunihiro and Tendō 2003). What is noticeably different from the 1960s studies is the status of the kin network. The role played by siblings in the 1980s dropped dramatically, whether in terms of direct childcare assistance or informational and emotional childcare assis-

Table 1.2 Frequency of wives' visiting their parents' homes per year by their attitude towards "neighboring"

	(%)					
	0	1~2	3~4	5+	*unknown*	*Total*
Positive	20.1	45.5	6.0	27.3	1.1	100.0
Neutral	10.0	45.1	15.3	27.7	1.9	100.0
Negative	8.9	41.5	7.3	40.5	1.8	100.0

Source: Masuda (1960)

tance. The kin network was compressed to include *only* their own parents (Ochiai 1993: 116). This was not due to a weakening of the relationship between siblings; rather, there were no more than one or two siblings on each side among the cohort who became parents in the 1980s. The parents (of infants and small children) in the 1960s belonged to the pre-transitional cohort in terms of fertility transition, whereas the parents in the 1980s belonged to the post-transitional cohort. The fertility transition occurred in Japan between1950 and 1957 (Ochiai 1997). The main cause of the decline of the kin network in the 1980s was demographic: there was a lack of siblings to help one another, even if they wanted to.

On the other hand, urban mothers in the 1980s with children had set up extensive, active neighborhood networks. The reason for this becomes clear if we juxtapose the frequency of childcare-related interaction with neighbors with the family type based on the distance from the couple's parents. The shorter the distance from their own parents, the weaker the interaction with neighbors (Table 1.3). In other words, the kin network had a complementary relationship with the neighborhood network (Ochiai 1989a, 1989b, 1993).

To the extent that can be known from this study, the urban Japanese family of the 1980s, in comparison with the family of the 1960s in the same life stage (the period of caring for infants and small children), had lost most of the linkage with siblings, so that the kin network was minimized to include only their own parents. To compensate for this, mothers of the 1980s developed neighborhood networks while their children were still infants.

Table 1.3. Frequency of childcare-related interaction with neighbors by the distance from their own parents

	Living with the husband's parents	Living with the wife's parents	Living next to the husband's parents	Living next to the wife's parents	Living near to the husband's parents	Living near to the wife's parents	Isolated nuclear family
Almost everyday	13.3	10.3	31.1	43.3	37.6	53.6	54.3
2~3 times per week	30.0	34.5	28.9	23.3	36.4	28.1	19.8
3~4 times per month	24.0	17.2	22.2	16.7	7.8	6.3	13.7
Almost never	32.7	38.0	17.8	16.7	18.2	12.5	12.2
Total	100.0	100.0	100.0	100.0	100.0	100.0	100.0

* "Living next to": in ten minutes distance; "Living near to": in ten to forty minutes distance

Source: Ochiai (1989b Chapter 5: 106, 1993: 117)

The mutually complementary, or mutually exclusive, relationship between the neighborhood network and the kin network could already be seen in the 1960s. However, the important difference is that in the 1960s, a very strong kin network existed even in urban areas, so that an observable change took place in the nature of the network as the children grew older: mothers in the 1960s depended on their kin network when their children were infants and toddlers, and developed their neighborhood network as the children grew older. By contrast, in the 1980s, the kin network was weakened by the parents' own lack of siblings, so that many families with small children could not receive assistance from relatives. Responding to necessity, these families developed neighborhood networks much earlier (Ochiai 1993).

Despite this, it is not the case that the Japanese family of the 1980s was fully successful in reconfiguring the system of networks for caring for infants and small children. In many cases, it was not possible to adequately develop a neighborhood network to compensate for the loss of the kin network. Makino Katsuko (1981, 1988) has described the social problems that frequently affect childrearing today as "parenting anxiety," that is, "an emotional condition of longstanding, vague fear regarding children and childrearing," as indicated in Table 1.4. A comprehensive look at the findings of Makino's many studies and follow-up studies by other researchers shows that the main factors that prevent parenting anxiety are "the cooperation of the husband" and "the extent of the mother's own social network." Or, to put it the other way around, parenting anxiety in the 1980s occurred when mothers and children, unable to form an adequate social network, became isolated.

What, then, are the kinds of social networks that contemporary Asian families – other than Japanese families – have? Are there kin networks, and are they active as in Japan in the 1960s or as in Japan in the 1980s?

RESEARCH METHODS

The target population for the collection of new data for this study was the urban middle class in five societies in East and Southeast Asia, namely Thailand, China, Singapore, Taiwan, and South Korea. For Japan, we use previous findings for comparison because the research had already been completed by project members employing the same framework used in this research project. The urban middle class, a totally new social group in some of the areas we investigated, is creating new lifestyles and working as the agent of social change. The research method common to our studies of each of the five societies was interviews with middle-class residents in the research area. With respect to household duties and care for children and the elderly, we asked residents, through semi-structured interviews, about task sharing within each family, social networks where support could be obtained, and family consciousness. In addition, we conducted hearings at facilities providing care to children and the elderly as well as at central and local government offices. Finally, we conducted questionnaire surveys in China and Thailand. While not covered in this book, our study included interviews and questionnaire surveys dealing with carework for the elderly, which will be published in a later collection. Also, although Wongboonsin and Park are members of this project, most of the research results they present in this book rely on their independent projects.

We must emphasize that although we refer to the societies discussed in this book as South Korea, China, Taiwan, Thailand, and Singapore, these terms do not imply that the data discussed are representative of these societies as a whole. The subjects of the study mainly belonged to the urban middle classes in those societies, and additionally, they were limited to the particular locations indicated below. In Singapore, the ethnicity of the subjects was limited to ethnically Chinese residents.

The research outlines for each society are as follows:

China

Area: Mainly in Beitang District, Wuxi City, Jiansu Province (as well as case studies in Beijing and Shanghai)

Method:

(i)   Questionnaire survey with ordinary households as respondents (stratified random sampling by selecting four communities in Beitang); 400 questionnaires distributed and 400 collected; August 2002

(ii) Semi-structured interview with households (thirty two cases) selected from respondents in (i) above and other households (eight cases); August 2002

(iii) Questionnaire survey with elderly persons as respondents (random sampling by selecting twenty households having members aged sixty or older from four resident communities in the district); eighty questionnaires distributed and forty-eight collected; August 2002

(iv) Hearings conducted at central and local government offices, ward committees, the local office of the All-China Women's Federation, daycare centers, nursery schools, nursing facilities for the elderly, maternity clinics, pediatric hospitals, etc.; April, May, and August 2002

Thailand

Area: Suburbs of Bangkok (mainly in Khet Khrong Samwa)

Method:

(i)   Semi-structured interview with residents of detached house residential districts and town house residential districts, etc. (twenty-nine cases); August and September 2002

(ii) Hearings conducted at central and local government offices, daycare centers, child-centers, elderly care centers in hospitals, etc.; August 2001 and August-September 2002

(iii) Questionnaire survey with residents of detached house residential districts and town house residential districts, etc. as respondents; 106 questionnaires collected; August and September 2003. *Joint investigation carried out with *Comparative Research on Change in the Asian Family and the "Invention of Tradition"* Project[7]

Singapore

Area: Not specified

Method:

(i) Semi-structured interview with families of Chinese descent (twenty-four cases); December 2002 to January 2003

(ii) Hearings conducted at welfare facilities for the elderly; July-August 2002

Taiwan

Area: Taipei

Method:

(i) Semi-structured interviews with ordinary households and individuals (twenty cases); February 2003

(ii) Hearings conducted at government offices, women's foundation, social welfare foundation, childcare facilities, care facilities for the elderly, etc.; February 2002 and February 2003

South Korea

Area: Busan and its surrounding areas (Yangsam), Daegu and its surrounding areas (Gyongsan)

Method:

(i) Semi-structured interview with single mothers and households with small children, single women, elderly persons, elderly persons living in care facilities (forty-two cases); August 2002 and August 2003

(ii) Hearings conducted at central and local government offices, postpartum centers, daycare centers for children under three (*aga bang, nori bang*), kindergarten, nursery schools for children over three (*eorini jip*), elementary schools and junior high schools, various institutions caring for the elderly, including public welfare centers and apartment houses for the elderly called "silver towns"; September 2001, August 2002 and August 2003.

Japan

Area: City of Nara

Method:

Questionnaire survey with fathers and mothers who have small children as respondents (343 cases for mothers; 270 cases for fathers)

SOCIO-ECONOMIC CONDITIONS IN THE SIX SOCIETIES

Before analyzing each society separately, let us take a look at the characteristics of the six societies under study. Table 1.4 lists the socio-economic indicators of six societies during the research period. The variation is huge, from a city-state, Singapore, to the most populous country in the world, China. The composition of populations reflects the different economic structure of each society. The proportions of urban population are highest in Singapore, followed by South Korea, Japan, and Taiwan; and

Table 1.4 Socio-economic conditions of six societies

	year	China	Thailand	Singapore	Taiwan	South Korea	Japan
Total population (million)	2000	1242.6	62.7	4.1	22.3	46.1	126.9
Male population (million)	2000	640.3	31.1	2.1	11.4	23.2	62.1
Female population (million)	2000	602.3	31.6	2.0	10.9	23.0	64.8
Prop. of urban population (%)	2005	40.5	32.5	100.0	65.1	80.8	65.7
Prop. of rural population (%)	2005	59.5	67.5	0.0	34.9	19.2	34.3
GDP per capita (US dollar)	2003	1100	2273	21195	17400	11059	33819
Real economic growth rate (%)	2003	9.1	6.7	0.5	4.3	3.1	2.7

Source: United Nations, *Statistical Yearbook* 2006 for Japan, Korea, China, Thailand and Singapore.
Directorate-General of Budget, Accounting, and Statistics, Executive Yuan's homepage. http://www.dgbas.gov.tw/mp.asp?mp = 1 for Taiwan.
(Proportions of urban and rural population are for 2003. The real economic growth rate and GDP are estimates for 2006.)

the proportions of rural population are highest in Thailand and China. The Gross Domestic Product (GDP) per capita is highest in Japan and Singapore, followed by Taiwan and South Korea; a wide difference separates the top four from Thailand, and China trails the others significantly. China's remarkable recent economic development notwithstanding, those societies that experienced earlier development continue to reap the advantages of their early growth.

What position is held by the "urban middle class," the focus of this study, in each of the societies? It has been given many names, but the concepts and realities of the middle class vary from society to society, making it difficult to specify a definition that can be applied for cross-regional comparison. Michael Hsiao and other pioneers of comparative research on the middle class in East Asia developed the following classifications of social class: capitalist (employers of twenty or more employees), the new middle class (professionals), the old middle class (small employers with and without employees), the marginal middle class (routine non-manual employees and personal service workers), the working class (technicians and supervisors, skilled workers and semi- and non-skilled workers), and farmers/farm labor (farmers and agricultural workers). The second through the fourth of these classes are grouped together as the "middle classes" (Hsiao 1999: 8-9). In Japan, starting from the wide definition developed by Hsiao, Hattori Tamio and others created an operational definition of the middle classes as encompassing people with "administrative/managerial, professional and technical, and clerical" occupations as well as "a part of service and sales workers" (Hattori, Funatsu and Torii 2002:10). All of these categories are based on type of occupation; other approaches take into account income, job status, type of industry, lifestyle, and subjective perception of class affiliation.

Determining the size and proportion of each social class for the societies in question is complicated by problems of definition and measurement. For purposes of this discussion, we will place "professionals and technicians" in the "new middle class," and define the "middle class in a larger sense" as this group plus "managers" and "clerks." On this basis, we can describe the proportions in each society of the various categories, based on occupation statistics. Statistics were taken from 2001, the year this study commenced, or a time close to 2001. These figures show the percentages of people belonging to the "new middle class" and the "middle class in a larger sense," respectively, as follows: South Korea (2000), 16.1 percent and 30.4 percent; China (2000), 5.6 percent and 9.9 percent; Taiwan (2001), 23.8 percent and 39.0 percent; Singapore (2001), 28.4 percent and 55.3 percent; Thailand (2001), 7.7 percent and 18.3 percent, and Japan (2000), 13.5 percent and 35.5 percent.[8]

For China, studies that attempted to consider characteristics beside type of occupation were also conducted by Lu Xueyi from 1999 to 2001 at the Institute of Sociology of the Chinese Academy of Social Sciences. When income level was given central consideration (along with type of occupation, lifestyle, and subjective self-assessment), the middle class was calculated at 7 percent of the overall population, and 8 to12 percent of the population of large cities. However, the final figure arrived at by Lu's group for the middle class was 20 percent (Lu 2004). As calculated by the overseas office of Nomura Securities in Singapore (Nomura Singapore), when membership in the middle class and above is defined in economic terms, as persons belonging to a household having an after-tax yearly income of 3000 dollars per household member, the middle class makes up 3.5 percent of the total population of China and 31.7 percent of the total population of Thailand (both in 2004).

In studies comparing the growth in population share of the "new middle class" since the 1960s, Hattori et al. have contrasted the sudden, rapid growth in countries like South Korea and Malaysia with the longer, steadier growth seen in the Philippines and Thailand. Patterns of formation of the middle class are closely related to the growth of the urban industrial and modern sectors and their ability or lack thereof to attract excess rural labor to the modern sector. Thailand and the Philippines have been distinguished by the growth, from an early period, in the "sales and service workers" that include the "marginal middle class" (Hattori, Funatsu and Torii 2002:16–23).

DEMOGRAPHIC CONDITIONS

We now turn to the issue of demographic conditions, which exert a critically important influence on the family. From a demographic perspective, the development of a society is strongly affected by the change from a state of high fertility and high mortality to a state of low fertility and low mortality, known as the demographic transition. Based on a comparison of the average life expectancy at birth (an index of mortality) and the total fertility rates shown in Table 1.5, all six societies have already experienced mortality and fertility transition. Population increase has also nearly stopped. In all six societies, fertility rates are below the replacement level, and, in particular, South Korea, Singapore, Japan, and Taiwan have the lowest fertility rates in the world.

Although current fertility rates are not so different in these six societies, the differences in the period of their demographic transitions have resulted in notable differences in their age structures. The timing of the decline in total fertility rates is shown in Figure 1.5. This decline, for the five societies apart from Japan, ended in the 1970s and 1980s, more or less simultaneously in all societies. Japan stands out for having experienced this decline much earlier, in the 1950s. Figure 1.6 shows how the current age structures of the populations of the six societies reflect this difference in time period of fertility decline. For example, while Japan is already an aged society with a high proportion of aged people, the other five societies are still at the so-called "demographic dividend" or "population bonus" stage; that is, they have a high proportion of their population in the economically productive age groups.

Table 1.5 Demographic conditions

	China	Thailand	Singapore	Taiwan	South Korea	Japan
Population growth rate (2002)	0.9	0.9	3.5	0.8	0.9	0.2
Life expectancy at birth (2001)	72	69	80	77	75	81
Total fertility rate	1.8 (2002)	1.82 (2000)	1.26 (2003)	1.34 (2002)	1.17 (2002)	1.29 (2003)
Proportion of population 0-14	23%	22%	21%	20%	21%	14%
Proportion of population 65+	7% (2002)	6% (2001~2)	7% (2000)	9% (2002)	7% (2000)	19% (2002)

Source: Governmental statistics for each society.

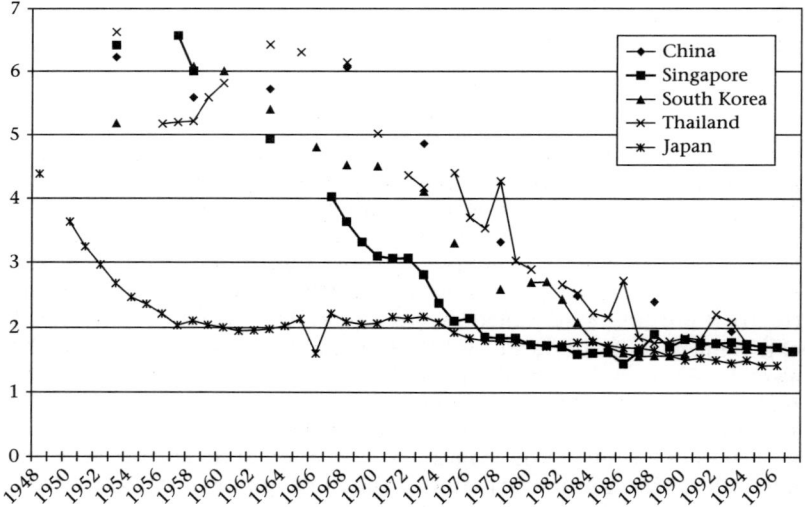

Figure 1.5 Fertility decline in Asian societies (TFR)
Source: United Nations, *Demographic Yearbook*

The period of "demographic dividend" is advantageous for economic development, because the dependent population of children and the elderly is relatively small. This period is also good for family formation, because much effective help is available from the kin network due to the large number of siblings who survived to the prime of life. As shown above, a comparison of the makeup of social networks related to

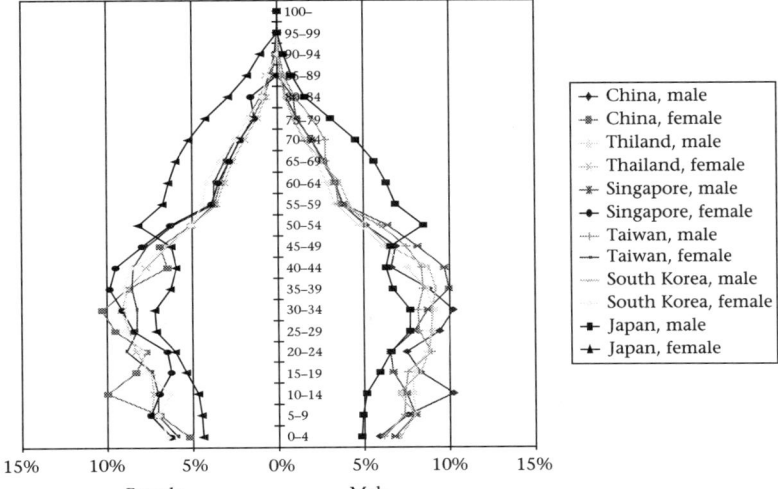

Figure 1.6   Age structure of Asian Population
Source: Governmental statistics of each society

childcare in the 1960s and 1980s in urban Japan reveals that in the 1960s, the kin network was dominant, while in the 1980s the strongest network was the network of neighbors. The explanation for this is that during the period of "demographic dividend" in Japan in the 1960s, each one had an average of four siblings who survived to adulthood, but this later declined to only two (Ochiai 1997). The weakening of the kin network was compensated for by the activation of a network of neighbors (Ochiai 1993). This kind of relationship between demographic conditions and social network structures will be kept in mind in this book's analysis of the six Asian societies.

GENDER AND LIFE COURSE

The research for this book uses as its theoretical base the idea of gender. Gender is a complex phenomenon that cannot be separated from the many cultural aspects of a society. Here, we will focus our attention on the gender division of labor, an important concept in this book, to compare the way in which women work in the different societies as revealed by statistics on women's employment.

We must, of course, keep in mind the problems with statistics on women's labor themselves. Labor statistics only reflect work that the government considers to be work. Easily left out of the "labor force" are people who pursue economic activities in the so-called informal sector.

Since in some Asian societies, a significant portion of labor falls into this category, and since many of the agents in these cases are women, women's labor tends to be under-reported.[9] "Household labor" also tends not to be viewed as labor in official statistics, which in itself is part of the mechanism of "housewifization" that makes household labor invisible, as Maria Mies pointed out. In other words, statistics on women's labor have the effect of making a large portion of that labor invisible, but having properly understood this situation, it is possible to use formal statistics of women's labor as a starting point for comparison.

Figure 1.7 shows the labor force participation rates for women by age, according to official statistics for the six societies, including Japan. The first thing to note is the high participation rates for women in some of these areas. In the broader Asian context, Japan's rates are not high at all. Moreover, the high rates of female participation in the labor force in developed countries like the United States and Sweden are similar to those found in Thailand and China.

Next, we note that the patterns for the age-specific rates of female labor force participation in these societies can be classified into three types (Figure 1.7). We define Type 1 societies as those in which high participation rates are maintained throughout the productive years. China and Thailand belong to this type. In Type 2 societies, women's rate of

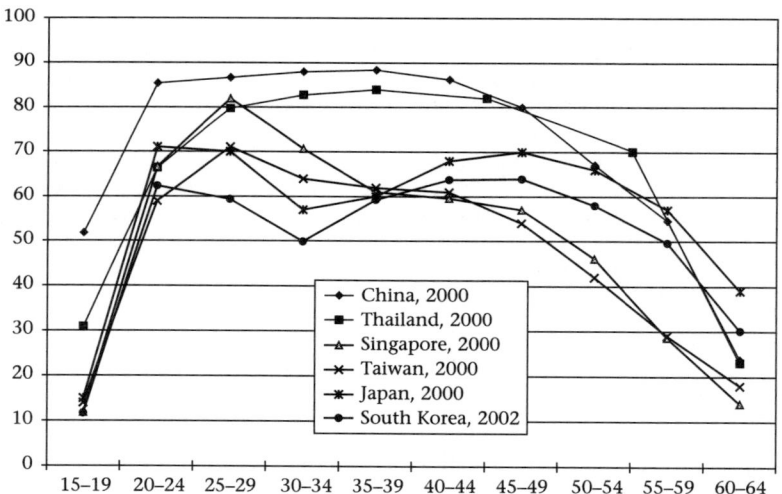

Figure 1.7 Female labor force participation rates by age in six societies
Source: China: National Bureau of Statistics, *2000 Census;* Thailand: National Statistical Office, *Report of the Labor Force Survey;* Singapore Dept. of Statistics, *Census of Population 2000;* Taiwan: Executive Yuan, *Human Resource Survey;* Korea: National Statistical Office, *Economically Active Population Survey;* Japan: Statistics Bureau, *Labor Force Survey.*

labor force participation gradually declines beginning in the thirties age brackets. Singapore and Taiwan belong to this type. Type 3 is where, after a temporary decline from the late twenties, the rate begins to climb again, thus showing an M-shaped curve. South Korea and Japan belong to this type. Women living in societies belonging to the first two types continue to work during the period of childbirth and childcare. This holds true for China and Thailand. In Singapore and Taiwan, female labor force participation rates remain high for age groups likely to be mothers of infants but begin to decline for age groups likely to have somewhat older children. From the perspective of housewifization, we can say that it hardly occurs in Type 1 societies, and in Type 2 societies the housewifization that does occur is not linked to the gender-determined childcare role that houswifization implies in its modern-family incarnation. This study focuses on the three types of female life courses defined by these societal types and analyzes the childcare support networks in each society.

FAMILY, HOUSEHOLD, AND RELATIVES

The structure of household and kinship is important information because families and relatives are the major providers of informal childcare support in many societies. Table 1.6 shows the varying size and structure of households in the six societies. We have taken the data on household structure, calculated by independent methods for each society, and expressed it in a form best suited for meaningful comparison. The proportions of households with more complex structures than nuclear family households (stem family households, extended family

Table 1.6 Size and structure of household

	China 1999	Thailand 2002	Singapore 2000	Taiwan 2000	South Korea 2000	Japan 2000
One person household	6.3	11.8	8.2	21.5	15.5	25.6
Nuclear family household	70.9	55.5	75.6	55.1	69.3	60.1
Stem, Extended and Joint family household	22.8	32.1	12.0	15.7	15.3	13.9
Other	0.01	0.6	4.1	7.8	–	0.4
Mean household size	3.6	3.8	–	3.3	3.1	2.7

Sources: China: *Demographic Year Book of China*, Thailand: http://www.nso.go.th/eng/indicators/house_e.htm, Singapore: *Census of Population 2000 Household and Housing*, Taiwan: *Household and Housing Report of Year 89*, South Korea: *Social Indicators of Korea 2003*, Japan: *Census Report*.

households, joint family households) are 12 to 16 percent for Japan, Singapore, Taiwan, and South Korea; more than 20 percent for China; and even greater than 30 percent for Thailand. By comparison, nuclear families make up more than 70 percent of households in Europe and America. Although Thailand, like other Southeast Asian countries, is sometimes referred to as a nuclear family society, the data shown here indicate a different pattern. However, one of the insights of this study is the limit of the concept of "household," which will become apparent when we reach the main analyses of this book. In almost all of the societies studied, interactions with relatives outside of the "household" were strong, and close daily contact with relatives was so common that there was no clear dividing line between "family" and "relatives."

According to anthropologists, China has a joint family system with a strong patrilineal descent group. Japan and South Korea have stem family systems, but while the Korean family has been based on a patrilineal descent group, the Japanese kinship system is far from one of strict patrilineality. In Japan, there are no patrilineal kin groups. Instead, Japan's system is based on a stem family known as the *ie*, with frequent use of adoption (especially of spouses of children) (Kurosu and Ochiai 1995; Guan 2005). In contrast to the tighter kinship organizations of East Asia, Southeast Asian kinship systems are characterized by their "loosely" structured bilateral networks. The "family" in these societies can be described as a network without clear boundaries centering on the individual and expanding and contracting according to circumstances. Mizuno Kōichi, a Japanese anthropologist specializing in Thailand, has called this the "family circle" or "network family" (Mizuno 1981).[10] Therefore, the complex families in Thailand represented in Table 1.6 can be loose networks rather than tight groups like the traditional Japanese family with its stem family structure.

As noted in an earlier section, our approach regards the family as part of the social networks centering on an individual. This methodology enables us to treat relatives as another part of the social network and to treat the family and the relatives in continuity with each other. It has the advantage of being applicable both to the tightly structured East Asian kinship organizations as well as to the loosely structured kin networks in Southeast Asia. In this study, we will reexamine gender and childcare in Asia and reconsider the appropriateness of stereotypical categories of the household and the family that have been traditionally used.

STRUCTURE OF THE BOOK

In short, this book provides a comparative regional analysis of patterns of childcare, taking individuals and their social networks as the unit of analysis. By noting the diversity in women's life course patterns in East and Southeast Asia, it refutes the stereotype of Confucian sameness. Our central question is whether the housewifization of women would occur in contemporary Asia that is experiencing modernization and globalization at the same time.

The structure of this book is as follows. Chapter 1 gives an overview of the theoretical framework and research methods, as well as the social background in the societies under study. Chapter 2 is a comparative analysis of the findings for the common topic of the study, namely gender roles and childcare networks, for each region. In Chapters 3 and through 8, either changes in gender roles, childcare practices, or both are considered. In some cases a single society is examined; in others several societies are compared. Chapter 4 and Chapter 6 utilize other data sources than the ones described in this chapter, although they are closely related to the other chapters. Chapter 5 considers the housewifization challenges facing highly educated women in the suburbs of Bangkok, and Chapter 7 considers the key issues and policies concerning Singapore's considerable numbers of foreign domestic workers. Chapter 8 considers housewifization, a trend common to several of the societies studied, from a theoretical perspective. Chapter 9 summarizes our findings as a whole.

Throughout the book, we hope to propose a common basic framework to understand the transformation of gender roles in rapidly changing contemporary Asia.

*This chapter is partially based on the introductory chapter of Ochiai, Yamane and Miyasaka, ed. (2007).

NOTES

1   The results of the "International Comparative Survey on Gender Equality" conducted by the Gender Equality Bureau, Cabinet Office, Japan.

2   Grant-in-Aid Scientific Research (A)(1) funded by the Ministry of Education, Japan. The members consisted of Miyasaka Yasuko (project leader), Ueno Kayoko, Emiko Ochiai, Onode Setsuko, Kiwaki Nachiko, Kobayashi Kazumi, Hashimoto (Seki) Hiroko, Fujii Wasa, Fujita Michiyo, Yamato Reiko, Yamane Mari, Hong Sang-Ook, Kua Wongboonsin, Park Keong-Suk, and Zhou Weihong. For Japanese publication, please refer to Ochiai, Yamane and Miyasaka eds. (2007) and Ochiai and Ueno eds. (2006).

3   It is essential to note Mies's view that the relegation of women's reproductive labor to the informal sector, with little or no financial compensation, is one of the essential aspects of "housewifization." In this view, anyone performing marginalized labor can be described as "housewifized," even if that person performs wage labor or happens to be a male. Mies's concept of "housewifization" in this way extends beyond the usual definition of the word "housewife." However, it is very important to keep in mind the significance of the extended meaning of the term, especially for Asian societies that have a high share of people, especially women, working in the informal sector. As a result, many women who appear to be merely housewives and are counted as such in official statistics actually perform informal labor.

4   See Ochiai 1989a, Sekii et al. 1991, Ochiai 1993, Kiwaki 1998, Yamato 2000, and Yamato 2004.

5   In Japan, too, there has been a lively debate about the issue of intimacy. Interestingly, while Western theorists such as Giddens tend to see sexuality as the core of intimacy, in Japanese discourse on this subject has focused on care (see, for example, Saito 2003). This has the interesting implication that Western and (East) Asian concepts of intimate relations differ from each other.

6   Our project also covered carework for the elderly, which will be a topic in the next publication.

7   Grant-in Aid Scientific Research B(1): Comparative research on Change in the Asian Family and the "Invention of Tradition" (2003-2005, Hashimoto Hiroko, project leader) funded by the Ministry of Education, Japan.

8   The sources of data are follows: South Korea, the Statistics Bureau homepage; China: Lu (2004); Taiwan: *Statistical Yearbook of the Republic of China*; Thailand: National Statistical Office, *Report of the Labor Force Survey*; Singapore: Department of Statistics, *Yearbook of Statistics Singapore* 2002; Japan: Statistics Bureau, *Census* 2000.

9   Under-reporting of female labor was also a major problem in national census studies made in Europe and America between the nineteenth and early twentieth centuries (Nyberg 1994).

10 This term (*kazokuken*) is standardly translated as "family circle," but we appended the term "network family" to convey the meaning more precisely.

2

Gender Roles and Childcare Networks in East and Southeast Asian Societies

EMIKO OCHIAI, YAMANE MARI, MIYASAKA YASUKO, ZHOU
WEIHONG, ONODE SETSUKO, KIWAKI NACHIKO, FUJITA
MICHIYO AND HONG SANG OOK

INTRODUCTION

This chapter focuses on gender role changes related to childcare through comparative studies of women's life course patterns and the structures of social networks in each society. The societies this chapter discusses are China, Thailand, Singapore, Taiwan, South Korea, and Japan, the six societies covered by our project. This chapter provides a comprehensive overview of the results of the entire project.

Our hypothesis is that the crucial factor behind a change in gender roles is a change in childcare practices. A child is taken care of by various agents in any society. However, the available kinds of agents and their relative importance are different in each society and change over time. In other words, the structures of social networks for childcare vary among societies and evolve historically. The salient feature of modern childcare is the concentration of caring roles on mothers. We assume that this phenomenon exists at the core of the "housewifization" of women that often takes place in the process of modernization. This chapter interrogates whether mothers are becoming the primary agents of childcare in contemporary Asia.

All Asian societies under study are facing tremendous social changes. They are rushing to catch up with the process of modernization at the same time that they are being swallowed by the tide of globalization. Our question, then, put differently, is whether Asian societies are constructing a civil society with the gendered modern family as its unit, or whether they are heading in a direction that Western societies did not experience in the modernization process.

In this chapter, we will examine in detail each society under study, then make comparisons and synthesize the findings from different societies. For each society, we will try to delineate the actual childcare practices that people experience everyday based on interviews, observations, and questionnaire surveys. Our focus is on who the agents of childcare are in the society under consideration, whether they are effective, and how people combine different types of agents in different situations. Then, we will examine the effect of childcare practices on women's life course and the changes taking place. As Bott has demonstrated, the nature of the family network and the family's internal structure are mutually related (Bott 1957).

As indicated in Chapter 1, the concepts of "life course" and "social network" were coined to overcome the limitations of treating the "family" as a group with clear boundaries and rigid membership rather than as a flexible network. The agents of childcare are not necessarily restricted to family members. We consider the child, not the mother, as the Ego, or the central individual of the childcare network. His or her network includes various kinds of agents inside and outside of the family, and the child's mother is only one of them. We avoid the modern assumption that the mother should be the primary agent of childcare. More generally, we need to be wary of cultural biases when conducting a comparative project covering such diverse societies.

The societies treated in this chapter are ordered by the type of female life course proposed in Chapter 1. The first are China and Thailand, which are Type 1 societies in which the high levels of labor-force participation rates for women are maintained throughout the productive years. The next are Singapore and Taiwan, Type 2 societies where women's participation rates decline unidirectionally from their thirties onwards. The last are South Korea and Japan, Type 3 societies with an M-shaped curve. Do societies with the same pattern of female life course have a similar structure of childcare networks? We will examine the six societies in turn with this question in mind.

FEMALE LIFE COURSE AND CHILDCARE NETWORKS IN THE SIX SOCIETIES

(1) China
GENDER AND LIFE COURSE

The female labor-force participation rate in China traces a reversed U-shaped curve. Specifically, labor-force participation rates for women between the ages of twenty and the early forties reach 90 percent (Figure 2.1). In a questionnaire survey conducted in the city of Wuxi in Jiansu Province, we asked both women and men what an ideal life course for women would be. Eighty-one percent of women and 71 percent of men chose "combining work and marriage/childbirth/childcare." "Temporary retirement followed by reemployment" came in second, but was chosen by only 9 percent of women and 10 percent of men. Thus, in both consciousness and in actual practice, "combining work and marriage/motherhood" is taken for granted in our Chinese sample. This is a result of the socialist ideology of the People's Republic of China and of specific policies implemented in the 1950s to increase production. Figure 2.1 gives estimated figures for female labor-force participation rate patterns in China from the 1950s to the present. As the figure shows, the reversed U-shaped curve pattern established in the 1950s has continued to the present day. We can surmise that the socialist revolution led to a great increase in female labor-force participation rates, since, as Sechiyama notes (Sechiyama 1996), women in northern China traditionally were not highly engaged in agricultural activities. In societies where female labor participation had been low prior to modernization, modernization itself could not lead to housewifization; to the contrary, in a country like China, which elected to modernize on the socialist model, the result was "de-housewifization." Moreover, the relatively youthful age of compulsory retirement – fifty-five for women and sixty for men – creates an environment for intergenerational reciprocal aid that allows both husband and wife to work while leaving their children in their parents' hands and, after their own retirement, to choose to look after their grandchildren to support the double-income of their children's generation.[1] In addition, the endowment insurance system – which requires workers to continue working until retirement age to receive a pension – is a compelling factor supporting the double-income practiced by married couples. The fact that the wage difference between men and women is

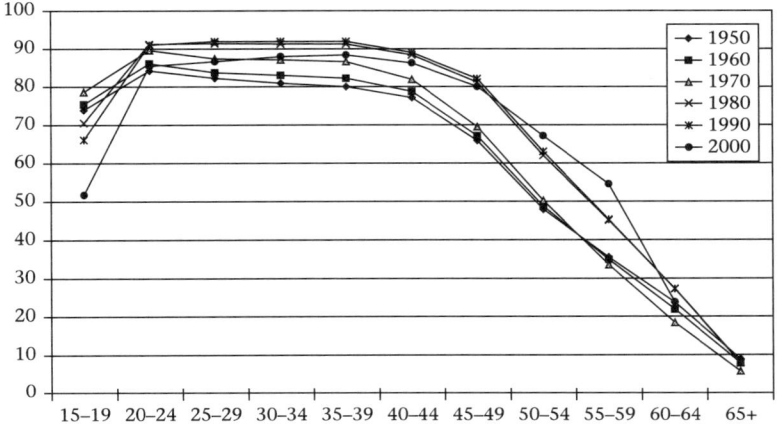

Figure 2.1   Female labor force participation rates in China
Source: China's National Bureau of Statistics, *2000 Census*. 1990; State Statistical Bureau, *Population Statistics of China*. 1950–80: ILO, *Economically active population. Estimated and Projections*, Geneva, 1986. (Estimated)

relatively small due to the absence of a family wage system (that is, a system that compensates heads of households more generously than other workers for the same work) is yet another factor supporting wives' continued workforce participation.

CHILDCARE NETWORKS

The combination of work and childcare in China is supported by flexible role sharing between husband and wife, informal aid through kin networks, and formal aid such as childcare leave and nursery schools. In addition, when it is difficult to obtain childcare support from relatives, especially in urban areas, people hire, at low wages, maids (*ayi*) or babysitters (*baomu*) from rural areas. The rise of the market economy and the relaxation of migration between rural and urban areas drive this phenomenon.

Public policy supports the continued employment of women with children. The most common type of formal childcare support is daycare centers such as those in company offices, municipal wards, or villages. Another leg of the formal support structure is the "childbirth insurance system." At present, the basic maternity-leave system grants ninety days of leave, at 100 percent of salary, after childbirth. The government's promotion of a "late marriage, late childbirth" policy to restrict fertility adds another sixty days of leave for mothers aged twenty-three or older.[2]

In the informal childcare support structure, flexible role sharing between husband and wife as well as between relatives is particularly notable. In our findings, role sharing with respect to housework and childcare transcended the gender division of labor, being determined according to the circumstances and time available of the husband and wife or grandmother and grandfather. Role sharing was especially common for cooking. In our survey, quite a few women noted that "my husband does more cooking than I do."

Based on the data that emerged from the interview surveys, childcare support networks can be divided broadly into three groups: (1) a combination of nursery school and support from parents and other relatives, (2) nursery school as the main source of support, and (3) other resources.

The first group included many cases where grandparents, especially the wife's parents, offered support. If the wife's parents had jobs, other relatives, such as the wife's maternal grandmother or the wife's sisters, might be asked for help. There were also cases where one or both of the wife's parents were called to live with the couple to help with childcare. Grandparents would travel to other cities and even other countries to take care of their grandchildren. In another case, a couple sent their child to one of their parents' homes. The Chinese government recognizes this phenomenon by including in its household statistics a special category of household called a "skipped-generation household," which consists of a grandchild living with grandparents and neither of the parents present (Zheng 2003).

The second group included many cases in which childcare support from the child's grandparents was not available due to the grandmother's employment or the grandparents' poor health.

As an example of the third group, if the husband or wife or both worked at a factory, there were cases in which the couple managed childcare themselves by working different shifts. In another case, the couple relied partly on support from a neighbor and partly on maids. The third group also included the hiring of maids or babysitters or the wife bringing her child to her workplace.

The above cases demonstrate that childcare support is expected first and foremost from grandparents, and when such support is not available, couples then turn to other relatives or nursery schools, and, if necessary, may even turn to maids or babysitters from rural areas. What we find here is an inter-generational division of childcare roles that follows a cycle: married couples work while having their children cared for by others; they then retire early and, by taking care of their grandchildren, support their own children's working-couple lifestyle.

The frequency of types of household structures, as deduced from the questionnaire survey, is as follows: households with only husband and wife (6 percent); nuclear family households (65 percent); stem family households (27 percent); and joint family households (4 percent). Of stem family households, 80 percent of couples lived with the parents of the husband. The nuclear family household was not the isolated nuclear family in the Parsonian sense, because nearly all couples lived close to relatives such as parents, children and siblings; they were, in fact, modified extended family households having a kin network in close proximity.[3] Our interviews revealed many variations of this situation, including: mothers and their sons' families, who had lived together in a joint-family household before the construction of urban housing projects, now living in the same or neighboring housing unit of a housing complex and regularly visiting each other; mothers and their sons' families living in adjacent rooms in collective housing units and sharing meals daily; dividing an old house in an older part of town between the (grand)parents and the son's family, and thus living as two adjacent households. When we asked women in households with only a husband and a wife and women in nuclear family households (a total of 228 women) to name a relative or relatives with whom they interacted more than once a week, the results were: "own sibling" (28 percent); "own parent(s)" (28 percent); "spouse's sibling" (20 percent); and "spouse's parent(s)" (16 percent). Even in China, where the patrilineal principle of kinship organization (*zongzu*) prevails, relatives on the wife's side form an extensive and tight-knit network outside the household.[4]

The questionnaire survey also touched on "childcare anxiety" – defined as anxiety produced by a mother's sense of isolation from other adults during the period of childcare and her worry that she is not performing childcare well – and found that the rate of such anxiety among Chinese women was low compared to that expressed by Japanese women. When the responses by Chinese women under age forty to questions about parenting are compared with those of mothers of infants and toddlers in Nara, Japan in 2002, the share of women agreeing with statements suggesting "childcare anxiety" are as follows: "My child is irritating and I get frustrated" – China, 24.6 percent, Japan 58.5 percent; "I feel pressured, as if I am raising the child by myself" – China, 17.8 percent, Japan 33.3 percent; "Childcare is almost unendurable" – China 15.1 percent, Japan 50.6 percent (Miyasaka and Fujita 2004: 141). Many people we met in China stated that "childcare problems do not exist here." Childcare anxiety is virtually non-existent in China with the presence of both formal and informal childcare support networks, the one-child policy, and the high employment rate for women.

While it is not rare for Chinese couples to leave their children at one of their parents' houses or at a daycare center (nursery school or kindergarten) until they reach the age of three to five, once children start school, many Chinese couples prefer to support their children's schoolwork by monitoring their homework. In China, the common belief seems to be that while it really does not matter who takes care of a child during infancy, educational problems will arise if the parents do not look after their own child at home by the time the child starts elementary school. Zhou Weihong, one of the authors of this chapter, has named this belief the "school-age myth," distinguishing it from the "three-year myth"– the notion, common in Japan, that children should be looked after by their own mother until reaching the age of three.

FUTURE PROSPECTS

Do full-time housewives exist, then, in China, which has been a society of double-income families up to this point? In the late 1980s, with the beginning of rapid economic development, the so-called *funü huijia* ("women should return home") dispute – which called on women to go home to solve the emerging problem of surplus labor – did take place (Ochiai 1988). But despite this earlier pressure to force women from the workforce, full-time housewives continue to be extremely rare. In this study, we were able to interview several unemployed wives who were laid off, but their self-perception was not necessarily of being a "housewife"; instead, some labeled themselves as merely "unemployed" (Ochiai 2005a and Chapter 8 of this volume).

While some women have left the workforce following the loss of a job, others have made a choice to be full-time housewives. The Japanese and Chinese media have begun to report the emergence of "voluntary full-time housewives" in major cities such as Guangdong, Shanghai, and Beijing.[5] According to these reports, some upper-class women have chosen to become "full-time mothers" for the sake of their children's education. In the interview survey conducted by Zhou and Ochiai in Beijing, there was one woman who became a housewife at age thirty-six after resigning from her position as a company executive. Although her resignation was for business reasons, she nevertheless believed that becoming a housewife would be beneficial for the family since her child was about to enter elementary school (Ochiai 2005a and Chapter 8 of this volume).[6] In one Beijing graduate program, female students responded that they would, of course, like to find challenging and rewarding jobs, but at the same time, they would like to take care of their own children themselves without relying on their poorly-educated parents. Some of the male students also expressed the opinion that, if economically possible, having a wife who was a full-time housewife would be a good option. In this way, the well-educated class placed strong emphasis on home life and, especially, on their children's education.[7] In sum, the shift towards "housewifization" of mothers in China is most evident in the two extremes of city dwellers – the lower middle class and the highest class.

(2) Thailand

GENDER AND LIFE COURSE

Families in Thailand, as in many Southeast Asian societies, have traditionally been characterized by a "bilateral system" rather than by either matrilineality or patrilineality. Many Thai women live with or close to their parents even after marriage, and daughters are often given priority for inheritance of farmland. In addition, in the area of production activities, Thai women have continued to be viewed as key laborers. Historically, Europeans who visited Southeast Asia during the Age of Exploration remarked on the high level of economic activity and the sexual freedom of Southeast Asian women (Reid 1993: Vol. 2, Ch. 4). Figure 2.2 shows the changes in female labor-force participation rates in Thailand from the 1960s to the present. As Figure 2.1 showed for China, a reversed U-shaped curve has been retained. However, unlike in China, this pattern is not the result of post-housewifization due to modernization, but a "tradition" extending back several hundred years. Have these practices been affected by the remarkable recent growth of a new urban middle class with middle-class values or attitudes?

CHILDCARE NETWORKS

The characteristics of Thailand's childcare support network that emerged from our study show that although childcare at home centers on the mother, the father (husband) also plays an active role. There are men, for example, who say, "I raised my two children all by myself, including changing diapers" (Ochiai 2003a: 99). In a time-use survey conducted for the first time in Thailand in 2001, it was found that among married men and women in Bangkok, women spent an average of 2.0 hours per day on childcare while men spent 1.4 hours – a difference of only 0.6 hours (NSO 2002), a relatively small difference by international standards.

Relatives dominate the informal network supporting the husband and wife. Affirming, in the interview survey, the statistics showing that extended family households including stem and non-stem kin account

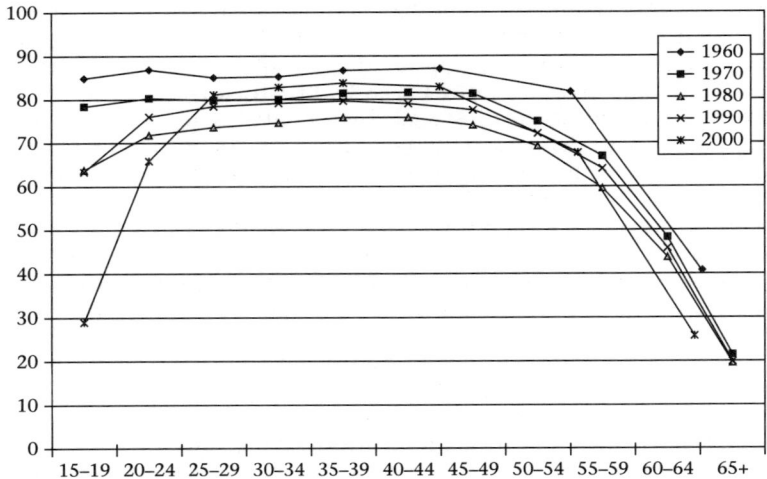

Figure 2.2   Female labor force participation rates in Thailand
Source: NSO, *Population and Housing Census.*

for 30 percent of families in Thailand (See Table 1.6 in Chapter 1.), we found cases in which the parents or siblings of the husband or wife, living under the same roof, took care of the couple's children. We also found cases of aunts and uncles providing childcare by taking in nieces and nephews coming from a distance. In the "family circle" (or "network family") society found in Thailand and other Southeast Asian countries,[8] children are often cared for by grandparents and close relatives, and the practice of adoption by either relatives or non-relatives is common. Hence, Thailand can be said to be a society where the function of surrogate parent has developed quite extensively (Hashimoto 2004a: 210–11 and Chapter 5 of this volume).

Our research indicates, however, that the role of relatives in providing a childcare support network is not as extensive in Thailand as in China. This study has identified a "revised multi-household compound" in which relatives live close to each other – an urban version of the "multi-household compound" found in Thailand's rural areas[9] – but this urban residential form appears to have little effect on families' ability to draw on their relatives' support for childcare. Since relatives begin to form these residential clusters only when they can afford to buy houses, which may occur after their childrearing years, the "revised multi-household compound" is useful mainly for taking care of the elderly, and not particularly useful for childcare (Ochiai 2003b: 98).

Domestic workers fill some of the demand for childcare. There are two hiring patterns for live-in maids: employing rural relatives and bringing in women from other countries such as Myanmar. The former pattern is most common among families of average or slightly below average income who live in townhouses, and the latter pattern is common among those of above-average income who live in detached housing (Hashimoto 2004a: 212). Using maids for childcare is not seen as ideal, however. Cost and supply difficulties have increased. Moreover, recently Thai parents have demanded high-quality childcare, and therefore generally do not perceive maids as childcare support resources but rather as servants hired to do housework.

Formal support resources such as daycare facilities are in short supply in Bangkok. Although there are childcare centers operated by municipal districts in addition to the daycare facilities managed by the city of Bangkok, such childcare centers do not exist in the new residential areas where we conducted our study (Hashimoto 2004a: 211 and Chapter 5 of this volume). The shortage of daycare facilities for children between birth and two-and-a-half years has become a particularly serious problem. According to the Social Welfare Division of the Social Welfare Department of the Bangkok Metropolitan Administration, only private – and no public – daycare facilities exist for this age group. Because it is believed that parents or relatives should look after their children, there has been no public support for childcare. Although some private daycare facilities (at the nursery school level) exist, most of these facilities are not cheap and only the upper-class can afford them. Another type of private daycare may be performed by a neighbor whom parents pay to look after their children at the neighbor's home; such businesses are unstable, however, and most of them go out of business fairly quickly.

Women returning to work after maternity leave report that they must often leave their children in the care of out-of-town relatives, hire a maid, or take a childcare leave without pay because they cannot find adequate childcare (Hashimoto 2004a: 211). A mother's childcare problems do not end, however, even when her child reaches the age at which daycare facilities accept children. To illustrate, a thirty-four-year-old female company employee noted that after she picked up her child at kindergarten at 3:00 p.m., she took her child back to her workplace, where the child played until 5:00 p.m. And because all the mothers at her workplace did the same, the workplace became something of a daycare center (Ochiai 2003b: 97 and Chapter 5 in this volume).

FUTURE PROSPECTS

In this study, we met more than a few women who became full-time housewives when their children were young. As in the case of China, these housewives could be divided into two types. Hashimoto named one type "a passive housewife" to indicate those women who, despite their desire to work, decided to leave the workplace due to a shortage of childcare support. Hashimoto named the other type "a positive housewife" to indicate those women who willingly became full-time housewives to care for their families and to provide childcare (Hashimoto 2002b; Hashimoto 2004a: 213–14 and Chapter 5 of this volume).

An example of the "passive housewife" is Mrs. T. She has thought about working, but at the same time would feel guilty about her child coming home from school to an empty house. Moreover, since she felt uneasy about hiring a stranger to work at her house, and because wages for domestic workers were too high for her to afford, she concluded that the best option would be for her to remain a housewife.

On the other hand, Mrs. Sot is a "positive housewife." Although a graduate of a prestigious national university, she became a full-time housewife after giving birth because she believed that "childcare is specialized work, and it is not an easy task." She now sends her child to a prestigious elementary school. The "positive housewife" is grounded in the view that the role of the mother is to educate the child. Nevertheless, this type remains an exception in Thailand (Hashimoto 2004a: 213–14).

Kua Wongboonsin of Chulalongkorn University found that the female labor-force participation rate in Bangkok in 1998 and 1999 traced a shallow M-curve with a slight dent for the age group thirty to thirty-four (Wongboonsin 2002: 97–101 and Chapter 6 of this volume). However, that dent disappeared in the year 2000. Wongboonsin explains in Chapter 6 of this volume that the disappearance was the result of women choosing to suppress fertility rather than leaving the workplace due to the severity of the unemployment situation at the time. The total fertility rate in Bangkok in 2000 was a record low of 1.17 (Wongboonsin 2004a: 202).

It is hard to predict what kinds of changes female life course patterns – for which "working continually for one's lifetime" has been the dominant practice up to this point – will undergo in Thailand, where the new middle class is still in the process of formation. With the end of the demographic dividend period, reliance on kin networks as a resource for childcare support will likely become more difficult, and without improved access to daycare facilities, the number of "passive housewives" may increase rapidly. The new middle class is not monolithic, moreover, and differences in educational background and income levels within the middle class may produce differences in the quality standards demanded for childcare as well as ability to market childcare. We suggest that these differences may be an important factor in determining the trend of housewifization in Thailand. However, for various reasons it seems likely that Thailand will not follow the same pattern as Japan. In Thailand, performing housework and childcare is not an inherent part of gender identity for women, and while the ideals of love, family, and motherhood are closely linked, in reality there is a great deal of cooperation between husband and wife in matters of childcare. In addition, neither a family wage system nor making women into full-time housewives is a goal of government policy (Onode 2003c).

(3) Singapore

GENDER AND LIFE COURSE

The distinctive feature of female labor-force participation in Singapore is its high rate throughout the twenties and steady decrease after the thirties. Women's employment rates during the childcare period are high, and the number of women leaving the workplace for childbirth or childcare is low, even among those surveyed in our study. However, this pattern is not a traditional one. As Figure 2.3 shows, labor-force participation rates in Singapore for women in their 30s and older were at a very low, uniform level of about 20 percent in 1970. After 1970, these rates rose rapidly, largely as a result of government policies. Having separated from Malaysia in 1965 to become an independent republic, the government of Singapore initiated a new economic development plan in 1971. In order to bring about industrialization, policies were implemented to make systematic use of female labor (Tamura 1999a). Women were encouraged to pursue higher education, childcare facilities were created, and female domestic workers were invited from abroad. Although Singapore is not a socialist country, it resembles China in having experienced "de-housewifization" as a result of strong governmental initiatives in the process of modernizing.

Childcare in Singapore can be divided into a "first stage" and a "second stage." The first stage is the "nurturing period," and few women leave the workforce during this period. The second stage is the "education period," and many Singapore mothers believe they are needed at home to help direct their children's education. Commercial educational

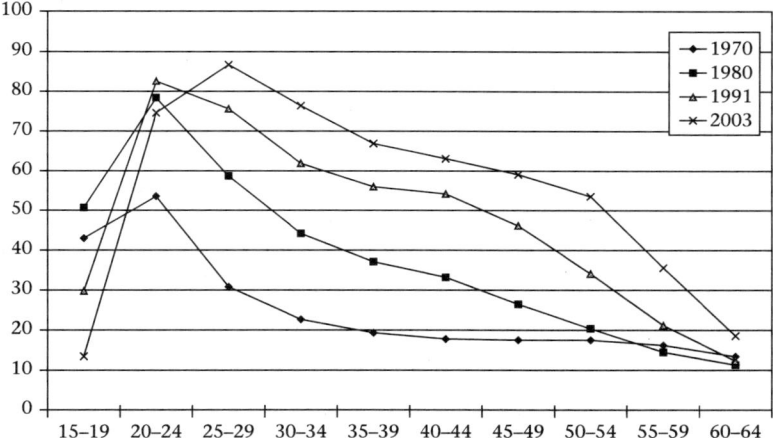

Figure 2.3 Female labor force participation rates in Singapore
Source: Singapore Dept of Statistics, *Yearbook of Singapore, 2002*. Quah, Stella, 1998. *Family in Singapore*. Singapore Times Academic Press. Saw, Swee-Hock 1984. *The Labour Force of Singapore*. Singapore Dept of Statistics.

facilities outside of school, similar to Japan's extramural tutoring programs or "cram schools" (*juku*), have not been widely developed in Singapore, and some mothers believe they must help guide their children's education. Once their children enter elementary school, some mothers take on this task, leaving the workforce around the age of thirty-five. Although, as we shall see below, some families use grandparents and after-school care, we have begun to observe that highly educated mothers may prefer to guide their own children's education because they are not satisfied with the educational quality of these forms of care.

Two factors contribute to mothers' continued workforce participation during their children's early years: the lack of a strong norm for motherhood and the outsourcing of childcare. In the absence of a motherhood norm (e.g. a widely held belief to the effect that "a child should be looked after by his or her own mother"), it is natural for mothers to continue to work while relying on some form of outsourcing of childcare. Mothers do not feel guilty about continuing to work, and working mothers are not the subject of public criticism. This study included questions about motherhood norms, but many informants, when asked their view on, for example, whether "mothers should quit their jobs and raise their children personally," did not even understand what the question was supposed to mean.

In addition, Singaporeans do not particularly believe that "meals should be prepared at home by the wife or mother." Singapore has numerous inexpensive, high quality restaurants, and it is common for Singaporean families to eat at a food court on a daily basis. Nuclear families do indeed live apart from other relatives, but the typical double-income family in Singapore has dinner, prepared by a maid, at the home of the husband's or wife's parents, and eats breakfast and lunch at a food court; meals are almost never prepared at home by the wife or mother. Relying on outside sources for housework and meals is an important factor enabling both husbands and wives to work during the early childcare period.

CHILDCARE NETWORKS

The basic characteristic of childcare in Singapore is "outsourcing." One method of informal support is relying on kin networks, including grandparents. Other methods include employing maids in the home and leaving the child to "nursing mothers," or, as Singaporeans call them, "foster parents," during the work week. Methods of formal support include daycare centers and, once the child enters school, after-school care.

In Singapore, many families hire maids. As in Thailand, where the hiring of maids has global or international dimensions, many of the maids in Singapore are "FDWs" (Foreign Domestic Workers), young female workers from the Philippines, Indonesia, or Sri Lanka. Since an estimated 100,000 to 170,000 FDWs are now living in Singapore (Yap 2000: 70; Huang and Yeoh 2003: 82),[10] by dividing that number by the total number of households, we find that approximately 11 to 15 percent of households are currently employing FDWs.

There are two types of maid: live-in and live-out. Maids are in charge of general housework, and their work consists of simple jobs such as cooking, washing, and cleaning. Some maids, after winning their employers' trust, plan and purchase items for meals. Maids do not, however, play an important role in childcare. Although they may perform simple tasks such as picking up a child at the school bus stop or feeding a child at home, they are not often put in charge of tasks related to education and nurturing. This is particularly true of maids recruited from Indonesia and Malaysia, many of whom are neither fluent in English nor have attained a high level of education, leading parents in education-conscious Singapore to believe that maids are not suitable for childcare. In addition, reports of incidents of child abuse committed by maids have made some of the Singaporean parents we interviewed uneasy about leaving their children alone with a maid.

For these reasons, many families, especially when their children are still infants, use both kin networks and maids as childcare resources, relying on maids for housework and grandmothers for childcare. For example, at Mrs. B's house, her twenty-month old daughter is looked after by Mrs. B's mother-in-law from Monday to Friday, while cooking and other housework are done by a live-in maid in her twenties. In this instance, there is no notion of the maid bringing up the child. Indeed, the role of the grandmother is not only to love and educate the child, but also to supervise the maid at the same time. When the parents bring the child to the grandmother's home to be cared for, the housework there is also done by maids. The grandparents are given economic assistance from the couple for helping with the childcare, enhancing a reciprocal relationship between the generations.

The bonds among Chinese Singaporean relatives are strong, and it is not uncommon for twenty or more family members to gather every weekend to eat and chat together (e.g., sons and their wives and children as well as grandsons and their wives and children gathering at the grandmother's house). For that reason, childcare, hiring of maids, and household management are coordinated not just by nuclear families but also by the kin network.

Not all families have such extensive resources. Double-income families without kin networks or maids turn to nursing mothers as childcare resources. The nursing mother system is one in which infants (prior to entering nursery school) are boarded at the home of a nursing mother for a fee during the workweek. Parents using this system generally leave their child at the home of the nursing mother on Monday and pick the child up on Friday. Our interviews with parents who relied on this system around ten to fifteen years ago did not detect negative feelings such as loneliness or guilt; the nursing mother system was perceived as simply one common method of childcare support. In recent years, however, perhaps because the notion of complete reliance for childcare on someone outside the kin network has been viewed less favorably, the use of nursing mothers has decreased.

Let us now turn to public childcare support. There are two types of daycare centers in Singapore: public and private. The public ones are built next to community centers. Some private daycare centers add value to their services by enhancing their educational functions. A combination of kin network and daycare centers appears to function well for many parents. In these cases, grandparents may bridge the gap between the end of the daycare session and the parents' return from work. After-school care for elementary school students is also hospitable and sufficient in Singapore. The operating hours are long, meals are provided, and financial aid is granted by the government. This system is a strong indication of the country's support for double-income families.

An example of the effective use of this system is seen in the case of Mr. D. A thirty-year-old office worker, Mr. D goes to work after dropping his children off at "after-school care" at 7 a.m. Because the children attend the afternoon class session of an elementary school that operates on a two-shift system, the children spend time at "after-school" care in the morning (something of a misnomer) and go to school by school bus in the afternoon. They study and play sports during that time. After attending their elementary school session, they return to after-school care and stay there until their father comes to pick them up after he leaves work at 7 p.m. The cost for such care is 260 Singapore dollars per month (approximately 172 U.S. dollars) per child, of which 150 Singapore dollars (approximately 100 U.S. dollars) are covered by government aid.

Public childcare support for up to twelve hours a day, as illustrated above, can only be found in Singapore. After-school care is available even during long vacations such as summer break, and because meals are provided, parents can leave their children without feeling burdened. If there is any "job" for parents, perhaps it is monitoring the child's homework. Thus, Singaporean parents rely on the outside for daily childcare, while keeping an eye on the child's schoolwork themselves.

FUTURE PROSPECTS

How will the life course of Singaporean women change from here on? Figure 2.3 shows significant increases in female labor-force participation rates in the last thirty years and indicates that the tendency for continuous employment has increased with the rise in the employment rate for women, especially those beyond their thirties. Moreover, for reasons such as the economic slump and increases in educational expenses in recent years, Singaporean women are likely to be increasingly oriented towards continuous employment. If an education industry offering after-school tutoring develops in Singapore as it has in Japan and South Korea, that would permit the outsourcing of one of the tasks some middle-class mothers take on – the guidance of their children's education. That, in turn, might further strengthen women's preference for continuous employment.

(4) Taiwan
GENDER AND LIFE COURSE

In Taiwan, as in Singapore, female labor-force participation rates have risen (Figure 2.4). However, the situation of working women in Taiwan is not uniform.

Two types of female life course, reflective of women's educational levels, exist in contemporary Taiwan. Highly educated women tend to continue working, after marriage and childbirth, until retirement age, while less educated women are more likely to leave the workforce to raise their children. The employment rates of married women vary significantly by educational background. In 2000, 41 percent of married women with a junior high school education or below were employed, compared to 55 percent of high school or vocational school graduates and 71 percent of college graduates and those with post-graduate education (Ministry of the Interior Statistics Bureau 2001). Our interviews underscored this data, indicating the high motivation of women who were employed and, in particular, the belief of well-educated women that it was natural for them to work throughout their lives. Although continuously employed women tended to agree with the statement that "mothers should stay close to the child until he or she reaches the age of three," even working mothers who agreed with that statement while not behaving that way themselves neither felt shame nor expressed self-recrimination.

Employment conditions have facilitated highly educated women's sense that it is natural to work throughout their lives. Wage differences

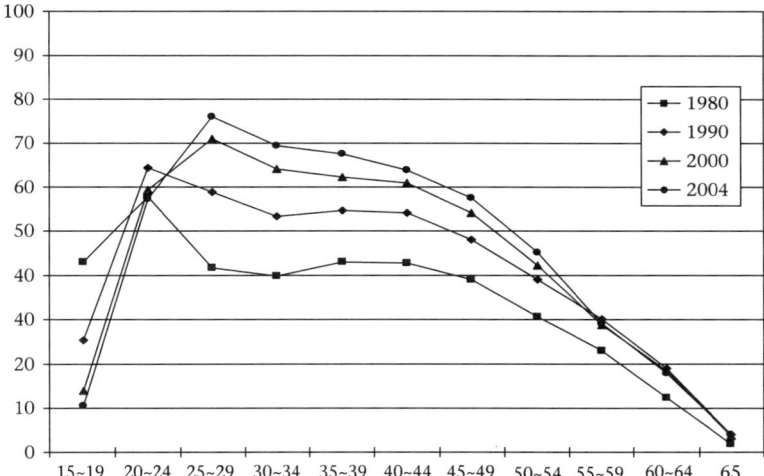

Figure 2.4   Female labor force participation rates in Taiwan
Source: Executive Yuan, *Human Resource Survey 2004*

between male and female employees have decreased, and opportunities for women in managerial positions have expanded. Middle-aged women who are not well educated, however, are often not satisfied with the employment conditions available for them, and even those who have the desire to continue to work tend to waver between work and carrying out family roles.

CHILDCARE NETWORKS

Aggregate data for 2001 of all married women regarding the method of childcare for the youngest child indicate that 72.3 percent answered "my husband and I take care of the child ourselves," which was followed by "parents and relatives" (approximately 20 percent), "babysitter" (6.5 percent), and "daycare centers and others" (0.5 percent) (Ministry of the Interior Statistics Bureau 2001). Different types of childcare support patterns emerge, however, when we examine the method of childcare according to the women's educational background. The response "my husband and I take care of the child ourselves" was selected by 84 percent of women with no more than a junior high school education but only 36.6 percent of women with at least a college degree. In these cases, although the husband helps his wife, she is the primary childcare giver. On the other hand, 37.5 percent of college graduates or higher but only 14.1 percent of junior high school graduates or lower cited "parents and relatives" as caring for the couple's youngest child. Moreover, 24.1 percent of college graduates relied on babysitters for childcare, but only 1.7 percent of junior high school graduates did (Ministry of the Interior Statistics Bureau 2001). Considering these numbers along with the above-mentioned employment rate of married women by educational background, a clear contrast emerges: highly educated women continue to work with the support of relatives and babysitters, while poorly educated women are more likely to take care of the child themselves by becoming full-time housewives. "Daycare centers and other" forms of childcare for children under the age of two are very limited in number, and only 1.2 percent of college-educated and 0.1 percent of junior high school-educated mothers use these resources. According to the Bureau of Social Affairs of the Taipei City Government, there are no public daycare enters, and city officials have no data for private facilities called "infant care centers" for children between the ages of one month and two years.

Several variations can be found in childcare by relatives. Some couples rely on their children's grandparents who live with them; some rely on grandparents who live away from them; and some rely on the couple's siblings who cooperate with childcare. In many cases, the first two types and the third type overlap. Such childcare support comes from both the husband's and wife's sides. In our interview survey, many Taiwanese expressed the view that the child "living away from his or her parents (for a long period of time)" is much preferable to the child "being looked after by babysitters and childcare facilities before he or she can even walk."

Several patterns can be found among the cases in which the grandparents live with their son or daughter to care for their grandchildren. In some cases, the grandmother performs housework while also looking after the grandchildren by herself (type i); in others, the children's aunt and uncle live with the grandparents and are involved in childcare (type ii); in yet other cases, maids take care of the child along with the grandparents (type iii). Maids, who come from countries such as Vietnam, are common in middle-class families. Because maids are generally in charge of housework while the grandmother looks after the grandchildren, maids who perform childcare are supervised by the grandmother. It is often a family's need for care of the elderly, and not childcare, that prompts them to hire maids, often of foreign nationality, due to the governmental policy of permitting the employment of foreign maids mostly as caretakers (see Lan 2006 and Ochiai 2007).

We would like to introduce a classic example of childcare support from relatives, in this case from the couple's parents and siblings (types i and ii). The couple has two children – an eighteen-year-old son and a sixteen-year-old daughter. Both children were born in Taipei, but for the first five years of life, they lived with and were raised by their father's parents in the central part of Taiwan. At that time, their father's younger sister, the children's aunt, still lived at home with her parents and, hence, also took care of the children. The couple visited the children's grandparents' home on weekends to see their children. The son returned to Taipei when he entered kindergarten and the daughter returned to Taipei when she entered kindergarten. The couple had to make these arrangements because they were both busy office workers at that time, and the husband had no relatives living in Taipei. This suggests a norm for the father's family to care for children, rather than the mother's, as we see in some other countries. At the time of the interview, the younger sister who took care of both her niece and nephew was living together with her brother and his wife and teaching at a nearby public kindergarten. Moreover, the husband and the aunt (i.e. his younger sister) were taking care of the six-year-old son of another sibling, their youngest brother, in the husband's home. The youngest brother, like his siblings, was living in Taipei, but his son would return home permanently only when he entered elementary school. The six-year-old child was living with his uncle and aunt because his grandparents had become too old for childcare and private kindergartens near the youngest brother's house had inferior facilities and an insufficient teaching staff and were too high in cost. On the other hand, the public kindergarten where the aunt was working was lower in cost and the conditions were good in every other respect. The six-year-old boy accompanied his aunt to kindergarten everyday, and he visited his parents on weekends. All three children as well as their parents have had no worries whatsoever about living separately during the children's early years. They take cooperation between families and relatives for granted.

FUTURE PROSPECTS

In sum, the most effective childcare support for working women was found to come from relatives such as parents and siblings. These relatives could be on the wife's as well as the husband's side of the family. This cooperation facilitates women's employment. Comparing the age-specific rates of female labor-force participation in 1989 and 2000, the proportion of employed women between the ages of twenty and fifty has increased, and the slight dent evident in 1989, which was suggestive of an M-shaped curve, has vanished. Looking at women who are eager to work as well as those who actively support them, we believe that the trend will not reverse any time soon. However, as the experience of Japan between the 1960s and 1980s shows, support from relatives, especially siblings, diminishes rapidly with the end of the "demographic dividend" (Ochiai 1993). When the generations with fewer brothers and sisters reach the childrearing years, the lack of this support will create a serious problem. We also expect an increase in demand for a variety of childcare facilities even in Taiwan.

(5) South Korea

GENDER AND LIFE COURSE

South Korea, like Japan, is a society with an M-shaped pattern of female labor-force participation by age. The historical changes in the shape and height of the M-curve seen in Figure 2.5 are very similar to those of Japan, which we will discuss later. But unlike in Japan, there is no evidence of a major drop prior to 1963. With male-centered forms of agriculture

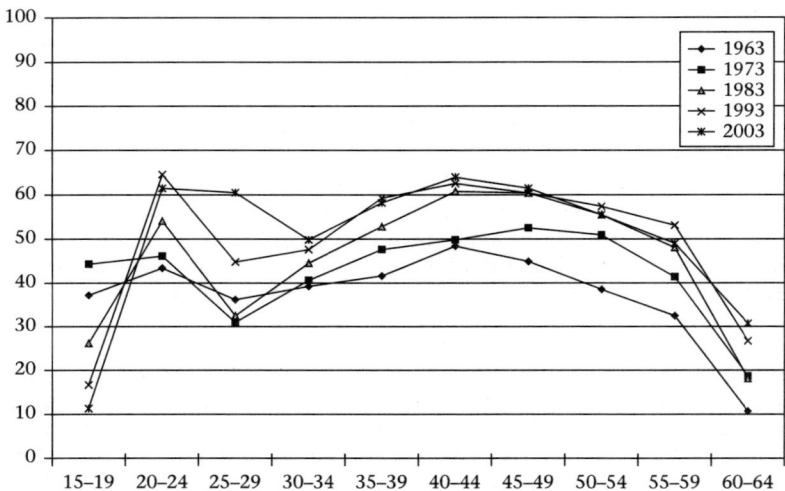

Figure 2.5 Female labor force participation rates in Korea
Source: Statistics Bureau, *Annual Report of Economically Active Population.*

similar to those of northern China, and with the wide diffusion of Confucian morality, a sharp spatial divide existed between men and women in traditional Korean society, with the result that female participation in labor was not extensive. There was, then, no room in Korean society for "housewifization." To the contrary, from the 1970s onwards "de-housewifization" began to take place.

Industrialization in South Korea has produced a life course for married women characterized by their absence from the workforce during the period of childcare. This is a new development. According to the Korean Women's Development Institute, cohorts of women who married before 1970 were most likely to follow one of three life courses: "working throughout one's lifetime," "never working," or "working after completing child-rearing." The life course of entering the workforce after graduation and then discontinuing work for marriage or childrearing as well as the life courses described by the "M-shaped" and "latent M-shaped" models were followed by only 12.3 percent of all women at that time. This changed radically in the next decades, increasing to 52.8 percent for cohorts who married in the 1980s (Park 2004: 73). The labor-force participation rate for women with high school, college, and postgraduate degrees had been remarkably low before 1990. Its rise in the 1990s was accompanied by a reduction in the previous disparity in female employment rates according to educational background.

The M-shaped life course model describes a pattern of leaving the workforce and returning at some later time. The main reasons cited by Korean women for stepping out of the workforce were marriage or pregnancy and childbirth. Women noted that the first good occasion to reenter employment was when their last child was around five years old and the second when the child was about ten. Reasons women cited for reemployment included the reduction in childcare demands as the child became older, their desire for self-fulfillment and establishment of self-identity, and economic necessity. Mothers typically reenter the workforce following the childcare hiatus in a manner easy to coordinate with family life (e.g. part-time work or self-employment). Their family role then changes, coming to include support of school expenses and the family budget. Some women, however, reenter the workforce under greater exigency, such as divorce or major changes in their husband's job; in addition, in the late 1990s, the International Monetary Fund crisis in South Korea wreaked havoc on many families' incomes, driving many women to seek to reenter the workforce.

Women who choose to become full-time housewives to devote themselves to childcare are often torn between childcare and self-fulfillment. To be sure, women who are oriented towards self-fulfillment often return to work later. But the Korean employment system makes it difficult for women (and men) to enter a professional occupation after a hiatus, and many highly educated women are frustrated by the inability to find jobs commensurate with their level of education. Some of these women turn to graduate studies in education both for self-fulfillment and to enhance themselves as mothers.

CHILDCARE NETWORKS

Childcare is basically assigned to the mother, but, compared to Japan, which also has an M-shaped pattern of labor-force participation, mothers have a wider variety of childcare support resources, including relatives, friends, communities, and institutions. Husbands and relatives often participate in the actual childcare, while communities and friends provide mothers with informational and emotional support such as childcare information and counseling. Support from relatives can come from either the husband's or the wife's side of the family; in either case, grandmothers play an important role. Relatives on the wife's side, even if living separately from the wife, tend to build a particularly firm relationship that integrates childcare into their daily lives. Mothers remain the basic coordinators of their children's care, and even when husbands and relatives look after children, it is often considered to be done "in support of the mother."

South Koreans relocate frequently; even when moving to a completely new region, however, full-time mothers tend to create social networks with other full-time mothers in the area. Our interviews uncovered no instances of the social problem identified in Japan as "mothers' loneliness" and "childcare anxiety," despite South Korea's being, like Japan, a "Type 3" society (that is, one characterized by an M-curve in women's labor force participation rates).

Of the nineteen cases of informants in the childcare stage of their lives whom we met through the interview survey, there were only two cases in which the informants hired a maid. While it is not uncommon for double-income families living in or around Seoul to hire live-in Chinese maids of Korean descent, the two cases in our survey both hired live-out, middle-aged South Korean maids. The typical salary rate for maids is 20,000 won (19.9 US Dollars) for a four-hour shift; by comparison, the average monthly salary for laborers is 1,880,389 won (1,874.4 US Dollars) (Statistics Bureau 2003).

Facilities for infants are few in number; this is another reason many mothers believe they have to stop working. Families with infants who wish to continue earning two incomes feel they have to enlist the help of the grandparents or relatives on either the husband's or wife's side or hire a babysitter. And yet, services for infants are certainly not cheap if mothers allot half of their monthly salaries to baby-sitting expenses.

Small-scale daycare centers for children aged one to three, called *aga bang* and *nori bang*, are used by some double-income families and single-parent families. The question of whether and how to have people outside the family care for one's child becomes moot when the child reaches the age of three. At that age, children attend kindergarten (schools with educational programs) or *eorini jip* (Children's House; programs that focus on child welfare), regardless of the mother's status as a full-time housewife or employee. The competition for enrollment of children among kindergartens and *eorini jip* is keen, and both of them provide a variety of educational programs. In addition, a variety of "academies" (*hagwon*) for children aged three or older offer lessons in music, art, and individual tutoring (Kobayashi 2004: 20). Each of our informants spent between 400,000 won (399.7 US Dollars) and 1 million won (996.7 US Dollars) each month on childcare and educational services that included *eorini jip*, kindergarten, and "academies."

South Korean parents are very concerned about their children's education. Once a child reaches the age of five or so, many mothers' main roles change from childcare to educational management and earning money to purchase educational services. Since the late 1990s, an increasing number of mothers have undertaken temporary "educational emigration" (*gyoyuk imin*) to Canada or the U.S. to provide an opportunity for their children to learn fluent English. The fathers, who remain in South Korea to work and send money to their wife and children, are known in in the media as *gireogi appa*, "goose fathers," because they are said to resemble migrant geese, who work hard to support their children and then fly over the ocean to see them (Kobayashi 2007: 56). Reports of fathers who are unable to bear the loneliness committing suicide are occasionally heard. This phenomenon is an extreme example of the thoroughgoing and substantial role of the mother as the child's education manager.

Returning to the question of childcare for children under three years of age, how do mothers for whom childcare facilities are limited and who wish to work full-time manage? In these cases, as the example below indicates, childcare requires much more than simply support from one's husband or relatives but rather a complete sharing of daily activities.

Mrs. A, who has worked as an elementary school teacher since graduating from college, lives in a nuclear family of three persons: she is married to a corporate researcher and they have a six-year-old daughter. Although her husband helps greatly with housework and childcare, Mrs. A's everyday life would not work out without assistance from her mother who lives nearby. The six-year-old daughter lived at the house of her maternal grandparents until she was thirty-six months old. The family eats breakfast separately – the husband at his workplace, Mrs. A at home, and the daughter at the grandparents' house. At dinner, Mrs. A and her daughter eat the meal prepared by Mrs. A's mother at the grandparents' house, while the husband eats at his workplace again. Mrs. A's mother drops off and picks up her granddaughter at school, and she also looks after the child after 5:00 p.m. Mrs. A pays her mother 300,000 won per month in return for this help and care.

As we have seen above, South Korean society continues to be characterized by a gender-based division of labor, and yet we witnessed, in full-time double-income families, instances of childcare arrangements common to Type 1 and Type 2 societies, such as leaving a child at the grandparents' house (although South Korean normative practice is different from China's in that the couple pays their parents for childcare support), equal performance of childcare by the husband and wife, and outsourcing of cooking (Yamane 2004: 30–3).

FUTURE PROSPECTS

Is the life course for middle-class South Korean women headed towards change? An examination of age-specific labor-force participation rates suggests an affirmative answer. Figure 2.5 shows a general rise in female labor-force participation rates, a rise in the bottom of the M-shaped curve after 1973, and a shift in the point at which the curve bottoms out to later age cohorts (thirty to thirty-four years). Because this shift of the low point of the M-curve is partly a result of couples marrying later, however, it is not necessarily an indication of the "disappearance of housewives" phenomenon observed in Northwest Europe or North America. Indeed, it is not easy to predict the trajectory of changes in middle-class women's life courses and childcare support we observed in this study. On one hand, if employment conditions continue to stagnate, Korean families may need to adopt childcare support systems characteristic of Type 1 and Type 2 societies in which female labor-force participation rates remain high for age cohorts that include women with infants and small children. On the other hand, barring international barriers to migration, the phenomenon of "educational emigration" – the extreme case of women's role as "educating mother" – may accompany the intensification of educational competition as more and more people achieve higher education.

In the end, drastic economic, social, and familial changes will likely produce changes in women's life courses and childcare support, but these will not necessarily follow a unidirectional trajectory.

(6) Japan

GENDER AND LIFE COURSE

Japan, like South Korea, has preserved the norm and the reality of a gender-based division of labor. However, gender roles in Japan underwent a dramatic change during the process of modernization. Figure 1.4 in Chapter 1 puts the estimates by Umemura Mataji (Umemura et al. 1988) for the prewar period in graph form, and combines them with statistics for the postwar period. In 1880, not long after the Meiji Restoration of 1868, labor force participation rates in the upper half of the 70 percent level were maintained continually for women from their twenties to their forties, with absolutely no indication of women leaving work for marriage or childbirth. Preindustrial Japan was a society where women worked a great deal, even by international standards (Saitō 1996). This is the same reversed U-shape curve found in present-day northern Europe, the United States and – in Asia – China and Thailand. Japan was in a continuum with Southeast Asia as a society with a high rate of female labor.

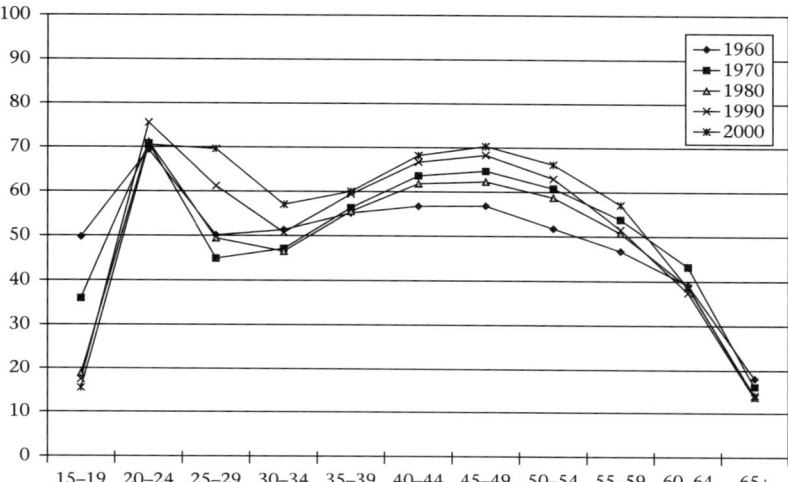

Figure 2.6   Female labor force participation rates in Japan
Source: National Center for Research on Social Security and Population Issues, *Population Trends*, 2006.

During the period of rapid economic growth from the late 1950s to mid-1970s, the notion that "men go to work while women do the housework and childcare" became established at the national level. The M-shaped pattern of labor, in which the female labor-force participation rate declines during the childbirth and childrearing period, also developed during that era, and even though the bottom of the M-shaped curve has tended to rise in recent years, the curve still bottoms out for women in their early thirties (Figure 2.6). Although the norm of the gender-based division of labor as illustrated by the saying noted above has been weakened with a certain progress in gender equality policies since the 1980s, the "myth of motherhood" – a discursive notion that mothers are necessary to raise very young children – remains, continuing to be the main reason why women stop working after giving birth. Unlike the other countries studied here, this abandonment of the workplace has been met with some ambivalence, a phenomenon labeled "childcare anxiety" in Japan. Although many women feel compelled to raise their children on their own, they also are disturbed by the possible consequences of leaving the workplace and their adult social networks. Mothers who become isolated after losing most or all of their social networks during their child-rearing years suffer from "childcare anxiety" which manifests itself as erratic behavior, including child abuse. Such mothers are made anxious not only by being isolated by the societal expectations that they leave work to raise their children but also by the fact that the new jobs women are able to take after the completion of childrearing are overwhelmingly part-time jobs with low income and little opportunity for promotion. Thus, leaving work during the childbirth and childcare period is not only isolating but is also linked to the marginalization of middle-aged women in the workforce.

CHILDCARE NETWORKS

In a survey conducted in the city of Nara in 2002, we found that childcare expectations and the basic demands of motherhood have been maintained. The childcare network was fairly limited; mothers in the childrearing years only received childcare support from the husband (65.1 percent) and the parents ("mother's own parents" [62.1 percent] and "parents-in-law" [31.4 percent]). Childcare support from parents was more common from the wife's side of the family. No more than a very small percentage of respondents cited relatives and neighbors, friends, and institutions. When it came to "babysitters" and "short-term childcare facilities," a mere 0.9 percent of mothers cited these as a source of support. There was significant resistance to "leaving the child somewhere all day" in terms of perceived norms as well. When the responses of "feel resistance" and "feel a little resistance" are combined, not only were mothers reluctant to leave their children with "close neighbors and friends" (84.3 percent), "daycare and other facilities" (53.6 percent), and "babysitters" (84.9 percent), but notable numbers also felt misgivings about "family and relatives besides the husband" (35.6 percent) and "husband" (21.4 percent).

In the area we investigated, few husbands performed housework and childcare. Only 7.2 percent of husbands did at least thirty percent of the family's housework. Although husbands generally took on childcare more than housework, even then, only 22 percent of husbands did at least thirty percent of childcare (Onode 2003a).

The childcare support networks of full-time housewives and full-time working wives also differed. The general setup is as follows: for women working full-time, in addition to their husband and their own parents, two formal connections were sources of support: "daycare and other facilities" and "colleagues from work" (the latter being limited to providing emotional support and information). In contrast to this, full-time housewives received substantial support from their husbands and the parents on both sides, with emotional and informational support coming from informal connections with friends and neighbors. The main factor determining this difference in childcare networks between working mothers and full-time housewives is the division between types of childcare facilities provided by government policy. In Japan, the most representative childcare facilities are nursery schools (daycare centers) and kindergartens. Nursery schools are public social-service facilities intended for working couples and single-parent families, and were established during the rapid economic growth period as the result of a movement for more adequate childcare resources. Kindergartens, on the other hand, are educational facilities first created as part of the modern educational system, and only during the rapid growth period did they become mass institutions available to the general populace. Even today, these institutions differ in their target clientele and in their nature: the great majority of children at nursery schools have mothers who work, while the great majority of children at kindergartens have mothers who are housewives. While some nursery schools care for infants and toddlers, kindergartens accept only children aged three and older; they do not provide care on a regular basis for the children under three in the full-time housewives' families. When we examined the use of childcare services for the first child, 85.7 percent of full-time working wives used nursery school (*hoikuen*), while 45.6 percent and 32.4 percent of full-time housewives used kindergarten (*yōchien*) and private infant school (*yōji kyoshitsu*), respectively. Moreover, 33.3 percent of housewives said that they had "never used" childcare services. Thus, it can be inferred that the children of full-time housewives may be divided into those who receive childcare service and those who do not receive it at all. In households with full-time housewives, the use of childcare services depended on the husband's income, and the higher the husband's income the more frequently a household would use childcare services. Only 0.4 percent of the total number of families use the "Family Support Center," a childcare-aid project mainly for housewives which the government has put a great deal of effort into in recent years (Yamato 2003).

For all practical purposes, in the urban and suburban regions of Japan today, the only providers of substantial childcare support (actually taking charge of the children) are the mother's husband and parents. Even in South Korea, also belonging to the third type of society in terms of women's work patterns, there is greater availability of support from friends and from neighbors; by comparison, childcare support in Japan is exceptionally weak. For that minority of families in which both parents work full-time throughout the childrearing period, systematic institutional support is available from nursery schools (daycare centers). For the majority of families, in which the mother is a full-time housewife, childcare support comes from the husband and parents supplemented by friends and neighbors, but again, informal connections with friends and others in the neighborhood tend to provide only emotional and other limited support. They are not able to provide the most needed service of actually taking charge of children. For those full-time housewives whose husbands have large salaries, it is possible to pay for childcare service in order to get time "away from the children," but when the husband's salary is low, such opportunities are limited. Those women who can rely neither on their parents or parents-in-law for support nor on their husbands' cooperation may have no choice but to go it alone with whatever meager childcare experience they have. From the 1990s on the mass media has portrayed the problem of child abuse in increasingly sensational terms; we need to understand that in the background of all this is the serious isolation of many housewives caused by the present structuring of society.

FUTURE PROSPECTS

Although the rise of the bottom of the M-shaped curve in the graph showing the age-specific rates of female labor-force participation is primarily due to the increasing age of first marriages, other factors have contributed to the continuous employment of women through the early childhood years. The government has targeted men's taking of childcare leave at 10 percent of those eligible, and family-friendly companies that emphasize balancing work and childcare have been encouraged. Strong efforts have been made in recent years to support childcare for double-income families as part of the measures to stem the declining birthrate since the 1990s.

In addition, a new image of men that differs from the "work-oriented" stereotype has emerged, and our study at Nara showed a high tendency for family-oriented husbands to perform more housework and childcare (Onode 2003b). In light of these findings, we suggest that the husband's participation in childcare may increase. Moreover, the Japanese problems of "childcare anxiety" and "isolation," which have persisted since the 1970s, may abate with improved governmental childcare policies that support community childcare as well as childcare facilities for full-time housewives and that promote improvements in the labor environment allowing people other than parents, such as relatives and local residents, to participate in childcare.

CHILDCARE NETWORKS IN COMPARATIVE PERSPECTIVE

Comparative framework
Now that we have considered separately the results of our studies of gender roles and childcare networks for each society, we can compare these results by society. Taking the "individual unit approach" described in Chapter 1, we take the child himself/herself as the Ego; the various individuals and groups, which we will call "agents," support the child's upbringing by providing childcare. The childcare network is formed by these individuals and groups and centers on the child. The field studies of the different societies showed a variety of individuals and groups acting as agents providing childcare. In most societies, the most prominent categories of childcare-providing agents were: mother, father, relatives, domestic workers, and institutions. The relative importance of each category varied from society to society.

Table 2.1 shows the relative effectiveness, according to society, of the various categories of agents in fulfilling their roles. The ratings A, B, C, and D indicate, respectively, "very effective," "somewhat effective," "present but not so effective," and "completely ineffective." Specifically, these assessments mean the following: "very effective" – giving regular, daily care, including evenings; "somewhat effective" – acting as a substitute for the regular caregiver, or being the caregiver for certain delineated periods of time; "present but not so effective" – acting as the caregiver for irregular, temporary periods or only available for a limited

Table 2.1 Comparison of Childcare Networks

	Mother	Father	Relative	Domestic worker	Institution and facility
China	A−	A	A	C (B for large cities)	A
Thailand	A−	A	B	B	B (D for children under two-and-a-half)
Singapore*	A+	B	A	A	A
Taiwan	A	B	A	B	B (C for children under two)
Korea	A+	C	B	C	B (C for children under three)
Japan	A+	C (B for dual-career family)	C (B for dual-career family)	D	B (C for children under three with non-working mothers)

The ratings A, B, C, and D indicate, respectively, "very effective," "somewhat effective," "present but not so effective," and "completely ineffective."
* The samples for Singapore only include ethnic Chinese.

group of people in society; "completely ineffective" – providing no care at all. The ratings for the agent categories in each society were determined by compiling the results of interview and questionnaire studies, which were then assessed by the heads of the investigations in each society and by the members of multi-society investigations. A- and A+ are only applied in the case of the mother in order to indicate the relative intensity of concentration of care work by mothers compared with other societies, although in both cases (that is, both A- and A+) the mother is a "very effective" provider of childcare. Although the mother is rated as A- in China, that does not necessarily mean that Chinese mothers are less effective in childcare than Chinese fathers, who are rated as A.

What does this table tell us about the social network for children in the six societies studied? We will begin by taking a look across societies at the roles played by the various categories of agent in different societies, and then considering the different patterns of social network for each society.

Relatives
To begin with, the most effectively functioning network in most societies, apart from the mother, is made up of relatives. In the five societies other than Japan, the network of relatives is "very effective" or "somewhat effective" in performing its functions. In every society it is extremely common for grandparents, aunts, and uncles to take charge of the

children and care for their daily needs from morning until dinnertime (often in coordination with kindergarten and school hours). Beyond that, apart from Japan, it is common for the children to spend nights with relatives and for this practice to continue for several years. In China, the arrangement by which grandparents and grandchildren form a household together is known as the "skipped-generation household." This is done for various reasons, such as when the grandparents, who live in the same city, live near a better kindergarten than the parents do. In Thailand, where migration from the countryside to the city is common, children are sometimes left with their relatives in the countryside for many years while their mother and father work in the city. In South Korea, many families in which the husband and wife both work depend on the mother's relatives to help.

Within Asia, the relationship of mutual dependence between relatives appears to be stronger in China, Taiwan, and Singapore than in Thailand and South Korea. In ethnic Chinese communities, meals and housework are regularly shared between relatives, including collateral relatives. A high level of dependence is the rule, and the custom of twenty or thirty relatives gathering each weekend is strongly entrenched. Taking care of relatives' children is considered so natural that it probably should not even be thought of as "assistance." Indeed, traditionally it is said to have been standard practice for children to be cared for by their grandparents, with little idea that childcare must be done by the mother. This poses a fundamental challenge to research methodologies based on the modern European custom of seeing the mother as the primary caretaker. The informants themselves say that childcare by grandparents goes together with care for the elderly by their children. These practices are incorporated into a family system which has as a fundamental principle the exchange of care between generations. Confucianism can be considered the ideological expression this system. What is interesting is that China, Taiwan, and other Chinese societies in Singapore and elsewhere, which are considered to embody a patrilineal family system, actually have a bilateral kin network from the perspective of childcare. Traditionally, it was standard in Chinese society for the grandparents on the father's side to care for children, but at present, at least, the grandparents on the mother's side play an equivalent or even greater role. Looked at in this way, connections between relatives in Chinese society are indeed strong, but the tight structure seems to be lacking which would be brought by a strict patrilineal family system and the strong group identity of joint-family households. To the contrary, the boundary between immediate family and relatives is vague, and the actual functioning of the network of relatives in Chinese society is better understood as extending to both the mother's and father's relatives, expanding and contracting in response to conditions. The Chinese sociologist Fei Xiaotong famously described Chinese social relationships, and particularly family relationships, with the term *chaxu geju* (literally, diffentiated-ordered associations). The term evokes the idea of a system of relationships with the individual in the center, extending like the ripples from a stone dropped in the water, and getting weaker the further they are from the center. This certainly is an apt description of the conditions observed in this study (Fei 1947).

Relatives are an important agent for providing childcare in Thailand and South Korea as well. However, this network seems weaker in these two countries compared to Chinese society, for different reasons. In Thailand, the main reason is probably the geographic distance between the grandparents, aunts, and uncles in the countryside and the couple who have migrated to Bangkok. In Thai farming villages, labor and tasks of daily life are performed cooperatively by a group of families living on the same compound, and the immediate family network overlaps, without clear boundaries, with a network of more distant relatives, forming what Japanese anthropologists have called the "family circle." Migration to the cities severs those ties at least temporarily. The present investigation has shown that these relationships are eventually reconstructed to some extent in suburban residential areas outside the city center, but because it takes a number of years to buy houses in adjacent areas so that relatives can regroup in the new location, this network did not seem very effective for families at the life stage where they required childcare, though it may help with the later care of the elderly. By contrast, we can see that Singapore, a city-state, and China, where free migration between the city and rural villages is not permitted, clearly have the conditions necessary to further reinforce already-strong family networks (Zheng 2003).

In South Korea, in contrast with China, childcare is not commonly felt to be a shared responsibility of family and relatives. Rather, the role of childcare agent is clearly ascribed to the parents. In some cases, the parents even pay money to the grandparents for taking the job of childcare. This difference from China seems to be grounded in the absence in Korea of the traditional joint family system found in China. The traditional Korean family system centers on a stem family, which has its own family line, considerably independent from the patrilineal kinship group in which it is situated. If we understand the Chinese family system in terms of *chaxu geju* or the "ripple" system, the resemblance between the Thai and Chinese systems becomes apparent. Compared to these, the stem family system may be characterized by a group identity that draws a line between the stem family and the network of relatives, and encloses the children and other members within the boundaries of the core "family."

The role of relatives in the Japanese family is also important, but compared to the other societies it is distinctly smaller. What might be the reason for this? Japan traditionally has had a stem family system as strong or stronger than that of South Korea. The relation between siblings is hierarchical, and the *ie* (household) is clearly independent of the network of relatives. Of particular importance is the fact that the traditional Japanese family system functions to break the connection with relatives outside the immediate family. Also significant are the demographic conditions described in Chapter 1. As elsewhere, when Japan was benefiting from the demographic dividend or population bonus in the 1960s, relatives were highly effective providers of childcare assistance, with sisters contributing nearly as much to childcare as parents did (Morioka et al. 1968; Ochiai 1993; and Chapter 1 of this volume). Nowadays, the generation raising children in Japan has two or fewer siblings. The decrease in the number of relatives brought about by the end of the demographic dividend made the weakening of the kin network critical. The five Asian societies other than Japan discussed in this study, presently in the middle of the demographic dividend period, still have the period of greatest strength for kin networks to look forward to, but with fertility rates already dropping, this will inevitably be followed by the weakening of those networks. It cannot be expected that the childcare systems existing at present, which depend on current conditions, will continue to function adequately in the future.

Domestic workers
In many societies, another important source of childcare comes from domestic workers. And indeed, even in pre-modern and early modern societies in Asia and Europe, the main social networks supporting families were made up of relatives and domestic workers (Fauve-Chamoux, ed. 2005). In Japan, domestic workers were called "serving girls" (*gejo*) in the early-modern Edo period (1603-1868) and "housemaids" (*jochū*) and "nurses" (*komori*) from the modern Meiji (1868) era onwards. In both Asia and Europe, female domestic workers were sometimes relatives brought from rural areas and sometimes strangers. The practice of hiring domestic workers ended in Europe in the early twentieth century and in Japan by the 1960s, with the newly-born "housewife" taking on full responsibility for housework.

Outside of Japan, domestic workers continue to be a normal and widespread presence in Asia today. However, it would be a mistake to view this simply as the persistence of a longstanding traditional custom. In particular, there has been a dramatic change in the typical nationality of domestic workers, who were once mainly from within the country but now often are of foreign nationality. Singapore and Taiwan, in taking in young female domestic workers from Southeast Asian countries like the Philippines and Indonesia, have been transformed into societies that take in cross-border migrants as a standard practice.

And while not as extensively as in Singapore and Taiwan, South Koreans and Thais, while continuing to employ native citizens, are also bringing in domestic workers from abroad – older ethnically Korean women from China to South Korea and young women from the neighboring Southeast Asian country of Myanmar to Thailand. While globalization has been accompanied by a revival in the employment of domestic workers in the United States and Europe as well, in present-day

Asia the transformation to a global system has taken place with little or no intermediate period of reduced employment of domestic workers.

In China, the huge economic gap between urban and rural areas provides the basis for hiring domestic workers from rural villages. The same pattern occurred in Japan prior to the rapid growth period, but in China the enormous rural society functions almost like a foreign country. The employment of domestic workers, then, usually takes place across national boundaries or between areas in the same country with great differences in economic development.

While some domestic workers commute to their jobs, most live with their employers. In Singapore, for instance, high-class condominiums are usually built with a small maid's room near the front entrance, where the Filipina maid typically lives and which she decorates with photographs of her family and Christian images. In the courtyard of the condominium, children can often be seen playing together under the watch of the various maids employed by their families.

Domestic workers, then, play an important role in providing childcare. However, in recent years there has been a common trend in many societies for this role to be reduced. As these societies place more and more importance on education, parents become uneasy about leaving childcare to maids. Instead, there is a growing preference for a division of labor. In Singapore, for example, the mother has the main responsibility for childrearing, while the maid plays a supporting role by cleaning house, doing laundry, shopping, cooking, and the like. In Taiwan, the primary reason maids are hired is to care for the elderly, not to raise children. It is also very common for the grandparents to monitor the maid's childcare activity.

In Singapore, there is also a category of childcare provider known as "foster parent" or "nursing mother." This practice consists of hiring a non-relative to take custody of the children on weekdays and evenings. The parents of the children become "weekend parents." Unlike with domestic workers, in this case it is the children who go to live with the foster parent; but the phenomenon of marketing childcare is common to both situations. In the past this practice was widespread, and there have even been government services for introducing "foster parents," but it seems no longer to be popular. As with domestic workers, there seems to be a growing resistance to paying strangers to care for one's children.

In comparison with other societies of Asia, Japan stands out for the almost complete absence of hired domestic workers. There has been a dramatic growth in employment of Japanese helpers to care for the elderly, but there is little use of helpers for childcare. As in other societies, the use of nurses and housemaids was standard practice in the past, but the ubiquitous "helper" (*otetsudai-san*, a new name for housemaid) vanished with the onset of rapid economic growth. Even in the global era, unlike in Europe, America, and other areas of Asia, there is no sign that Japanese will begin to hire foreign domestic workers. Practically speaking, this is because governmental policy forbids the hiring of unskilled foreign laborers, but there is probably resistance to this at the family level as well. This subject stands out as a particular quality of the contemporary Japanese family.

Institutions and facilities
In considering institutional childcare, we can broadly divide the societies of study into three types. The first type includes societies where institutional care is provided to all families regardless of the social class of the parents or the employment status of the mother. China and Singapore belong to this category. In China, socialist policies have led to the successful creation of public facilities providing childcare for small children. It is possible to leave one's children in such facilities from infancy onwards, and "full care" with a boarding house system is also available. In Singapore, public and private daycare are available, as well as "after-school care" for schoolchildren.

In the second type of society, adequate childcare facilities are available for older children, but are not available at the same level for smaller children and infants. In Japan, postwar childcare policy has been to provide childcare support to families in which both parents work. Social movements with slogans demanding "as many childcare facilities as mailboxes" brought about lasting results. However, there are no facilities available to provide continuous childcare for families with full-time housewives until the children enter kindergarten, an educational institution. By comparison, in South Korean society availability of institutional care depends on the age of the child. For children aged three and over, there are numerous kindergartens, which are educational institutions, and *eorini jip*, which are social welfare institutions, enabling parents to choose from many facilities offering a variety of programs. Facilities for children under three (*nori bang* and others), on the other hand, are lacking, forcing working couples to rely on relatives for help. In Taiwan, there are nursery-care centers for children under age two, but these are not widely used. Childcare support for working couples mainly comes from informal sources such as relatives and babysitters. However, recently there has been a movement to create prototype childcare facilities, and private kindergartens have begun to create classes for smaller children.

The third and final type of society is that in which childcare facilities are undeveloped, particularly for small infants. Such is the case in Thailand. In Thailand, there are no public facilities available for children under the age of two-and-a-half, while private facilities for such children struggle due to a lack of public funding. In some cases, when informal care from relatives is unavailable, the lack of childcare facilities forces the wife to quit her job and become a full-time housewife. In this final type of society, the idea that childcare should come from the family probably impedes the systematic creation of facilities, but the real problem is a lack of funds. Still, as the problem of inadequate childcare facilities has grown, the government has finally started to move. In the 2004 elections for governor of Bangkok, almost every candidate promised to create adequate childcare facilities.

Mothers and fathers

Finally, we will consider the mother and father in their roles as caregivers. At the beginning, our program of research contained the unspoken assumption that "parent = provider of childcare," but it became clear as we proceeded that this was a Japanese bias. In many societies, it was observed that the parent is only one agent playing a limited role within a varied network of childcare providers.

In the ethnically Chinese societies of China, Taiwan, and Singapore, it is not so much the parents as it is the grandparents, aunts, uncles, and cousins who are the main providers of childcare. Children are brought up in a wide family network, and the parents' role is only a part of it.[11] Thai society is traditionally a "network family" society. However, because of the unique geographical circumstances in the area investigated in the study, namely the Bangkok suburbs, the kin network is limited, which has the effect of strengthening the tendency for parents to become the main agents of childcare.

In contrast, South Korea and Japan are both societies in which the parents, and particularly the mother, are expected to be the main providers of childcare. In South Korea, when both parents work it is common for the grandmother on the wife's side to be a major care provider. Support from relatives comes with the understanding that childcare is primarily the responsibility of the parent (the mother). This contrasts markedly with China, where, when the grandparents are unable to care for their grandchildren because they are still working, they are often expected to contribute the funds needed to hire a caregiver.

Another factor in making the parents only one of many agents is the externalization and marketing of housework and childcare. The classic case of this is Singapore, with a high development of two important elements: imported labor from neighboring Southeast Asian societies and well developed childcare facilities. While there is a difference in degree, the absolute quantity of childcare by family members is reduced as well in China by a large number of public childcare facilities and by the presence of domestic workers from the countryside. The same effect results in Thailand from the marketing of housework (in practices such as eating out) and the presence of domestic workers.

Let us now look at the differences between the roles of mothers and fathers. In China and Thailand, there is relatively little difference in roles based on the gender of the parent. In China, this is explained partly by tradition – in southern China, women's workforce participation has been high – as well as by the socialist policy promoting women's work. Chinese men are skilled in housework and play a role in childcare nearly equal to that of mothers. In Thailand, the effect probably comes from the traditional bilateral structure of society. In contrast, we find in Taiwan and Singapore a tendency for the mother to be more involved in childcare than the father, although the presence of the family network and of domestic workers prevents this from being manifested in a much greater concentration of maternal childcare duties.

It is in South Korea and Japan that we find a clearly defined role of the parent as the caregiver as well as a strong gender division of labor. Differences exist between these two societies, however. In Japan, as indicated by the "three-year-old myth" (the idea that a mother must care for her child personally for the first three years to avoid problems), there is an emphasis on the mother's role in "caring" for the child during infancy. In South Korea, in addition to the "caregiver" aspect, there is a strong ideal of the mother as an agent of education. In both of these M-curve societies, "gender equality" has become an issue invoked as a reason to do away with the concentration of childcare responsibilities on the mother. To put it conversely, it can be argued that it is precisely when the boundaries of the nuclear family and the stem family become clearly established and the ideal of motherhood and the concentration of childcare responsibility on the mother become actualized that "gender equality" in childcare becomes a social issue.

But in South Korea and Japan, too, there are signs of a change in the gender division of childcare roles. In South Korea, with the Asian economic crisis bringing a decline in the economic force of the husband, cases have begun to appear of husbands and wives sharing childrearing and housekeeping responsibilities equally. In Japan, studies of families raising children have shown that men interested in raising a family actually did a great deal of housework and childcare (Onode 2003b). The effective promotion of labor and childcare policies could make possible a new movement in the direction of joint childcare for couples.

REGIONAL PATTERNS OF CHILDCARE NETWORKS AND WOMEN'S LIFE COURSE

Returning to Table 2.1, a comparison among societies of social networks related to childcare shows two kinds of society: societies in which several categories of effective childcare networks exist together, and societies in which virtually no effective childcare networks exist. Types 1 and 2, in which both members of the couple work during the childrearing period, represent the former type, while Type 3, in which the mother leaves work during the childrearing period, is the latter kind.

Among Types 1 and 2, China and Singapore are notable for having an impressive four different categories of networks that provide childcare in a very effective manner. In the first place, in both societies, generous institutional childcare is available from infancy to school age, as a result of government policies of incorporating women into the labor force. In addition, ethnically Chinese society itself is distinguished by wide, strong networks of collateral relatives that perform an effective function in childcare. In both Singapore, which is a city-state, and China, where migration is limited, many relatives live in the same city, and this situation probably has the effect of tending to strengthen kin networks (Zheng 2003). Furthermore, effective use is made of the cheap labor of domestic workers, whether from abroad (Singapore) or from economically disadvantaged parts of the country (China). The contribution of the father to childcare is stronger in China. While men in China typically participate in housework and often are skilled cooks, in Singapore, the large role played by maids diminishes the relative amount of childcare performed by both the father and the mother.

In these societies, with their abundance of childcare networks, it is difficult to find evidence of a "childcare problem." In fact, we were unable to find any books in bookstores in China with titles referring to "childcare problems" – although there are many books that deal with "educational problems."

Thailand and Taiwan, Types 1 and 2, both fall in the same category as China and Singapore, but they are somewhat different. The lack of institutionalized childcare, and in particular the lack of a developed system of public facilities, caused by the government's unwillingness to view childcare as a proper object of public funding, is leading to a "childrearing problem." For example, in Thailand, there is a striking absence of facilities where children aged two-and-a-half and younger can be left. With no public facilities existing for children of this age, and with private facilities either extremely expensive or unstable and likely to go bankrupt, one study found that only 1.6 percent of its subjects had ever used childcare facilities for one-year-olds (Richiter et al. 1992). Even when children become old enough to enter nursery school, there are many cases of parents bringing their children to work between the end of kindergarten and the end of the workday. New phenomena such as mothers being forced to become full-time housewives and declining birthrates due to the deliberate avoidance of having children are emerging. In 2000, the Total Fertility Rate in Bangkok reached a record low level of 1.17 (Wongboonsin 2002).

In Type 3 societies, in which the mother leaves work during the childrearing period, childcare support is quite weak compared to societies where both partners work. Both South Korea and Japan belong to this type. While one now sees fathers taking their children out on holidays, the contribution of these fathers falls quite short of what is done by fathers in China and Thailand. Public facilities are well-established in comparison to Thailand and Taiwan, but there are cutoffs to these services based on the child's age (South Korea) and the employment status of the mother (Japan), so that some categories of families raising children have no access to institutional support. There also are differences between the two societies in terms of involvement of relatives and domestic workers. Unlike Japan, which employs almost no home helpers, in South Korea babysitters are frequently used. In addition, in Japan, the kin network shrank to include only the grandmother following the end of the demographic dividend, while in South Korea, watching each other's children and sharing support with others in the kin network continues to make a significant contribution to childcare.

Moreover, South Korea also differs from Japan in that it has networks of working and non-working women who share childcare duties.

Among all the societies investigated in this study, only in Japan was "childcare anxiety" in mothers with young children found to be a major problem. There are some signs of a similar trend in South Korea, but they are by no means widespread. Japan, having passed through the demographic dividend stage, now has a decreasing absolute number of relatives and has no government policy for bringing in domestic workers from outside the country. It stands out in this study as extremely deficient in childcare networks in comparison with other Asian societies. With widespread "childcare anxiety," steadily declining birthrates, and little growth in the employment of women, highly inadequate childcare networks were shown to constitute a serious structural problem.

CONCLUSION

This chapter has examined the patterns of childcare networks and women's life course in six societies in East and Southeast Asia. Our initial hypothesis was that the crucial factor behind a change in gender roles is a change in childcare practices.

The structure of childcare networks differed in each society, and concerning that structure a great variety of agents was found to perform the networks' important functions. The most immediate causes of the diversity in childcare network structure can be found in the differing traditions including kinship structures and family and gender practices. In ethnic terms, Chinese societies are characterized by flourishing, active interaction between relatives that transcends the boundaries of the single household. It is more the case that childcare responsibility belongs to all the relatives than that relatives "help" the parents. The Thai family, structured as a "family circle" in which the distinction between "family" and "relatives" is not sharply defined, resembles the Chinese family in some respects. In Thailand, with its bilateral family structure and tradition of both sexes performing labor, sexual division of labor for housekeeping and childcare is weak even today.

Conversely, in the stem family systems in South Korea and especially Japan, the tendency is for the family to grow distant from collateral relatives. These societies place strong emphasis on the responsibility of the parents for childcare. It is in this traditional kinship structure itself, as well as its transformation in the urbanization process, that we must look for the cause of the increasingly serious problem of isolation of mothers.

State policies exert an influence on childcare network structures on a par with traditional culture. Public childcare facilities play a prominent role in China and Singapore, in both cases as the result of national policies promoting an expanded, vital female labor force. China is, of course, a socialist country; modernization under the socialist model is not accompanied by housewifization. To the contrary, the promotion of female participation in the labor force has been accompanied by the planned development of institutional care for infants and small children. Singapore is a capitalist country, but because of its national policy of rapid development, the government has promoted the development of institutional childcare facilities along with the importation of domestic workers from abroad. By contrast, other Asian societies tend to be strongly "familistic," seeing childcare as the responsibility of the family; in these societies one consistently finds a shortage of childcare facilities, especially for children under two-and-a-half or three years old. "Familistic" policies are more likely motivated by financial considerations than by ideology.

Based on the findings discussed so far, the critical factors determining childcare network structure are essentially the same as described by Sechiyama's two axes for analyzing the four types of East Asian societies (Sechiyama 1996). However, Sechiyama's discussion focused on the differences in traditional ethnic culture and differences in the social system, that is, socialism and capitalism. In this chapter the field of study has been extended to Southeast Asia, where we find that even in a capitalist country, when governmental policies promote the addition of women to the labor force, the results can be much the same as under socialism. We attribute this to the strong influence of government policy more than to differences in the social system.

Another factor affecting the structure of the childcare network is globalization. Globalization means the integration of a society into a worldwide market economy, resulting in the dramatic movement of capital, products, and people. It is related to the "axis" of government policy, since the extent of globalization can be adjusted based on national policies. The extent to which national policy allows the importation of foreign domestic workers has a major influence on childcare. Japan is an extreme example of a country with a strong restriction on the importation of foreign domestic workers.

Let us now consider how the distinct structure of the childcare network in each society, formed by the elements described above, is related to the women's life course in that society. The findings discussed in this chapter show a clear, straightforward relationship: in societies with ample childcare networks, women continue working through the childrearing years (Types 1 and 2); in societies with inadequate networks women leave work during this period (Type 3). It can rightly be said that until now, societies in which most women were housewives were societies with few effective childcare-providing agents, so that the care role was concentrated on the mother. This result supports our hypothesis. In particular, the meagerness of the childcare network of Japan, in which demographic factors have reduced the kin network while government policy restricts the employment of foreign domestic laborers, has firmly reinforced the M-shaped curve pattern of women's employment. This explains the failure of de-housewifization to take place in Japan.

However, the experience in each society that led to the present-day structure of the childcare network and women's employment cannot be simplified into a simple, linear process. It is too simple to assert that the agents connected with childcare declined as a result of the social change of modernization, leading the mother to take on the primary role in childcare. In both Japan and South Korea, a large number of women are housewives, but the process leading to this state differed in the two countries. As we have seen in Chapter 1, Japan was a society in which women had always worked a great deal, and what took place in Japan was classic housewifization. In South Korea, however, traditional norms enforcing separation of the genders were very strong, and female labor-force participation was low. As a result there is little evidence of a transformation in which women heavily involved in activities other than housework quit those activities to become housewives.

Today, in the other four societies studied, many women work during the childrearing period, but the process by which this came about differs in each. Thai society has traditionally had a high female labor-force participation rate. In Thailand, the process of modernization brought almost no change in labor-force participation rates for women in their productive years. In other words, modernization took place without housewifization (at least until very recently). The childcare network structure in Thailand fundamentally sustains a pattern of relying on relatives and domestic workers, although some of the domestic workers, formerly nearly all from Thailand, now come from foreign countries. By contrast, women's labor-force participation rates in China, Singapore, and Taiwan have actually risen with modernization. In China and Singapore, in particular, state policies designed to effectively utilize the female labor force have been very effective. In these societies, modernization brought about not housewifization but de-housewifization, the effects of which continue today. The childcare facilities built according to national policy in China and Singapore led to major changes in the structure of the childcare network. The hypothesis of the U-curve pattern of women's employment, which says that economic development first "housewifes" women, then "de-housewifes" them, is an oversimplification of the situation in East Asian and Southeast Asian societies.

This study also brought some unexpected results: namely, that even in Type 1 and 2 societies, where childcare networks are well developed, we encountered a considerable number of housewives. We have already mentioned the cases in Thailand of women becoming housewives against their will due to a lack of childcare facilities. Even in China, it is said that due to reasons like unemployment, 20% of women in their forties living in housing complexes are full-time housewives. Furthermore, though their numbers are smaller, in several societies women become housewives of their own accord in order to manage their children's education or for other reasons. Some of the phenomena diverged from our hypothesis that the structure of the childcare network determines the pattern of women's life course. To the contrary, it was a change in gender role norms that led to such structural changes as the loss of the previously available option of using a foster parent in

Singapore and the viewing of the use of domestic workers for childcare as undesirable. Such phenomena suggest that in some cases the process works in the opposite direction: changes in the value system can change the structure of social networks.

"Housewifization" is still considered a minor phenomenon by researchers of the various countries covered in this study; very little research has been done, and quantitative comparison is difficult. More consideration must be given to defining the difference between house-wives and unemployed persons and determining the effect of class differences. However, the following general tendencies can be observed. Housewifization is a very limited phenomenon in China. In Thailand, it is also limited but is progressing at an unexpected rate. In Singapore, the effects of both rising labor-force participation rates for all age groups and a trend towards leaving work in mid-career seem to be vying with each other.

The mechanism for housewifization seems to share common features regardless of region. We will deal with this phenomenon further in Chapter 8.

* This chapter is based on Ochiai, Yamane, Miyasaka, Zhou, Onode, Kiwaki, Fujita and Hong (2004) and the concluding chapter of Ochiai, Yamane and Miyasaka eds. (2007).

NOTES

1 Sechiyama Kaku mentions that the relatively early drop in female labor-force participation rate among the older group is "one of the distinctive features of the areas with Chinese tradition" and is common to the People's Republic of China, Taiwan, Singapore, and Hong Kong (Sechiyama 1996: 264).

2 "Handling of Childbirth Insurance" http://www.harbor.com.cn/csi7/csi7.htm

3 The fact that migration between cities and between urban and rural areas is restricted due to the household registration system may be the key contributing factor in maintaining high-density kin networks in urban areas (Zheng 2003: 91).

4 In Jiangnan area, including the investigation area, the custom of men marrying into the wife's family exists. Jiangnan is stereotyped as a region with strong women, as men often do cooking and housework. However, because the importance of bilateral networks in Chinese society has also been reported in a study of the country's northeast region (Shutō 2003: 181–2), information here does not necessarily reflect regional characteristics.

5 "More and More Women are Becoming Full-time Mothers in Guangzhou," *Beijing Evening News*, November 4, 2002; "One-Child Policy at a Crossroads," *Asahi Shimbun*, November 29, 2003.

6 From interview in Beijing (July 2004) by Zhou and Ochiai.

7 From interview in Beijing (May 2004) by Miyasaka.

8 "Family circle" refers to the ways in which the family sphere, with Ego at the center, either expands or contracts depending on circumstances, and "family" is not a group with definite boundaries but a network. It is a concept used by Japanese researchers with respect to families in Southeast Asia (see Tsubouchi and Maeda 1977).

9   This concept was created by anthropologist Mizuno Kōichi (Mizuno 1981). It is a form of residence common in Thai villages in which households of mainly female relatives – i.e. household of mother, daughter, sisters, etc. – cluster together in the compound.

10 As shown by Ueno Kayoko in Chapter 7.

11 In the case of Taiwan, this statement might best be limited to the case of working couples.

3

A Comparative Study of Childcare and Motherhood in South Korea and Japan

YAMANE MARI, HONG SANG OOK

INTRODUCTION

South Korea and Japan exhibit a number of similarities in their definitions of gender roles and gender norms. In both societies, modern gender-based divisions of labor and an M-curve pattern of women's labor-force participation emerged with industrialization. In addition, the M-curve pattern, as well as strongly held norms regarding motherhood, have persisted in both societies even though gender equality has been on the political agenda since the 1980s. At the same time, however, modernization has produced significant gender role differences, particularly in the area of "motherhood." Numerous Japanese social historians since the 1980s have shown that motherhood – the rearing of children by their mothers – did not have the social value in early modern Japan that it would gain after industrialization. For example, within the samurai class of the Tokugawa era (1603–1868), fathers played a significant role in the education of their children (Ohta 1994). Children of the peasant class were brought up within broad social networks that included parents, grandparents, nursemaids, and local children's groups. Mothers were only one part of this network of childrearing agents, and the norms emphasizing motherhood had not yet developed (Miyamoto 1967). A large body of scholarship in social history contends that the assignment of value to motherhood, especially the stress on the emotional attachment of mother and child during the child's infancy and early childhood years, is a "modern" invention (Wakita, ed. 1985).

Compared to the case of Japan (as well as northwestern Europe and the United States), where the construction of motherhood was greatly altered by industrialization, contemporary notions of motherhood in South Korea have two dimensions: the principles of patrilineality and Confucianism rooted in the Choson period (1392–1910) and a modern sense of motherhood grounded in a gendered division of labor between the workplace and home. Women were valued in the premodern era when they bore sons as heirs to the headship of their *jip* (house and patrilineal line) and contributed to the social success of their husbands and sons through housework and childrearing. Indeed, rearing a successful son was a mother's only means of receiving public praise. Building upon these premodern norms of motherhood, Korean motherhood has, nevertheless, changed through the introduction of the Western and Japanese-influenced concept of *hyeonmo yangcheo juui* (principle of good wife, wise mother) during the precolonial and colonial period of the late-nineteenth and early-twentieth centuries (Sechiyama 1996), the development of a gender division of labor accompanying the rise of an urban middle class, and the stress on "scientific" motherhood following the period of rapid economic development (Lee 1999). Motherhood in Korea, unlike motherhood in Japan, where maternalism emerged alongside modernization, should thus be regarded in the dual context of premodernity and modernity.

The differing historical trajectories of motherhood in Japan and Korea affect the present situation of motherhood in those societies. Although Japan and Korea are often considered similar in terms of gender-related normative structures, there appear to be important differences between them concerning childrearing. For example, anxiety about early childhood care, which has been described as a structural social problem in Japan, is not viewed as a common problem in South Korea. South Korean mothers' "educational fever" – that is, their enthusiastic devotion to their children's success in educational competition – is not as evident among Japanese mothers. Another significant difference is in the attitude towards son preference. Son preference is not common in Japan but has increased in importance in Korea as the birthrate has declined since the 1970s.

The data suggest both commonalities and differences regarding childcare in these two societies characterized by M-curve patterns of women's labor force participation. This chapter will also consider possibilities for change as each society experiences a rise in the age of first marriage and an increase in rates of divorce and re-marriage.

DATA

This chapter is based on the findings of three studies:

Research Study A: South Korea[1]

    Area: Busan and surrounding areas (Yangsan), Daegu and surrounding areas (Gyongsan). Method: Semi-structured interviews with households that included young children or elderly members (forty-two cases total): August 2002 and 2003

    Object of analysis: nineteen mothers with young children

Research Study B: South Korea[2]
Area: Daegu city
Method: Questionnaire survey
Respondents: Parents of elementary, junior high, and high school students (725 cases for mothers, 640 cases for fathers)
Object of analysis: 334 mothers with young children

Research Study C: Japan[3]
Area: Nara City
Method: Questionnaire survey
Respondents: Parents with young children (343 cases for mothers; 270 cases for fathers).

HISTORICAL CHANGES IN HOUSEHOLDS, FERTILITY, AND FEMALE LABOR-FORCE PARTICIPATION

The number of extended family households declined in both Korea and Japan with industrialization. The revision of Japan's family law after World War II underscored the significance of the nuclear family, allowing the ratio of nuclear families to increase during the postwar period of rapid economic growth (see Table 3.1).

In contrast, the increased ratio of nuclear families was not tied to a change in national family policy in South Korea. The patrilineal family was embedded in South Korea's official family ideology between the Korean War and the 1990s, when that ideological position began to be revised. The ratio of nuclear families increased during those years, and this pattern has continued with industrialization (see Table 3.2). Few parents in either society share living quarters with either their own or their spouse's parents to whom they can turn for childcare assistance.

Table 3.1 Household Transition in Japan

						Households composed of relatives		
			Nuclear family					
	Total	Total	Couple	Couple and child(ren)	Father or Mother and child(ren)	Households including other relatives	Households composed of non relatives	Single-person households
1960	83.6	53.0	7.3	38.2	7.5	30.5	0.3	16.1
1970	79.4	56.7	9.8	41.2	5.7	22.7	0.3	20.3
1980	80.0	60.3	12.5	42.1	5.7	19.7	0.2	19.8
1990	76.7	59.5	15.5	37.3	6.7	17.2	0.2	23.1
2000	72.0	58.4	18.9	31.9	7.7	13.6	0.4	27.6

Source: Statistics Bureau, *Population Census of Japan*

Note: Extended family is included in "Households composed of relatives."

Table 3.2 Household Transition in South Korea

	Nuclear family			Extended family		
	Couple	Couple and child(ren)	Father or mother and child(ren)	Couple and parent(s)	Couple parent(s) and child(ren)	Other
1970	5.4	55.5	10.6	1.4	17.4	9.7
1980	6.4	56.5	10.0	0.6	10.4	16.1
1990	9.3	58.0	8.7	0.9	9.3	13.8
2000	14.8	57.8	9.4	1.2	6.8	10.1

Source: Korea National Statistical Office, *Social Indicators in Korea*

Table 3.3 Fertility Transition in Japan

	TFR	Sex ratios at birth
1950	3.65	106.1
1960	2.00	105.6
1970	2.13	107.1
1980	1.75	106.0
1990	1.54	105.4
2000	1.36	105.8
2005	1.26	105.3

Source: Ministry of Health, Welfare and Labor, *Vital Statistics of Japan*

Table 3.4 Fertility Transition in South Korea

	TFR	Sex ratios at birth
1970	4.53	109.5
1980	2.90	105.3
1990	1.59	116.5
2000	1.47	110.2
2005	1.08	107.7

Source: Korea National Statistical Office, www.nso.go.kr

Fertility transitions have occurred in both societies. These transitions are contingent on the historical periods in which fertility rates began to decline and the relative influence of kinship systems in the premodern period (see Table 3.3 and Table 3.4). In Japan, fertility decline occurred in two phases: an initial rapid decline in the 1950s as a result of the implementation of family planning policies after World War II, and a second decline in the latter half of the 1970s when the Total Fertility Rate (TFR) dropped below the replacement level of 2.1 births per woman. Between these two phases – a period of rapid economic growth in Japan – the

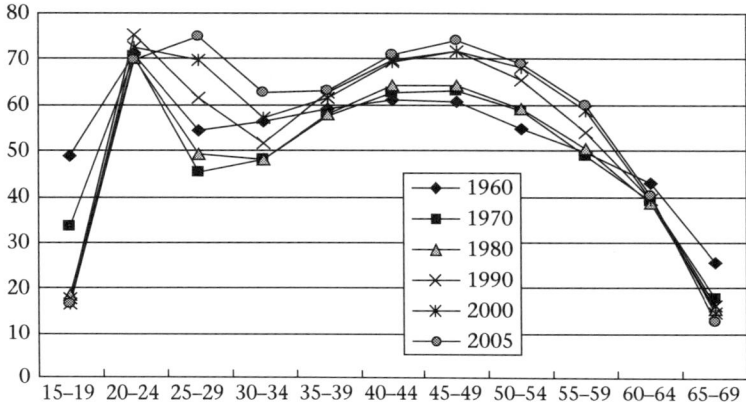

Figure 3.1   Female labor force participation rate by age in Japan
Source: Statistics Bureau, *Labor Force Statistics*

fertility rate was rather stable, remaining slightly above the replacement level. As the two-sibling generation born in the 1950s became parents during the latter half of the 1970s, they could not expect the same amount of abundant support from kinship networks as earlier generations could.

In South Korea, although a family planning policy was instituted in the early 1960s, the TFR remained 4.53 in 1970. Between the 1970s and the 1980s, a rapid decline in fertility occurred, and the TFR dropped below the replacement level in 1984. Because South Korea's fertility decline began twenty years after that of Japan, parents currently raising children are still in a "demographic dividend" generation, and thus are able to get assistance from their relatives.

Son preference also played a role in the decline in fertility rates in South Korea. In the 1980s, the imbalance of sex ratios at birth, especially for the third child, expanded along with a rapid decline in fertility. Differences between the basic kinship systems that predated both countries' modernization may have contributed to the differences in the sex ratios at birth observed in Japan and Korea. In South Korea, the patrilineal kinship system formed during the latter part of the Choson period emphasized primogeniture and maintenance of the family through the male line. The Japanese *ie*, on the other hand, was not a unilineal system. Developed during the Tokugawa Period, the *ie* system allowed for many variations in inheritance, including the succession of the first child of either gender (*ane-katoku*) as well as the last son (*basshi-sōzoku*). The adoption of non-kin also distinguished the Japanese *ie* from Korea's patriarchal, unilineal kinship system.

Another significant transition has been in female labor force participation rates. In Japan, housewifization and the emergence of an M-curve pattern accompanied rapid economic development between the latter

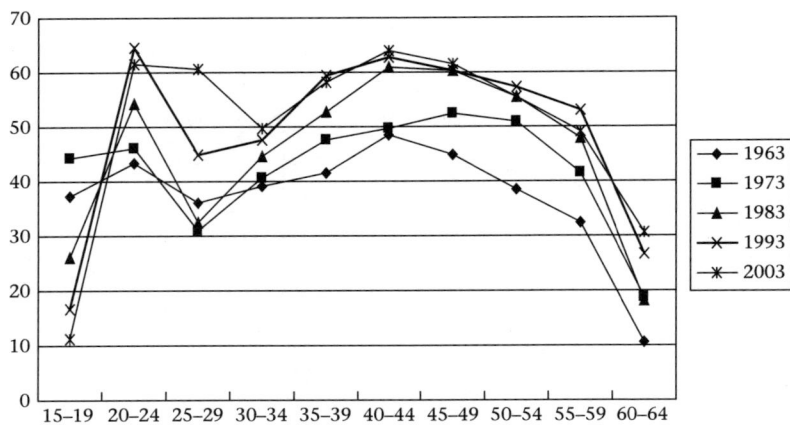

Figure 3.2   Female labor lorce participation rate by age in South Korea
Source: National Statistics Office, *Economically Active Participation Survey*

half of the 1950s and the beginning of the 1970s. Figure 3.1 shows that
overall labor force participation rates tended to be rather high in the
1960s, constituting more than 50 percent of women in their twenties to
fifties, despite the development of an M-curve for women between the
ages of 25 and 35.

South Korean female labor-force participation rates do not indicate a
similarly clear process of housewifization. Participation was relatively
low in 1963 (Figure 3.2). As participation rates rose in the 1960s and
1970s, an M-curve pattern began to emerge. According to Park's analysis
of the Korean Women's Development Institute data, an M-type life
course pattern[4] became dominant among cohorts of women married
after the 1980s. There has been a decline among recent marriage cohorts
of two categories: women who took their first job only after completing
their role as mothers and women with no work experience (see Table 3.5)
(Park 2004; Park and Yamane 2007).

WOMEN'S LIFE COURSE AND THE STRUCTURE OF GENDERED NORMS

The data collected in Nara indicated that 79.2 percent of mothers with
young children are housewives. The largest percentage of women who
work outside the home, 7.2 percent, are full-time teachers or civil sector
employees, followed by the self-employed (4.2 percent), part-time
company employees (3.7 percent), full-time company employees (3.4
percent), part-time teachers or civil sector employees (1.1 percent), and
others (2.3 percent).

Among those who quit work following marriage or childbirth, 44.4
percent retired at the time of marriage, 31.2 percent retired before the
birth of their first child, 4.7 percent retired between the birth of their first

Table 3.5 Women's Life Course Patterns by Marriage Cohort (%)

	Period of Marriage				
	<=1969	*1970– 1979*	*1980– 1989*	*1990– 1994*	*>=1995*
Simultaneously performing family and work roles	23.3	14.0	8.4	12.7	10.9
M-type	6.7	19.3	28.4	22.5	11.3
Latent M-type *	5.6	11.5	24.4	46.4	68.4
First job entry after child rearing	35.4	34.0	24.1	9.6	2.8
Family centered without work experience	29.0	21.2	14.8	8.8	6.6
Total	100.0	100.0	100.0	100.0	100.0

* Latent M-type means no re-entry into the labor market after maternity leave.
Source: Park (2004)

and second child, and 0.9 percent retired between the birth of their second and third child ("other," 2.6 percent; "don't know," 16.2 percent). The major reasons given for retirement included: "I wanted to concentrate on raising children" (28.8 percent); "I wanted to quit the job anyway"(19.7 percent); "I wanted to continue, but the company was not supportive of working mothers" (6.2 percent); and "I wanted to continue, but it was the norm for pregnant women to quit at my workplace"(4.7 percent). When those who were not currently employed were asked if they intended to go back to work in the future, 57.6 percent answered that they were "planning to work part time;" 7.9 percent answered that they were "not planning to get a job;" 7.6 percent answered that they were "planning to work at home;" and 5.6 percent of mothers answered that they were "planning to work full time" ("other," 4.4 percent; "don't know," 16.8 percent). Nara mothers' consciousness is evident in this data; the M-curve life course, which entails quitting one's job following marriage or childbirth and re-entering the workplace later as a part-time worker, is a common pattern (Kiwaki, ed. 2003: 107–108).

The Daegu-Busan interview data indicated three major types of life course patterns among our nineteen informants, all of whom were in the childrearing stage of their lives: (1) the continuous work type, i.e. mothers who continued to work following marriage and childbirth (five mothers); (2) the M-curve type (eight mothers); and (3) the interrupted-career type, i.e. mothers who withdrew from the workplace and did not reenter it (five mothers). The five mothers in the continuous work type fell into two distinct groups: women in female-dominated professional occupations such as teaching and nursing who worked both to support their families and to advance their personal career goals; and women who worked solely to make a living and did not see their employment as part of a larger career plan. The major reasons for a mother of the M-curve type to quit work were marriage and pregnancy/childbirth. The first occasion for her to re-enter the work force was typically when her child was around five years old; others did so when their children were around ten years old. The reasons for reentry into the workplace included: a decreased need for mothers to spend time in childcare as their children grew; self-realization or the establishment of self-identity; and economic concerns. The typical pattern for re-employment of mothers with young children at home was to work in a style that was easy to coordinate with family life, such as working part-time or being self-employed. Among the five mothers who did not have a job at the time of the study and wanted to work in the future, only one wanted to have full-time work while the other four wished to work part-time or be self-employed (Yamane 2004: 27; Yamane 2005: 83–4; Yamane and Hong 2007: 37).

As noted above, our data show that the M-shape life course is maintained in both societies. In addition, women in both societies who seek to reenter the work force usually chose a work style that is easy to coordinate with family life. The two differ in one important way – women in South Korea are more likely to chose self-employment as a re-entry work style. In South Korea, a society less corporate-based than Japan, self-employment continues to be a significant representative work style for men as well. This work style may allow childcare networks made up of relatives to be more common in South Korea than in Japan.

GENDER NORMS

Gender norms play an important role in the reproduction of the M-curve life course pattern in both societies. But mothers' attitudes toward these norms differ significantly in the two countries.

Among Nara respondents, 77.5 percent of mothers disagreed with the statement that "a husband should work outside the home, while a wife should stay at home and concentrate on housework." Also, more than half of these mothers – 56.8 percent – agreed with the importance of a "husband's equal participation in housework and childcare." At the same time, however, 62.3 percent of mothers agreed that "a woman should take care of housework and childrearing tidily even if she has her own job," and 64.5 percent of mothers agreed that "a mother is responsible for raising her children." Thus, although gender norms concerning the division of labor between the public and domestic spheres have significantly changed and norms concerning men's new roles have, to some extent, stabilized, previous norms regarding women's roles with respect to housework and motherhood persist (Table 3.6).

The Daegu data collected in 1998 contrast with the Nara data. In Daegu, most mothers agreed with all three questions regarding a gender-based division of labor: 70.6 percent of mothers with young children agreed with a "gender-based division of labor for the public/domestic spheres;" 80.2 percent agreed that was the "women's role to attend to

Table 3.6 Gender Norms (Nara data 2001, Japan) (%)

	N	Agree	Agree somewhat	Disagree somewhat	Disagree
A husband should work outside the home, while a wife should concentrate on housework	338	3.6	18.9	45.3	32.2
A woman should do housework and childrearing tidily even if she has her own job	338	19.2	43.1	29.5	8.3
A husband should participate equally in housework and childcare	338	17.1	39.7	34.2	6.7
A mother should be blamed for undisciplined children	338	16.9	47.6	23.7	11.8

Table 3.7 Gender Norms (Daegu data 1998, South Korea) (%)

	N	Agree	Agree somewhat	Disagree somewhat	Disagree
A husband should work outside the home, while a wife should concentrate on housework	334	39.2	31.4	23.7	5.7
A woman should do housework and childrearing tidily even if she has her own job	334	48.5	31.7	13.5	6.3
A husband should participate equally in housework and childcare	334	23.7	43.1	24.5	8.7
Whether a child is well brought up or not is up to his/her mother	334	26.3	41.6	19.2	12.8

Note: Only mothers with young children were selected for analysis.

housework and childcare;" and 67.9 percent agreed that mothers had a "responsibility for children." On the other hand, 66.8 percent of mothers agreed that the "husband's equal participation in housework and child-care" was desirable (Table 3.7).

Common to both societies is the coexistence of norms underscoring the difference between genders, on the one hand, and those supporting gender equality, on the other. Men's new roles in housework and child-

Table 3.8 Norms Related to Motherhood by Educational Background (Daegu data, 1998)
Statement: "The quality of a child's upbringing is determined by his/her mother"

Educational background	Agree	Disagree	Total(N)
Junior High School or less	51.1	48.9	100.0(45)
High School	68.1	31.9	100.0(138)
Junior College or more	73.3	26.7	100.0(146)
Total sample	68.1	31.9	100.0(329)

P<.05

Table 3.9 Norms Relating to Individuation—by Educational Background (Daegu data, 1998)
Statement: "I want to have my own world even if I somewhat neglect housework."

Educational background	Agree	Disagree	Total(N)
Junior High School or less	42.2	57.8	100.0(45)
High School	59.1	40.9	100.0(137)
Junior College or more	64.4	35.6	100.0(146)
Total sample	59.1	41.9	100.0(328)

P<.05

care seem to have acquired legitimacy, at least on an ideal level, though there is much discrepancy between the ideal and reality. Although the notion of a gendered division of labor between the public and domestic spheres has lost legitimacy to some extent in Japan, it still seems to be a legitimate norm in South Korea. Norms regarding motherhood as well as housework persist among women in both societies, with little discrepancy between ideals and reality.

Cross-referencing views concerning gender norms with mothers' academic background reveals an interesting difference between the Nara and Daegu respondents. Academic background does not appear to affect Nara mothers' views relating to gender norms, while it does produce significant differences in Daegu mothers' views. Mothers with higher levels of academic achievement tend to accept norms related to motherhood. The gap between junior high school graduates and high school graduates is particularly noteworthy (Table 3.8).

In the Daegu data, women's levels of consciousness relating to their self-realization and their ability to carry out their individual interests also vary significantly by academic background. Mothers with higher educational backgrounds tend to agree with the statement, "I want to have my own world even if I somewhat neglect housework."[5]

More highly educated Korean women appear to suffer from a "superwoman syndrome" that takes the form of a conflict between motherhood and self-realization because of their need to pursue individualization while being bound by strong norms related to motherhood.

Women's desire to pursue their own interests, together with the cultural value accorded to higher education, encourages the development of "educational fever" in South Korea. The Busan-Daegu interviews revealed that there are abundant educational resources for children aged three and over. Kindergarten and *eorini jip* (children's houses or daycare facilities) offer a variety of educational programs. There are also some *hagwon* (academies) for children aged three years or older, offering lessons in music, art, private learning, and so forth (Kobayashi 2004). Each of the informants spent approximately 400,000 won to 1 million won each month on childcare and educational services. The role of mothers shifts from a caregiving role to a management role when their children become old enough to begin educational training. Since the late 1990s, an increasing number of mothers have taken their children to Canada or the United States to study English. This "educational emigration," which is part of the process of globalization, underscores the substantial role of mothers as their children's education managers. The following case is a good example of a mother's extreme management role.

Case C, a housewife and mother of a six-year-old son living in Busan, graduated from a top-ranking university in Seoul and worked full-time at an insurance company in Seoul after giving birth. She quit her job because her husband decided to change companies and move to Busan after the Asian economic crisis began. C then decided to pursue graduate studies in education to learn educational methods for her only son. She spends one million won for her son's education. Despite the fact that she is an eager manager of his education, she does not seem to attach importance to being a good housewife. She hires a maid because she does not like housework. She hopes to go to Canada with her son in the future if the opportunity arises.

CHILDCARE NETWORKS

What kinds of childcare networks are built by housewives and working mothers in the two societies? In Nara, the childcare networks able to offer substantial support in circumstances such as a mother's illness were limited to the children's father or grandparents on either side, with childcare support more likely to come from the maternal grandparents (Table 3.10).

According to Yamato's analysis of childcare support network patterns by the mother's occupation, networks used by housewives and full-time working mothers differ.[6] First, on a substantive level, full-time working mothers receive a large amount of support from their parents and from nursery school. Second, on an emotional level, housewives' support networks are restricted to informal resources such as family, relatives, neighbors, and friends, while support networks for full-time working mothers include not only informal resources but also formal ones like the workplace and nursery school. Third, there are differences in the way the two

Table 3.10 Support Networks in Nara Data (Substantial level of support)

	Fulltime working mothers (n=35)	Housewife(N=262)
Husband	60.0	64.9
Husband's parent(s)	17.1	32.4
Husband's relative	2.9	0.8
Wife's parent(s)	71.4	60.7
Wife's relative	8.6	4.2
Neighbor	0.0	4.2
Friend	0.0	5.7
Institution	11.4	0.8
Babysitter, day-care center	0.0	0.8
Workplace	0.0	0.0
Other	2.9	0.4
No support network	0.0	1.9

categories of women use these childcare services. Most full-time working mothers use nursery schools, while housewives are split into two types – users of childcare services and those who never use them. Whether a mother uses a childcare service or not often depends on her husband's income. This means that a housewife whose husband's income is low has little opportunity to separate herself from her child. The rate for using a "family-support center," a childcare aid project that the government has put a great deal effort into establishing in recent years, makes up only 0.4 percent of the total. Because of this network structure, housewives who live apart from their parents and who cannot rely on support from their husbands have no choice but to care for their children alone and unaided (Yamato 2003: 8–29). Though it has been almost twenty years since the isolation of mothers was pointed out as a cause of child-rearing anxiety (Makino 1988, Yamane 2000), this structure continues today.

Table 3.11 shows the childcare networks used by twelve mothers with children under school age that appear in the Daegu-Busan data. As was the case in Nara, the major sources of substantial support were husbands and parents. Mothers tended to have a wider variety of support resources such as relatives, friends, and neighbors. As for support on both the emotional and informational level, support resources in Daegu tended to expand further than in Nara, and included friends and neighbors. Among the twelve cases, the phenomenon of "mother's isolation and childcare anxiety," viewed as a serious social problem in Japan since the 1980s, did not appear. Rather, we met women who actively tried to create social networks with other mothers. For example, we met a housewife who moved only a few months before who had already created a network with another housewife living in the same apartment building. She told us, "*Agi chingu ga eomma chingu* ("A mother will make friends with other mothers if their children make friends with one another"). Support from relatives comes from either the husband's or the wife's side, and when

Table 3.11 Childcare Networks in Daegu-Busan Data (Substantial level of support)*

	Case	Husband	Wife's mother	Husband's mother	Wife's relative	Husband's relative	Neighbor or Friend	Institution
Single income	C	■	■				■	
	J	■	■				■	
	L			■				
	N			■				
	A	■		■				
	B	■		■		■		
	E	■		■				
Double income	K	■	■					
	M						■	
	O	■			■		■	
	P				■		■	
Single mother	I							■

Note: Twelve mothers with children who were younger than school age were selected for analysis.

parents receive support from both, it is assistance from the mother's side that plays the more important role.

Unlike Japan, there is little difference between housewives and working mothers in South Korea in their use of childcare services. One reason for this is that access to childcare facilities is not differentiated by a mother's occupational status in South Korea. Looking at our twelve cases, we discovered a substantial support network of housewives and working mothers whose children went to the same kindergarten. The other reason for this seems to lie in the higher value of education in South Korea. Regardless of income level, parents of children aged three and older select some kind of educational services from a variety of choices.

The pattern of childcare networks for full-time working mothers differs from that of other mothers. In the cases of housewives, part-time workers, and self-employed mothers, childcare and substantial support are limited to support alone, because those wives and mothers undertake a major role in housework. When a mother decides to work full-time, however, the daily burdens that must be shared among the mother, father, and their relatives go beyond mere childcare "support."

An examination of some examples of full-time working mothers is informative. In one case, we see a mother's complete dependence on her own mother. Case A, who works as an elementary school teacher, has a nuclear family of three: she is married to a corporate research worker and they have a six-year-old daughter. She has worked as an elementary school teacher since graduating from college. Although her husband helps out greatly in terms of housework and childcare, her everyday life would not work without the help of her mother living nearby. Her daughter lived at the house of her grandparents until she was three years old. The family eats breakfast separately – the husband at his workplace, the wife at home, and the daughter at the grandparents' house. At dinner, the wife and her daughter eat a meal prepared by Case A's mother at the grandparents' house, while the husband eats at his workplace. Case A's mother is asked to drop off and pick up the daughter from kindergarten, and she also looks after the daughter after 5 p.m. Case A pays her mother 300,000 won a month in return for such help and care.

The second example is a case in which the husband participates equally in housework and childcare. Case O, living with her husband and two children, has realized an equal division of labor with her husband. After the husband changed companies because of the Asian economic crisis, the wife re-entered the workplace as a full-time worker when her second child was two-years old. She shares housework equally and flexibly with her husband. Because the husband takes a stronger role than his wife in childcare, the children would rather spend their time with their father. A new type of father, a "kind father taking care of his children," is emerging (Yamane 2005: 86–91).

CONCLUSION

Although there are many similarities between these two East Asian M-curve societies, there are differences in the nature of the "childcare problem" and the social strata that embody this problem. In Japan, strong norms regarding motherhood and housework continue to influence women's life courses. "Mother's isolation and childcare anxiety" have remained concerns since the Japanese "childcare problem" was first discussed in the 1980s. Housewives whose husbands' incomes are relatively low are most affected by these problems.

In South Korea, there are two manifestations of a "childcare problem." One is the instability of a woman's life course due to the desire for her to bear a son, based on the patrilineal principle. The other lies in the structure of gender-based norms, according to which mothers are torn between the norm of motherhood and the desire for self-realization. The social stratum that embodies this problem – what we call the "super-woman syndrome" – is that of mothers with higher levels of education. When we observed mothers' child rearing networks, we noted that mothers have a number of support networks. Childcare problems did not take the form of the "isolation and childrearing anxiety of the housewife" common in Japan.

How can each society's "childcare problem" be resolved? One possibility for Japan lies in the emergence of "new men" who are different from the "work-oriented men" of the last few decades. In our study of the Nara data, we saw that there was a strong tendency for family-oriented husbands to perform more housework and childcare (Onode 2003: 38–47). In light of this finding, there is a possibility that a husband's participation in childcare could increase under the proper working conditions. The second way to address the issue of childcare lies in developing the local childcare networking system including non-profit organizations that play an active part in the care of the nation's children. Although there are various childcare networks that receive support from the government, most of them remain housewife-centered activities. If non-profit childcare networks succeed in offering places for housewives, working mothers, and men to meet each other, they may help to solve the structural "childcare problem" in Japan.

In South Korea, the potential to change the structure of gender norms that cause the "super-woman syndrome" seems to be based on a new division of labor in childcare among full-time working mothers. In our interview data from Busan and Daegu, we encountered a few cases in which the women involved attained a level of equal participation in childcare with their husbands or relied heavily on the mother's parents. The Asian economic crisis and the demand for self-realization were seen as motivations for women to reenter the workplace as full-time workers. The structure of gender norms may change along with the substantial changes occurring in the area of gender-based divisions of labor.

One important issue for future considerations of this problem is whether or not the phenomenon of "mother's isolation and childrearing anxiety" will emerge in South Korea in the generation following the current demographic dividend generation. South Korea's transformation process is likely to be different from Japan's, however, since different socio-cultural factors are in play, including strong relationships between relatives based on a unilineal kinship system, the fact that access to childcare facilities is not dependent on the mother's occupation, and the relative ease with which childcare networks can be formed regardless of how upwardly mobile the mother happens to be. Considering these factors, South Korea's demographic transition may not result in social problems like the "childrearing anxiety" felt by mothers in Japan, at least not on a society-wide level. Nevertheless, it should be kept in mind that a demographic transition may result in a reduction of the labor force available for childcare in each household in the near future.[7] As South Koreans are not reluctant to hire domestic workers, an increasing number may employ such workers, thereby introducing a new pattern of housework and childcare.[8]

NOTES

[1] This research was conducted as a part of an international joint project under the title of "A Comparative Study on Gender in Asian Societies" in six societies of East and Southeast Asia. Members included Miyasaka Yasuko (project leader), Ueno Kayoko, Emiko Ochiai, Onode Setsuko, Kiwaki Nachiko, Kobayashi Kazumi, Hashimoto (Seki) Hiroko, Fujii Wasa, Fujita Michiyo, Yamato Reiko, Yamane Mari, Hong Sang Ook, Kua Wongboonsin, Park Keong-Suk, and Zhou Weihong. For details, see Miyasaka, ed. (2004), Ochiai, Yamane et al. (2004), and Ochiai, Yamane and Miyasaka, eds. (2007).

[2] This research was conducted in 1997–1999 as part of a project under the title of "A Comparative Study of Village Structure in Japan and Korea," supported by Grants-in-Aid for Scientific Research. The project leader was Kitahara Atsushi. Among the three surveys conducted during this project, the survey on the family was conducted by Yamane Mari and Hong Sang Ook. For details, see Kitahara, ed. (2000).

[3] This research was conducted in 2001–2002 as a project under the title of "Investigative research on gender relations and networks related to childcare," supported by Grants-in-Aid for Scientific Research. The members involved were Kiwaki Nachiko (project leader), Fuyuki Haruko, Miyasaka Yasuko, Nakatani Natsuko, Onode Setsuko, Yamato Reiko, and Yamane Mari. For details, see Kiwaki, ed. (2003). Nara has the highest proportion of housewives among Japanese cities.

[4] This includes the so-called "latent" M-curve pattern, which refers to women who have left the workforce due to marriage or childbirth with the intention of rejoining it later, though they have not yet done so.

[5] We do not have the same or correspondent variable in the Nara survey.

6   Since the number of self-employed and part-time employed mothers is small, this analysis focuses on the difference between housewives and full-time working wives.

7   We may see ominous precursors of the phenomenon even now in the fact that more mothers are asking for postpartum care through the *Sanhu joriwon* (a facility where mothers are given postpartum care) or the fact that double-income nuclear families living apart from their parents on both sides often hire maids to do household chores.

8   We should also point out that there is a discussion to ask for socialization of childcare as social policy asserting that the private sector is not enough to cover the demands of families bringing up infants and young children (Im 2003).

4

Korean Women's Life Courses and Self Perceptions: Isomorphism of "Family Centeredness"

PARK KEONG-SUK

INTRODUCTION

Korean women's family lives and economic activities have changed radically during the past four decades. They marry later – by 2004, their average age at marriage was 27.6, an increase from 23.3 in 1970 and 26.5 in 2000 (KNSO, 2005) – and have fewer children – their Total Fertility Rate (TFR) had plummeted to 1.16 children in 2004. Married couples' residential arrangements have also been undergoing change. Despite their low fertility rate, Korean mothers value their roles as parents, making great efforts to support their children's education, even at the cost of close bonds with their husbands. Thus, in order to prevent disruption in their children's education, many married couples live apart from one another during the work week or for even longer periods of time if a parent is transferred at work. Women's relationships with their parents and parents-in-law have also changed in recent decades. These relationships, which are an important component of Korean women's family and economic activities, are based on increasingly diverse patterns of intergenerational support. While the majority of newly married women and their husbands establish their own living arrangements, others take responsibility for caring for their elderly parents and, in some cases, provide substantial support for them. The converse has also become common; that is, many working mothers receive assistance from their parents or parents-in-law.

Korean women's economic activities have also been marked by great change in recent decades. Women's labor-force participation rate increased from 42.8 percent in 1980 to 50.2 percent in 2005. The age pattern of economic participation at the aggregate level indicates that women in their late twenties and early thirties – the period of women's lowest economic participation – are nevertheless more involved in economic activities than older cohorts had been. Scholars continue to debate, however, whether the rise in aggregate employment levels of women in their late twenties and early thirties reflects an increase in women balancing careers with their family roles. Although numerous studies have investigated the complex changes in contemporary Korean women's lives, important questions remain unanswered. In particular, many recent works have described Korean women's difficulties in balancing family roles and economic activities, but they fail to specify in detail the changes in women's perceptions about conflicts between family and economic activities.

This chapter analyzes empirically-grounded data to explicate the changes in Korean women's lives. It examines women's own interpretations and understandings of family roles and market labor to uncover the structural distinctiveness of gender relations in Korean society. The meaning of family roles and economic activities is not just the representation of social norms internalized; it is also the externalization of women's self-experiences over their life course. Inquiry into the ways women interpret their family and economic activities and the ways these meanings are related to collective cultural systems in Korean society provides important keys to understanding the distinctive structural-behavioral interplay in the formation of gender identity in Korea.

This study employs a life course analysis to discover the characteristic patterns of women's family and economic activities and to articulate the ways that women themselves interpret their lives. Using a nationally representative data set, it examines the sequential patterns of family roles and economic activities over the course of women's lives. In addition, it analyzes in depth interviews with Korean women residing in the Busan area to trace the interplay of meanings surrounding women's family and economic activities.

ARE KOREAN WOMEN'S FAMILY-CENTERED ATTITUDES DIMINISHING?

Contemporary Korean policy-makers and demographers contend that the very low fertility rate and the consequent rapid aging of the population are driven by women's decisions and actions. Many argue that delayed marriage – and the resulting decline in fertility – derive from Korean women's collective resistance against a society characterized by gender discrimination (Kim et al. 2000; Cho et al. 1997). Emphasizing the impact of social development, some also argue that Korean women's increasing aspiration for social participation challenges the prevailing social system divided by gender (Park 1999). Some scholars employ the rational choice model developed by Becker (1981) to suggest that Korean women's rational considerations for their own or their family's interests motivate their family roles and economic activities (Kim 2000). Some scholars add that many single young women, believing they will feel burdened by their family roles once they are married, delay assuming those roles until they find the ideal spouse. In these cases, very low fertility is regarded as the result of women's avoidance of responsibility for family-building. These perspectives emphasize the strong influences of individualization, growing autonomy, and increasing economic participation on Korean women's status in the family and labor market. They assert that women's expanded economic participation and individualized attitudes weaken their appreciation of family roles, accounting for delayed marriage, low fertility, and growth in family dissolution.

Other scholars place less emphasis on individualization, however. Some note that only a small portion of contemporary young women are influenced by economic activity to reject family roles. Many empirical studies of Korean working women also indicate that until the 1980s, female employees held more conservative attitudes about gender role division than did full-time housewives (Lee and Ji 1988; Park Min-Ja 1991; Chung 1991; Kim 2000). Moreover, until the 1980s women with a college education were less likely than women who had attained lower levels of education to have participated in economic activity (Park 1991; Min 2003).

Whether Korean women's autonomy has increased also continues to be debated. Family responsibilities and labor market barriers against women have long deterred their participation in the economy (Chang 2001; Yee 1996; Park 2002; Chung 1996; Nahm 2001; Shin 2001; Han and Chang 2000). The M curve – a dip in economic activity followed by an increase – appears to have flattened out on the aggregate level, leading some to emphasize an increasing trend of married women's building occupational careers with fewer job interruptions (Kim, 2000). Other scholars argue, however, that the apparent flattening of the curve does not reflect a rise in women's continuous employment in careers; rather, they assert, it signals changes in the industrial workforce, including an increasing demand for cheap labor – jobs often filled by married women (Kim and Kim 1996; Kang 2001).

To be sure, many contemporary unmarried young men and women do not hold normative (gendered) attitudes towards marriage. This does not necessarily mean, however, that young singles' lives embody individualism. Many Korean singles are emotionally and materially connected to their parents. Compared to many Western societies, couples' premarital co-residence is still limited in Korea. Ironically, some of the lowest levels of fertility occur in societies that stress family cohesion, such as Korea, Japan, and Italy, rather than in societies that place greater emphasis on the individual. As Billari et al. (2004) have argued, individualism does not, per se, deny the value of reproduction, as reproductive behavior can be part of self-fulfillment.

In sum, it is questionable whether economic participation, individualization, and autonomy are linked to changes in Korean women's family and economic activities. To what extent do those activities reflect changes in Korean women's gender identity and self-perception? This study aims to examine the characteristics and diversities of Korean women's experiences, employing a life course analysis to examine the patterns of family and economic activities and articulate the meanings of those activities for women.

DATA AND METHODS

This study employs both quantitative and qualitative methods. A quantitative approach is used to investigate characteristic patterns of Korean women's family and economic activities over the life course. Drawing on the timing and order of marriage, fertility history, and work history, I analyze the significant changes in life patterns and sequences of family and economic activities during recent decades, using as my dataset *The Fourth Survey of Korean Women's Economic Activity*, conducted by the Korean Women's Development Institute (KWDI) in 2002. The survey's respondents were Korean women between the ages of fifteen and sixty-four. Briefly describing the general characteristics of respondents as shown in Table 4.1, the mean age of respondents was 39. 3 years. Women from agricultural families made up 11 percent of the total sample. Women with high school educations represented 41.5 percent of the

Table 4.1 General Characteristics of Respondents

N	4,722
Mean age (year)	39.3
Agricultural family (%)	11.0
Educational level	
Middle school and below (%)	32.6
High school (%)	41.5
College level and above (%)	26.0
Educational level of husband	
Middle school and below (%)	27.2
High school (%)	40.5
College level and above (%)	32.2
First Marriage	
Marriage rate (%)	74.5
Age at first marriage (year)	24.5
Divorce rate (%)	3.9
Births	
Age at first birth (year)	25.8
Total births	1.6
Total period of births	4.5
Work	
Work experience (%)	73.1
Age at first job (year)	24.7

Source: Korean Women's Development Institute, *The Fourth Survey of Korean Women's Economic Activity*, 2002.

total sample, and those with college or more education 26 percent; 40.5 percent of the men married to the women in the survey had high school educations; 32.2 percent had college or higher levels of education.

I used a qualitative approach to interpret Korean women's experiences in family and economic activities. Employing in-depth interviews with twenty-eight women residents in the Busan metropolitan area in 2002 and 2003, I asked informants to narrate their life stories, including their history of family and economic activities. I took into consideration the informants' social and economic status and ages when selecting them. Interpreting women's narratives is a complex process, integrating life events to construct a whole life story, drawing out the themes women use to interpret their lives, and relating these themes to women's self-identity (see Table 4.2).

PATTERNS AND CHANGES IN WOMEN'S LIFE COURSE

Several distinctive patterns of the life courses of Korean women can be identified in the sequence of their marital history, fertility, and working careers. Excluding pre-adult women who had not yet joined the work-force or formed their own families, I divided respondents into six groups (see Table 4.3). The first category, labeled "work as single," refers to unmarried women with no fertility history who were involved in economic activities. The women in this group, with a mean age of 27.7 at the time of the survey, were younger than those in the other groups. The mean age for acquiring their first job was 22.3, and they had less than one year of interruption in their work history.

The second type, with a mean age of forty-eight, represents ever-married women with no previous job interruptions at the time of the survey. Tracing average tendencies in the timing of their life events, we note that they had their first jobs at age 20.7, married at 23.7, and had their first child at twenty-five. They had an average of 2.4 children over a period of 5.4 years. Women in this category worked longest as unpaid family workers. Older women in agricultural families and younger women in professional occupations were typically in this category.

The M-type, the third category, refers to women who experienced economic activities before marriage, interrupted their employment during their child-rearing years, and later resumed economic activities. The mean age of women in this category was 42.7 years. On average, they began their first job at age twenty, married at twenty-five, had their first child at 26.3, and bore a second child four years later. They had more than one job interruption, and those interruptions averaged ten years since their first job.

The fourth type, denoted as the "latent M-type," refers to women who stopped working after marriage or childbirth and had not returned to economic activities at the time of the survey. Their mean age was 37.6. Childbirth rather than marriage was more often the motivation for their first job interruption. On average, they started their first job at age 20.9,

Table 4.2 General Characteristics of Interview Participants, 2002

Alias	Age	Educational level	Marital status	No. of children	Work status
Lee, Soon-Hye	32	High school	married	1son, 1daughter	manufacturing worker
Lee, Kyung-Seong	43	High school	married	1 son, 1 daughter	manufacturing
Eom, Mi-Hyang	39	High school	married	2 daughters	manufacturing
Kim, Min-Kyung	38	University	married	1 daughter	Nursing
Sim, Hyun-Hee	36	University	married	1 son, 2 daughters	Agrarian
Choi,Myung-Moon	37	university	married	2 sons	Nutritionist
Kim, Kyung-Son	44	university	single	–	Teacher
Song, Mi-Jeong	37	High school	divorced	2 daughters	Part time in
Choi, Hee-Sook	40	High school	divorced	1 daughter	public
Yoon, Jeong-Mi	38	College	divorced	1 daughter	service
Sa, Mi-Kyung	31	College	widowed	2 sons	"
Chung, Sook-Kyung	35	High school	divorced	1 daughter	"
Oh, Kim-Joo	41	High school	married	1 daughter	Not in workforce
Kim, Young-Ran	30	University	married	–	
Oh, Sook-Jeong	51	Literate	widowed	1 son, 1 daughter	"
Lee, Young-Jai	30	High school	married	1 son, 1 daughter	"
Kim, Myung-Ah	37	High school	married	1 son, 1 daughter	"
Park, So-Young	38	university	married	1 son	"
Chai, Jeong-Ran	34	university	married	1 son	"
Chung, Kyung-Hye	42	university	Single	–	"
Im, Sen-Jeong	54	High school	married	1 son, 2 daughters	"
Kim, In-Seon	43	university	married	1 son	"
Park, Mal-Za	66	Literate	married	2 sons, 1 daughter	"
Park, Yoon-Soon	70	Literate	married	1 son, 1 daughter	"
Kim, Bong-Deok	76	Literate	divorced	1 son, 1 daughter	"
Jin, Kim-Wha	86	illiterate	widowed	1 daughter	"
Kim, Kyung-Sook	71	High school	married	3 sons	"
Im, Phil-Soon	77	Literate	widowed	2 sons, 3 daughters	"

Note: General characteristics refer to the women's status measured in 2002.

Table 4.3 Life Patterns of Korean Women, 2002

Mean characteristics		Type of sequence of family and economic activities						
		Work as single	Family and work together	M-type	Latent M-type	Work after childrearing	Family only	Pre-adulthood
	Age	27.7	48.0	42.7	37.6	48.9	49.5	19.8
M	Age at first marriage	-	23.7	25.1	26.2	23.2	23.7	-
	Age at first birth	-	24.9	26.3	27.4	24.6	25.1	-
	Age at last birth	-	29.3	29.2	29.8	28.6	29.2	-
C	Birth intervals	-	5.4	4.0	3.4	5.0	5.2	-
	Total no. of children	-	2.4	2.0	1.8	2.4	2.4	-
W	Age at first job	22.3	20.7	19.9	20.9	36.6	-	-
	Age at last job	27.0	46.7	41.5	25.4	47.0	-	-
	Total duration of working years	4.7	26.0	21.6	4.5	10.4	-	-
	% of job change	16.4	27.7	100	6.1	16.7	-	-
	% of job interruption (@)	10.7	0.0	100	2.0	8.3	-	-
	Total duration of job interruption	0.4	0.0	10.0	0	0.4	-	-
S	Sequence of life	W@W	WMCW	WM@C@CW	W@MCC	MCCW@W	MCC	..
	%	11.5	10.3	13.9	20.1	17.6	12.9	14.1
	% (married women only)	-	13.7	18.6	26.9	23.5	17.3	-

Key: M = marriage; C = childbirth; W = workforce participation; @ = work interruption

Table 4.4 Distribution of Life Patterns by Marriage Cohort

	Marriage Cohort				
Life patterns	<=1969	1970-1979	1980–1989	1990–1994	>=1995
Family & work together	23.3	14.0	8.4	12.7	10.9
M-type	6.7	19.3	28.4	22.5	11.3
Latent M-type	5.6	11.5	24.4	46.4	68.4
Work after childrearing	35.4	34.0	24.1	9.6	2.8
Family role only	29.0	21.2	14.8	8.8	6.6
	100.0	100.0	100.0	100.0	100.0

married at 26.2, and gave birth for the first time at 27.4. They had an average of 1.8 births over 3.4 years. Given their relatively younger age, they had the potential to reenter the labor market later.

The fifth type represents women with no work experience before marriage who entered the job market only after a period devoted to childrearing. Their mean age was 48.9. On average, they married at age 23.2 and had their first child at 24.6. They had an average of 2.4 children over a five-year interval between the first and last child. Their mean age when beginning their first job was 36.6.

The sixth type includes women with no work experience over their life course. The mean age of the respondents in this type was 49.5, the oldest among the six life-sequence patterns. Their average age at marriage was 23.7. Following the birth of their first child at age 25.1, they had a total of 2.4 children in a 5.4 year interval between the first and last child.

Focusing on ever-married women, there is significant variation in women's life patterns by marital cohort. Table 4.4 divides married women into cohorts designated by the era in which they were married: before 1970, in the 1970s, in the 1980s, between the years 1990 and 1994, and after 1995. The decade of the 1990s is subdivided to account for changes in marital and family behaviors after the economic crisis of the late 1990s. Interestingly, the proportion of women who continued to work without interruption had been declining prior to the 1980s but then began to increase rapidly for the marriage cohort of the 1990s. These trends parallel the changing compositional characteristics of the category. Before the 1980s, women who had continued to work without interruption had primarily been agricultural workers, and the decline in the proportion of married women who worked without interruption most likely resulted from the declining number of agricultural workers in the labor force as a whole until that decade. The increasing proportion of women who continued to work without interruption among the post-1990 marriage cohorts parallels the rise of women in professional occupations.

The number of women in the M-type category also increased until the 1980s before declining among women married after 1990. In addition to the increase in the number of women who married after 1990 who continued to work without interruption, this decline in the number of M-type women in that marital cohort is also likely due to the fact that these more recently married women have not yet reentered the workforce after leaving it for a period of time. Indeed, the great increase in the proportion of women in the "latent M-type" group among the same marital cohort supports this interpretation. The greatest number of women in the most recent marital cohort were either in the M-type or latent M-type categories. Women who entered the workforce only after marriage or childrearing or who had no job experience whatsoever were common in marriage cohorts of the 1960s and the 1970s, but these types were less common in marital cohorts of the 1990s and later.

These changes in the distribution of ever-married women's life patterns provide several important clues to the puzzle of recent changes in the age profiles of Korean women's economic activities. As noted above, the curve representing Korean women's economic participation during the last twenty years has flattened out at the aggregate level across age; this has often been analyzed as indicative of a decline in the incidence of job interruption with a resulting improvement in women's economic activities. But an analysis of individual women's life sequences suggests a contradictory explanation; that is, younger cohorts are more likely, rather than less likely, to experience M-type patterns of economic participation. These seemingly contradictory trends between aggregate and individual levels are the result of a simultaneous rise in the average age of marriage and the continued practice of women's employment interruption after marriage or childbirth. In other words, the aggregate rise in the number of women working in their late twenties and early thirties is not due to women's uninterrupted employment during their childrearing years, but rather to a rise in the average age of marriage.

While the M-type life course pattern remains most common among younger Korean women at this time, the number of women who continue in their careers without interruption has also been increasing among younger marital cohorts. This suggests that another significant generational change in Korean women's life patterns is likely in the near future.

THE MEANINGS OF FAMILY AND ECONOMIC ACTIVITIES FOR
CONTEMPORARY KOREAN WOMEN: THE CONTINUING PREVALENCE OF
THE "M-TYPE"

Why and under what circumstances do many young women choose to exit and reenter the labor market? Women's narratives of their life experiences provide several explanations for their job interruption. Most women's jobs are poorly compensated and menial. The first jobs of women with high school educations interviewed for this study included working in manufacturing, in unpaid family businesses, or as clerks, jobs typical for women with this level of education. These have particular drawbacks for married women with children. The physical demands of jobs in manufacturing make it difficult for many to manage family roles simultaneously. Part-time jobs as clerks in small service shops are very poorly paid. Most informants whose work-force participation was interrupted had not been offered paid leave for birth or childrearing. It is commonly believed by employees in small companies that employers would be deterred from hiring women if they were required to offer fringe benefits to working mothers or working parents. The poor compensation, lack of benefits, and menial nature of these types of jobs diminish their appeal to married women with preschool-age children, causing many to leave the workforce and refrain from reentering it during their childrearing years.

Interviewees who stepped out of the labor market addressed the influence of normative gender expectations on their choice to withdraw. An interesting contrast by respondents' age and economic status emerged in the ways in which they interpreted that decision. Kim In-Seon, a university-educated woman in her forties, introduced herself as a member of the "4-7-5" generation: in her 40s at the time of the survey, attending university in the 1970s, and having been born in the 1950s. She said that it was natural for women of her generation to resign from work at the time of marriage. Sim Hyun-Hee, thirty-six at the time of the survey, had been employed by a large company before marrying a man who worked in the same company. Like Kim, Sim explained her withdrawal as reflective of the "culture" during the time she was employed.

While Kim and Sim asserted that leaving their jobs was normative in the cultural context of their generation, Park So-Young and Chai Jeong-Ran, both in their thirties and highly educated, did not attribute their departure from the workforce to normative gender expectations; rather, they said it was motivated by particular circumstances that made it difficult for them to perform both their family and work responsibilities. Park had worked in a foreign company and did not directly perceive any discrimination in her company when she married. But she resigned from her job after marriage, thinking it would only be for a few years. Following graduation from a renowned college, Chai had entered a prominent financial company and did well enough to be promoted. She continued to work after marriage to a man from her university, taking only a three-month maternity leave when her son was born. Facing difficult childcare circumstances when her husband was transferred, burdened by the high cost of quality care, concerned about her child's education, and confronting an uncomfortable climate at work following her company's restructuring, Chai decided to leave her job.

Despite some differences in their motivations, the younger and older women's interpretations of their withdrawal from the workforce all emphasize the influence of normative gender expectations on women's decisions to resign. The narratives differ, however, in the ways in which these women view their responses to cultural norms or constraints. In their interpretation of their departure from the workforce, Kim and Sim expressed themselves passively, describing their withdrawal as natural in the context of the social value system. This suggests that Kim and Sim internalized patriarchal norms in defining their female self-identity. In contrast, Park and Chai's interpretation of gender norms was not patriarchal or natural; they viewed these norms from the perspective of women. Park and Chai did not perceive gender-divided norms as grounded in culture, but rather as conflicting constraints on their rational decisions. Job withdrawal was not interpreted as a passive response to gender norms, but as a decision based on cautious concern about the well-being of their families and themselves.

The interviewees' primary motives for returning to the workforce after a long leave were to supplement their children's education funds and to support their families' subsistence. Reentering the workforce for essential economic reasons was particularly evident among single mothers currently working in publicly supported programs. Yoon Jeong-Mi, thirty-eight, had worked in a kindergarten after completing college, abandoning that career when she married at age twenty-four. After her divorce, she was forced to take a variety of jobs simply to survive. Within a single year, she worked alternately as a bookseller, cosmetic assistant, teacher in a *nori bang* (baby care house), hotel maid, and church guide. Single parents like Yoon, trapped in a cycle of menial short-term jobs to survive, bounce between unemployment and work.

The experience of women in the M-type category with poorly compensated and menial jobs, their primarily economic motivation when they do seek work, and their weak ties to the labor market due to their frequent periods of unemployment suggest that many women in this life pattern do not view women's economic activities in a positive light. Rather, women in this group link women's economic activity primarily to their family's poor economic status. The statement by university graduate Kim Young-Ran, thirty, that "My friends who are married to men making a lot of money do not work" suggests that some women perceive women's economic activities as marginal or even detrimental to women's self-perception. This helps to explain why many middle-class housewives with high levels of education have had low levels of participation in economic activities until recently. Like their male counterparts, many highly educated women have strong aspirations for social achievement, but the realities of the workplace – inferior jobs and job opportunities for women and a resulting negative attitude towards those who take those jobs – makes the workplace an inadequate venue for them to realize their aspirations. In this mismatch between aspirations and opportunities, many highly educated women develop the strategy of achieving social status and self-achievement through their family roles.

The determined attitude of middle-class women like Park and Chai to withdraw from the workplace and develop their family roles can be interpreted from the perspective of the views described above. Park and Chai note that they left their jobs not because they did not want to work, but because childrearing was much more meaningful to them. Such statements as "Getting a job is not the only way that women can display their ability. Their ability can be realized within the family and through childrearing," reflect the strong need those women have for self-achievement. Their strong motive for self-achievement can be compared to the attitudes of older women with the same levels of education and economic status. For example, Kim In-Son, a woman in her forties with a university education, had only a brief experience in employment before her marriage, and Kim Kyung-Sook, seventy-one, lived as a full-time housewife after her marriage. Both women's life narratives indicated that they regretted spending most of their time only caring for their families and emphasized the importance of women's social activity and autonomy. In contrast, the life narratives of younger, highly educated housewives such as Park and Chai described their current status as housewives with no sense of regret or depression.

WORK IN SOCIALLY-VALUED CAREERS AND WOMEN'S SUPPORT NETWORKS

Although they are not the dominant group among women, married women with professional careers have been increasing since the 1990s. This change might signal a significant pending shift in women's perception about economic activities as a primary contributor to the construction of the self.

Women with careers maintain confidence and satisfaction about their jobs (interviews with Kim Min-Kyung, Choi Myung-Moon, and Kim Kyung-Soon). Great satisfaction with their jobs implies that economic activities are an important source of meaning in women's self-perception. The significance of economic activity in the construction of the self is related to the characteristics of women's jobs. Informants continuing economic activities without interruption for marriage and childrearing are employed in professional jobs such as teaching, nursing, and nutrition. Most professional jobs require qualification examinations, which women regard as lowering gender barriers. These jobs are also socially acknowledged, which also motivates women to continue to work without interruption.

Uninterrupted economic activities for married women require resources to substitute or supplement their family roles. Kin, particularly elderly parents, are a typical source of help (Choi Myung-Moon). Women prefer informal support from kin mainly because it is free or cheap as well as reliable. When my informants were not able to receive help from their parents, they had to use paid care givers. Informants with careers also addressed the supportive attitude of husbands, although many prior studies argued that Korean men's participation in family roles was very limited. Choi Myung-Moon, a food company nutritionist in her late thirties, emphasized her husband's supportive attitude regarding her job. She noted that "If I had to decide between my family or economic activity, I would choose my family roles. It was my husband's support that made me concentrate on my job."

Continual work over the life course is not just a recent phenomenon in Korean women's lives. Uninterrupted work was common for most elderly Korean women (Park Mal-Za, Park Yoon-Soon, Kim Bong-Deok, Jin Kim-Wha, and Im Phil-Soon). While younger women who performed both family roles and work gained a sense of individual identity from their work, older women did not experience economic activities in terms of self-achievement. Rather, they accepted work as their destiny. Moreover, they did not experience family and economic roles as clearly separated. With no support to carry out their dual roles, older women performed their economic activities while simultaneously taking their family roles for granted.

FROM OBLIGATION TO SUPPORT NETWORK: NEW VIEWS OF INTERGENERATIONAL RELATIONSHIPS

Many studies of contemporary Korean families note the prevalence of the extended family relationship (Chae 2002; Lee 2003; Park 2003). But these studies differ in identifying who, beyond the nuclear family, are members of the family. While some stress the still prevailing influence of the patrilinear relationship, others emphasize "a modified extended family relationship" including bilinear or matrilinear attachment (Cho 1997).

Most of my interview participants' concepts of the family were broader than the nuclear family as well. Lee Young-Jai and Sim Hyun-Hee (introduced earlier) noted that they felt much closer to the "*sijip*" (one's husband's family) than to the "*chin-jeong*" (one's natal family), explaining that their sense of affiliation to their parents-in-law was the result of their long interaction with their husbands' families. Lee Young-Jai, age thirty at the time of the survey, completed high school education, married at age twenty, and had two children. Her married life began with a mother-in-law, grandmother-in-law, and brother- and sister-in-law. While the beginning of marriage was difficult, she said that she managed to be recognized as a member of the *sijip*. Sim Hyun-Hee, thirty-six years old at the time of the survey and living in a rural area, had worked in a big company before her marriage. Upon marriage, she moved to her husband's rural *sijip* and began small-scale farming. Asserting that "it is the 1970s in my house," she regarded her family life as traditional. While she generally got along well with her mother-in-law, she expressed some discomfort with what she perceived as unfairness in the assignment of responsibilities and rights within the family. Although she and her husband assumed many family responsibilities, including living with the elderly mother, preparing for ancestor rituals, and giving crops to the husband's siblings, the family's eldest son, who was living apart from the family, was allowed to make key decisions and control the family's goods and property. Nevertheless, Sim accepted this situation, both because of her affection for her husband and because she expected that her children would be rewarded for her good behavior, noting the old saying that "supporting one's old parents brings glory to the (grand)children."

Except for these two women, the idea of the patrilinear family was not deeply instilled in the minds of those interviewed. Instead, most informants had closer affinity to their natal families than to their husbands' families. Close ties to their natal families had both emotional and material bases. Asked to identify whom they considered their family members, Chai Jeong-Ran and Park So-Young included their in-laws and natal families in addition to their conjugal families. Chai added that as the eldest child she had some obligations to her natal family as well as her husband's family. Her residential proximity to her parents also made her relationship with them more affinitive than with her parents-in-law who lived farther away. Chai, who sent some money to her parents-in-law every month for their living expenses, received financial assistance from her own parents. This assistance included their purchase of a house and appliances for Chai and her husband when they got married as well as financial support for Mr. Chai's business. Park also had a closer emotional affinity to her parents and continued to receive substantial help from them. She added that she felt the bond with her parents had grown following the death of her parents-in-law. Indeed, she and her husband rarely met with the husband's siblings other than on some memorial days. In contrast, she lived close to her parents whom she visited frequently. Her parents assisted her in many ways, including financial support to purchase a house, cooking and cleaning, and caring for the grandchildren.

Women's concepts of the extended family were linked to their attitudes towards care of elderly parents. Those identifying themselves as part of a patrilinear family, such as Lee and Sim, believed that caring for elderly parents was the children's duty or responsibility; at the same time, they emphasized that the family inheritance should, in fairness, be rewarded to the child who cared for the elderly and not be taken for granted as the right of the eldest son. In contrast, women more closely tied to their natal families were less enthusiastic about caring for their elderly parents-in-law. Chai, for example, said that despite her willingness to live with her elderly parents-in-law and to take care of them in times of critical need, she believed it was common for today's elders not to want to live with their children. She thought her own parents intended to move to a senior community in the future, adding that she was willing to give up any rights of inheritance to her brothers-in-law if they would assume the responsibility of caring for her parents-in-law.

In sum, informants interpreted their extended family relationships in diverse ways, including traditional culture and responsibilities, access to daily support, and affinity. In general, relations with one's parents-in-law were regarded as obligatory, not routine or customary but rather ritualized. In contrast, women preferred that relations with their parents become routinized as the basis of a useful support network. If relations with the parents-in-law were to become customary or regularized in everyday activities, "support" would take on the character of being enforced. Thus, the support by many contemporary women for the extended family is not due to their adherence to traditional patrilinear relationships, but rather to their interpretation of the extended family as a support network in the interest of the conjugal family.

THE ATTRACTION OF CHILDREARING AND EDUCATION

Childrearing and education are the most important family roles for young women. Many married women resign from economic activities when they give birth or have young children to care for. Informants' narratives indicated that women employed diverse sources of help in childrearing. Informants who received little or no help for childrearing – typical of M-type women – resigned their jobs when they were not granted maternity leave. Informants who continued to work during the period of childrearing relied on the support of their kin, particularly their elderly parents (Choi Myung-Moon and Lee Soon-Hye). Many mothers believed that their infant children's emotional development would be adversely affected if they were placed in public nurseries. Thus, middle-class women unable to care for their children themselves or with the help of kin would make use of high-cost private help (Kim Min-Kyung).

While women sought diverse networks of resources, including kin and private and public nurseries for infant care, they retained exclusive control of decisions about their children's education. Most informants were anxious about their children's education. One asserted that the mother's role increased with her child's age (Park). Women's concern for their children's education often encouraged mothers to begin their children's education earlier, sending them to preschool education centers that provided both learning and play programs.

Most informants, particularly middle-class women, explained their anxiety about their children's education as an attitude shared by most Korean parents, claiming that "Other women do as much as I do. I never do too much in comparison with other women." Chai, for example – who sent her six-year-old son to a kindergarten that had a native speaker of English, a special weekly talent program, and a variety of artistic and gymnastic tutors in skating, ice racing, ballet, Lego-building, and piano – stated that, "I never forced these lessons on my child, rather my child would absorb what he has learned. I just want to provide him with many experiences." Chai's daily schedule was arranged according to her son's education. Although 30 percent of the family's monthly expenses went to her son's education, she said this was not much compared to what families in Seoul's Kang Nam district spent. (Kang Nam is known for its large concentration of upper middle-class families who spend a great deal on their children's education.) Chai stated that in light of her son's talent, she wanted to send him to a science school and prepare him to become a scientist. Park's experience offered another example of women's anxiety over their children's education. She and her husband had a commuting marriage since early 2002, when her husband's workplace moved to a small city near Busan. She did not accompany her husband in order not to disrupt her son's education at a primary school that offered English lessons with a native speaker, swimming, and Tae kwon do. Compared to other families' children, she did not think that her son had too much work. Chai and Park also considered the growing phenomena of families' emigration to the United States for their children's education and the "goose father," a term used in Korea to describe the father who remained in Korea to earn funds for his children to study overseas.

Women in less affluent families shared concern for their children's education. Indeed, the reason many cited for seeking part-time work was their desire to supplement their resources for education. Many displayed a "guilty conscience" (Chung Sook-Kyung) if their economic situation constrained their ability to support their children's education. If their children did not perform well in school, they believed the cause was not the children's lack of talent but rather their not having received proper support from their parents (Yoon Jeong-Mi). These parents planned to invest more for their children if their economic condition improved (Lee Young-Jai).

My informants interpreted this strong desire to support their children's education as a parent's natural responsibility. They also regarded their wish to conform to social trends as a reason for spending more on their children's education. They worried that because other children attended private learning centers, their children would be isolated and fall behind if they did not attend. In a society where one's ability was highly valued and competition emphasized, it was imperative for parents to invest in their children's education from a very early age.

These broadly shared anxieties for children's education and the particularly active involvement of housewives in middle-class families with their children's education are related to the generational changes among increasingly highly educated women who formed their families since the 1980s. Educated women's high expectations for social achievement have continued to be constrained by the still limited opportunities in the workplace; as a result, most highly educated women have begun to view the family as an important domain to display their abilities. As obligation in the traditional (patrilinear) extended family weakened, women were increasingly able to maintain power to manage and decide family roles. In these circumstances, full-time mothers appeared in middle-class families, concentrating on intellectual tasks like children's education and relying, as did Chai, on part-time maids for household tasks. In this regard, women's concentration on their children's education displayed their aspiration for social achievement, finding its legitimacy in firmly grounded social beliefs about the esteemed role of motherhood.

GENDER ROLE ATTITUDES AND SHIFTS IN CONJUGAL RELATIONS

Most informants, regardless of differences in their economic status, emphasized the husband's responsibility for the family's livelihood. This opinion is suggested by the informants' comments: "The husband's sense of responsibility becomes weaker when his wife works to supplement the family's economy;" or "Women married to successful men do not have to work." As noted earlier, until the 1980s, Korean female workers had taken for granted their husbands' ignorance of family roles; only women were required to maintain their family responsibilities even when employed. The clear role division in families, except in the case of economic support, reflects the persistence, even in the recent past, of patriarchal practices in conjugal relationships.

A noteworthy change has recently emerged, however, when the husband fails to carry out his economic role of maintaining the family's livelihood. That is, women informants involved in economic activities to support the family rarely accepted that they alone should shoulder the dual roles of both earning money and taking care of their family. They often expressed their displeasure with husbands who were not supportive, causing, at times, spousal conflicts when they asked their husbands to participate in family tasks. In other cases, husbands did share family chores. For example, Mrs. Lee, thirty-two, employed in a textile factory, worked an eight-hour shift. She explained that her strenuous labor made it difficult to fulfill family roles simultaneously, but her husband understood her situation and shared various household chores and childrearing. Eom Mi-Hyang, thirty-eight, who worked twelve hours a day in the same factory, left most of the family chores to her husband. Chai and Kim Kyung-Son, who had (semi)professional jobs, also described their husbands' help in the family, including playing with the children. They noted that, "Just as working men need the support of their wives, working women need support from their husbands."

While economically active women regarded their husbands' participation in family roles positively, economically inactive women said that "their husbands were absolutely ignorant about household chores or childrearing" and rarely participated in family chores (Kim Myung-Ah, Oh Sook-Jeong). But these women added that they would rather accept their husbands' ignorance of these family chores if they made enough money. Moreover, middle-class housewives (Park So-Young and Chai) seldom expressed displeasure concerning their husbands' spending long hours at the office and rarely participating in family chores. Rather, these housewives accepted the tacit contract between the husband as bread winner and the wife as maintainer of the household.

FROM SERVANTS TO RULERS WITHIN THE FAMILY: CHANGES IN THE MEANINGS OF FAMILY-CENTEREDNESS

As noted above, my informants underwent diverse experiences in economic and family roles over their life course. Most of the married women in their thirties or forties worked in typical women's jobs from which they resigned at marriage or childbirth. Thereafter, they took on family roles such as childrearing, household chores, family meetings, and ancestor worship; they also frequently participated in economic activities to assist the family economically. Middle-class housewives in their thirties and forties who had worked in prominent companies before their marriages sometimes resigned their jobs later to concentrate on their children's education. Some middle-class women continued their careers in the professions, employing various resources, including their parents, husbands, and paid helpers, to supplement family responsibilities. Women who were single parents lived unstable lives with weak ties to both the family and the labor market.

The meanings through which these women interpreted their lives shed light on how they construct self-experiences. As Kaufman (1986) argued, life is a reservoir of many experiences and meanings, which together constitute self-identity. Self-identity is continuously reinterpreted. What the subject experiences is not directly meaningful; only experiences consciously or unconsciously chosen and memorized are interpreted in the interactive and purposeful context between the subject and society. Accordingly, the meanings of life experiences reveal the relationship between self and society. Tracing the ways in which informants interpreted their life experiences and the ways in which these experiences are tied to social status, generation, and a broader social context allows us to grasp Korean women's gender identity.

My process of interpreting the informants' narratives raised the issue of whether there is a common orientation, that is, a family-centeredness in and from which informants interpreted their experiences in a distinctive way despite the diversity of women's life courses and self-interpretations. While informants did not attach a rich variety of meanings to economic activities, they did discuss their families in richly meaningful ways. Meaningful relations to economic activities were rarely expressed by informants, who described a very solid sense of connectedness with their families.

Is the family-centeredness among contemporary Korean women in their thirties and forties any different from the earlier type of women's identity that was assumed to have been internalized under the influence of patriarchal family relations? Korean women in their thirties and forties shared more egalitarian opportunities for education and some have built careers in socially valued professions. This change in women's generational characteristics raises the issue of whether women's family-centered attitudes developed in a context different from the past. The evidence suggests that the family-centeredness of contemporary Korean women is achieved actively rather than being the product of internalized patriarchal family relations.

First, the way in which women interpreted their withdrawal from the labor force shows significant change. In the past, women interpreted their exit from the labor market as the result of the influence of cultural norms in which the self was just displayed as a passive adapter to the culture. In contrast, younger married women interpreted their job exit as a rational choice in the context of conflicting demands of the family and workplace. Similar conflicts may have prevailed in the past, but the manner in which contemporary younger women perceived these conflicts reflects significant change in women's self-perception. Claiming that they themselves identified conflicts between the family and economic activities and made their own decisions to favor their family roles, today's younger women asserted that their family identity was actively achieved by their own will and purpose.

Family-centeredness actively constructed in this way is also embedded in the meanings of family relations. Women's interpretations of their extended family relationships contained various meanings, including an obligation to support their parents or parents-in-law, a desire to receive household assistance, and emotional solidarity. Some informants held traditional family attitudes, carrying out family chores, attending family events, and supporting their elderly parents. But other informants interpreted traditional obligations to support their parents or parents-in-law as burdensome and did not make them part of their daily family interactions. Some women viewed the extended family in the context of its ability to be part of their support network. That is to say, these women interpreted and actively utilized extended family relationships as a source of help in childrearing, household chores, and financial support; as a result, they were more likely to attach emotional affinity to and prefer daily interactions with their parents. Women who viewed intergenerational relationships as part of a "support network" did not see the extended family itself as their primary orientation. Rather, they valued intergenerational relationships because of their usefulness to the conjugal family.

Women identify the rearing and education of children as their role. While my informants often used support networks that included parents and employed helpers to care for their infant children, they regarded their children's education as their exclusive sphere of responsibility. Indeed, the intense focus of women, particularly highly educated, middle-class housewives, on their children's education derived from their aspiration for social achievement through the family.

My informants' interpretation of conjugal relationships also revealed how they actively extended their status within the family. Informants shared the opinion that the husband's primary role was to support the family economically. At the same time, they believed that gendered role divisions with the family should be adjusted if the husband did not fulfill this role. While neither the spouses' educational equality nor wives' desire for self-achievement led to shared roles in their marriages, and despite middle-class housewives' agreement with the premise of gender-segregated identity, gender roles did change when women carried out economic activities. Regardless of the family's economic status, husbands were more supportive in the family when their wives were employed. This is a significant change from the patriarchal pattern in which women were obliged to fulfill their roles as housewives regardless of their contributions to the family economy. While contemporary young, married women emphasized the husband's responsibility to support his family, at the same time they also sought more egalitarian participation in family roles once they joined economic activities. The "goose father" living apart from his family to maximize his financial support for his children's education, many fathers' growing sense of marginalization and isolation within the family, and weakened spousal intimacy reflect shifts in power within the conjugal relationship.

Thus, the family-centeredness of contemporary Korean women, despite its seeming similarity to customary practices, is grounded in a significant change in women's self-construct. Young women's family-centeredness is not derived from their submission to patriarchal pressure; it is, rather, an orientation women actively construct as they pursue their own and their family's achievements. Family-centeredness embodies women's extension of their autonomy and influence vis-à-vis their elderly parents, husbands, and children. Family-centered women transform the meaning of the obligatory norms of support for their elderly parents into useful resources for financial and instrumental assistance to their own conjugal families. They reinterpret the hierarchical division of gender roles to emphasize the husband's responsibility both as the bread-winner and as a supporter of his children's education. These meanings parallel women's aspiration for status achievement in Korea's gender segmented society through their championing of the family.

A critical concern arises, however, concerning the contradictory consequences of family-centeredness on women's autonomy and gender equality. Although family-centeredness is an instrumental rationality for women to maximize their self-interest, its social consequences are paradoxical, potentially imprisoning women in gender divided systems that constrain their autonomy.

CONCLUSION

This study employs a life course analysis to examine the patterned characteristics of women's family and economic activities. In 2002, the life courses of married women fell into six categories, of which the most prevalent among recent marriage cohorts were the "M-type" and "latent M-type." A pattern that has increased since the 1990s was that of women with uninterrupted careers. Previously common patterns that have declined in recent decades include the category of women who took their first job after marriage or childrearing and that of women limited to roles within the family throughout the life course.

This study also examined the meanings though which Korean women interpreted their experiences of family and economic activities. Informants, the majority of whom had had some work experience, manifested a diversity of ways in which they linked economic activities to self-perception. Those whose careers were not interrupted actively sought their identity through their economic activities, while those in the "M-type" category common among women currently in their thirties and forties rarely displayed their active self through economic activities. Because women frequently undertook economic activity for subsistence or to cover the expenses of their children's education, and because most women's jobs were poorly compensated and their employment status unstable, many women had negative attitudes towards economic activity and themselves. The perception that need drove women to take meaningless jobs linked employment to economic class. As a result, many women transformed their self-identity into a family-centered identity once they proved themselves by having worked in prominent companies.

As other studies have also emphasized, this study finds a persistence of extended family relations among its informants. The extended family is not embedded in patriarchal relationships, however; it is, rather, manifested through its support network. Most mothers view their sense of responsibility for their children and their eagerness to support their children's education as part of the culture. Most regard mothers' sense of guilt when leaving their children in the care of others, their sacrifice to support and educate their children, and their serious consideration of emigration for the sake of the children's education not as a reflection of women's peculiar vanity but as characteristics common to all mothers. By making their children's education the focus of parenthood, many women in low-income families made great sacrifices to rear their children. The strong commitment to children held by most women raises questions about whether contemporary family changes and the demographic transition can be the result of a weakening family orientation among women. Indeed, women's exceptional eagerness to be involved in their children's education and the persistence of highly segregated gender roles among highly educated middle-class housewives illustrate that family-centeredness was not suppressed even by women's increasing educational equality and their desire for self-achievement.

Delayed marriage, very low fertility, and the continuing prevalence of the "M-type" pattern among married women reflect the high level of tension between Korean women's family roles and economic activities. As this chapter has shown, conflicts between family roles and economic activities are not generally caused by women's attaching greater value to work or by an increase in women's economic participation rate. Rather, conflicts result from a social setting with unequal labor opportunities, low levels of public welfare, and gender-divided social relations that coerce women's identity as home-makers.

As a result, family-centeredness has come to constitute the central part of Korean women's identity. It is embedded through life-long experiences of disadvantages in economic participation and a shared sense of uncertainty about women's own economic independence under the gender-segmented labor market. Family-centeredness is not just the repressive outcome of the gender-segregated society, however. Rather, it is actively constructed from a cautious concern for social achievement. In this regard, family-centeredness has an instrumental orientation.

Korean women have a strong aspiration to achieve status vicariously, through choosing their marital partner and crafting their roles as mothers; these account for Korean social phenomena such as the marriage market bubble, the "goose father," educational emigration, and family egoism.

Many policy-makers and scholars, describing Korea's current low rates of fertility and the rapid aging of the population as serious challenges to social sustainability, argue that population policy should be developed to enhance the family by imposing the role of "good mother" on all women. I take issue with this view. My concern is that women's family-centeredness, instrumentally developed in the intersection of status aspiration and gender segmented society, is responsible for the recent demographic change.

In suggesting future directions of family change, it is not easy to anticipate whether or to what extent women's family-centeredness might decline. Current social conditions have led to women's reinterpretation of the self as well as of economic activities and family roles. Women are still selective in terms of occupational and social status. Nevertheless, if more egalitarian culture extends to the workplace, social inequalities are reduced, social support systems are enhanced to support various types of families, then women's identity will also change in ways that are less instrumental and reproductive behaviors are more likely to be sustainable.

Housewifization and Changes in Women's Life Course in Bangkok

HASHIMOTO (SEKI) HIROKO

FROM A TRADITIONAL "WORKING COUPLE" SOCIETY TO THE EMERGENCE OF THE HOUSEWIFE

Southeast Asian countries, including Thailand, are bilateral societies with family structures and norms free of the patriarchal ideologies of some other East Asian societies. The Southeast Asian family structure is that of the "network family" or "family circle" (Tsubouchi and Maeda 1977). This type of family consists primarily of a married couple and their unmarried children, and thus they may appear at first glance to be similar to the classic "nuclear family" (or "modern family") of the West. Viewed from the inside, though, they are actually very different.

In network family societies, children are often raised by grandparents and close relatives, and adoption by relatives or even non-relatives is not unusual. In such societies, the "surrogate parenting" function is highly developed. Furthermore, in traditional Thai society, there was relatively little sense that housework and childrearing tasks should be divided according to the gender of the parent (Hashimoto 2003a: 71). The practice of living with the wife's side of the family after marriage and the equal division of inheritance among sons and daughters – thus guaranteeing the daughter's share of inheritance – made it possible for the Thai family to continue receiving support from the wife's relatives after marriage. A value system treating men and women as having equal worth was thereby fostered. The absence of strong norms limiting women to roles within the household in traditional Thai family culture, together with the assumption of household and childrearing labor by relatives and maids, made it possible for women to obtain employment outside the home. Arguably, this type of support system created by traditional family culture enabled women to work during their childrearing years, and at the same time sustained Thailand's high labor force participation rate for women.

Currently, influenced by urbanization and economic development, an urban middle class is steadily developing in the Bangkok Metropolitan Area (BMA). In particular, there has been a striking growth of the university-educated white-collar class. Centered around this "new middle class," the middle class now makes up over 30 percent of the total population of the BMA (Funatsu and Kagotani 2002: 204; Hashimoto 2002b: 24). This urban middle class, particularly the white-collar class, includes many people from regions outside the BMA. The majority of these families are "nuclear families" made up of a husband and wife and their unmarried children, whose family relationships can be expected to begin to take on the characteristics of the "modern family" as defined by Emiko Ochiai.

Kua Wongboonsin has described the appearance, starting in about 1998, of a dip in the curve graphing women's labor force participation rates in urban Thailand, including the Bangkok Metropolitan Area. The resulting pattern was a slight M-shaped curve. Wongboonsin has argued that the pattern of women's labor force participation in urban Thailand is becoming similar to that in Japan and Korea (Wongboonsin 2002: 96–9; Hashimoto 2003a: 54). As Wongboonsin has indicated, in the graph of women's labor force participation rates by age in the Bangkok Metropolitan Area, which had formed an inverse U-shaped curve, the section representing the thirty to thirty-four age group began to curve downward around 1998, and in 1999 a slight trough was observed with that age group marking the bottom of the curve (see Figure 5.1).

This M-curve pattern of labor force participation rates was a phenomenon particular to urban Bangkok; when Thailand as a whole is observed, the dip disappears. Wongboonsin suggests that this dip was probably the result not of restructuring and layoffs caused by economic recession, but of an increase in the number of women who quit their jobs temporarily to bear and care for children (Wongboonsin 2002: 98). This slight dip in the curve of women's labor force participation in Bangkok disappeared after only two years, however, reverting to its original inverse U-shaped curve from 2000 onward (see Figure 5.1).

When we consider the pattern in Bangkok of labor force participation rates for women in terms of their level of education, we find the M-shaped curve to be characteristic of university graduates (see Figures 5.2 and 5.3) (Wongboonsin 2002: 96–9; Wongboonsin 2004b: 120).

Furthermore, the slight dip in the curve peculiar to university graduates persisted even after 2000, when it had ceased to obtain for the total female labor force of Bangkok. Moreover, in 2002, after the slight drop in labor force participation rates for women in their early thirties, the pattern evolved to one where the dip extended to women in their forties. Based on the above discussion, it may be inferred that Bangkok women with high levels of education are beginning to develop an employment pattern in which they quit their jobs (temporarily) to raise children.

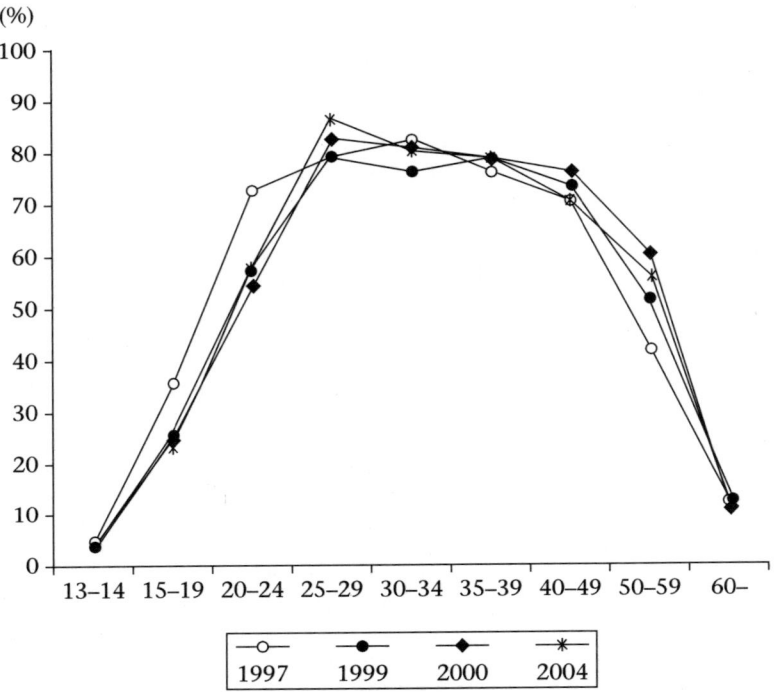

Figure 5.1   Female labor force participation rate, Bangkok Metropolitan Area, 1997-2004 (%)
Source: Wongboonsin, Kua, 2002, *Prachakonsat: Sara phua kantatsincai choeng thuraki* (Demography for Business Decision-making), p. 100, National Statistical Office, Report of the Labor Force Survey: Whole Kingdom Round 3 (Various Years: 2000–2004).

Wongboonsin's observations suggest that a "modern family" pattern bringing along with it housewifization, is developing among urban middle-class women with high levels of education. Why have highly educated women begun to choose this type of life course? In the next section, before we seek to explain these phenomena using data from the region studied, we will look at the present state of childcare availability in Bangkok and the other areas surveyed.

THE CHILDCARE SYSTEM IN THE BANGKOK METROPOLITAN AREA AND ITS KHLONGSAMWA DISTRICT

Despite the high labor force participation of married women, the absolute number of childcare facilities in urban Bangkok is insufficient, making it extremely difficult for women to work while raising children (Hashimoto

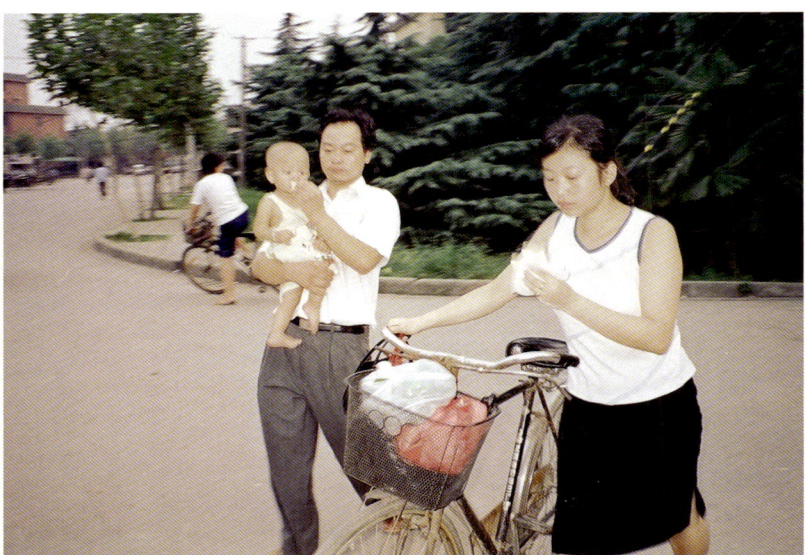

A couple returning home from work: They have probably collected their child from a childcare center or a relative's home. (Photo: Emiko Ochiai)

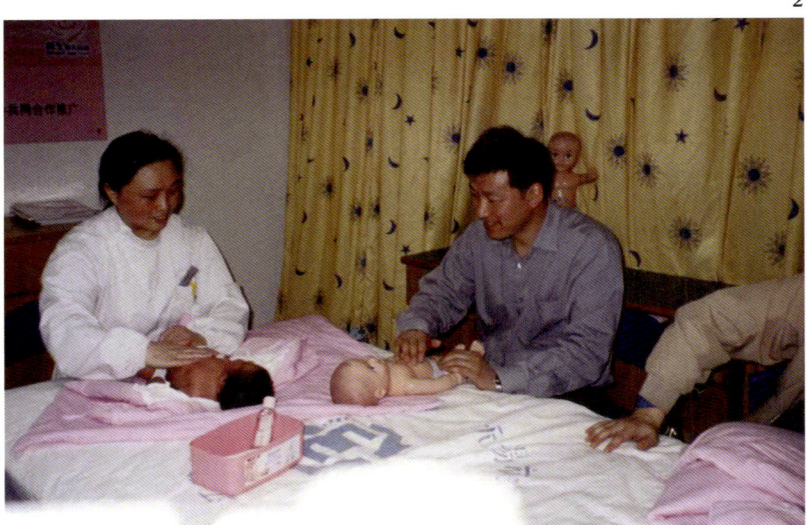

A new father learning techniques for massaging his newborn baby at a Mother and Infant Health Clinic (maternity hospital): The new mother's husband and mother spend the night following the baby's birth in the hospital. New fathers normally take time off work to prepare food and bring it to their wives, so many husbands can be found at the hospital. (Photo: Miyasaka Yasuko)

• CHINA •

3

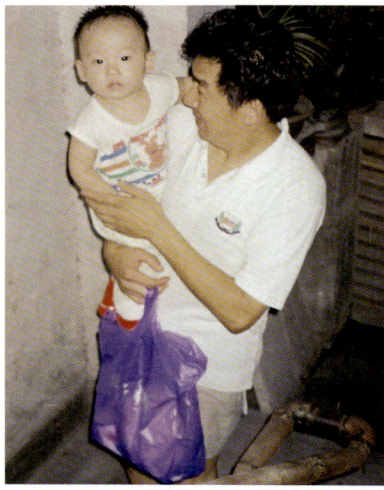

A grandfather takes his grandson back to his daughter's house after watching over him all day. (Photo: Emiko Ochiai)

5

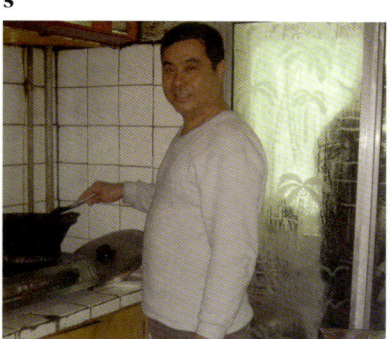

4

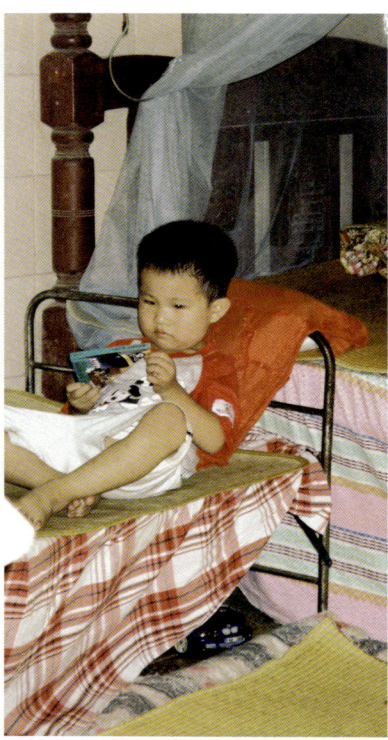

A grandchild staying with his grandparents: Many small children are cared for during the day by grandparents, aunts, and other relatives. Some stay throughout the work-week, returning home only on weekends, in some cases for several years. Here the child's bed has been set up next to the grandparents' bed. (Photo: Emiko Ochiai)

6

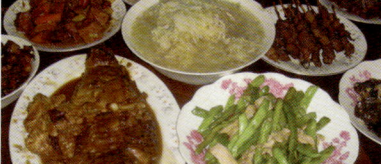

5 This man is a good cook. (Many Chinese men are good cooks.) (Photo: Emiko Ochiai)
6 Man # 5 prepared this meal by himself. (Photo: Emiko Ochiai)

7

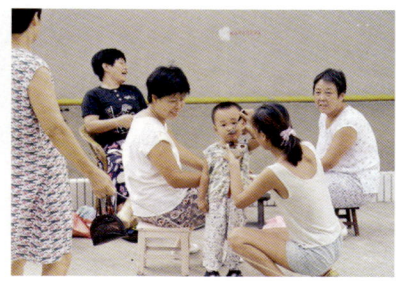

7 This child is raised within a neighboring network. (Photo: Emiko Ochiai)

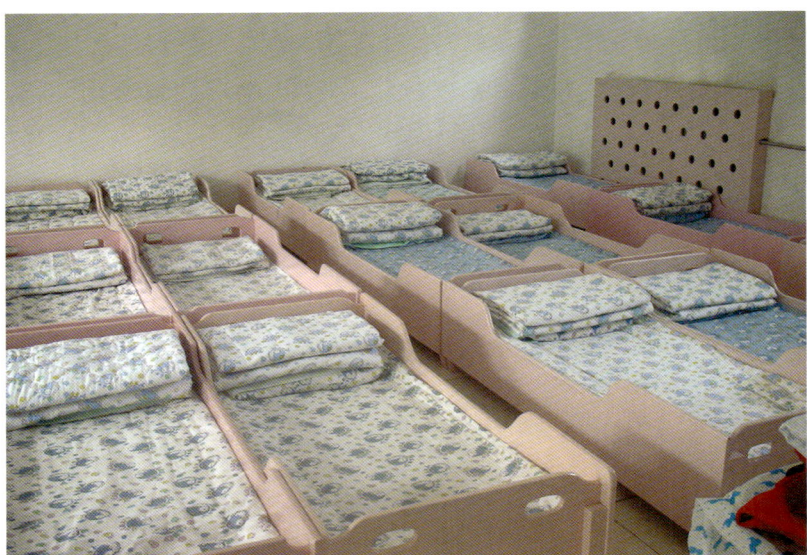

Beds for the kindergarten "full-time" class: Besides the "day class," which takes care of children during the day, a "full-time" class is available that provides care day and night during weekdays. (Photo: Miyasaka Yasuko)

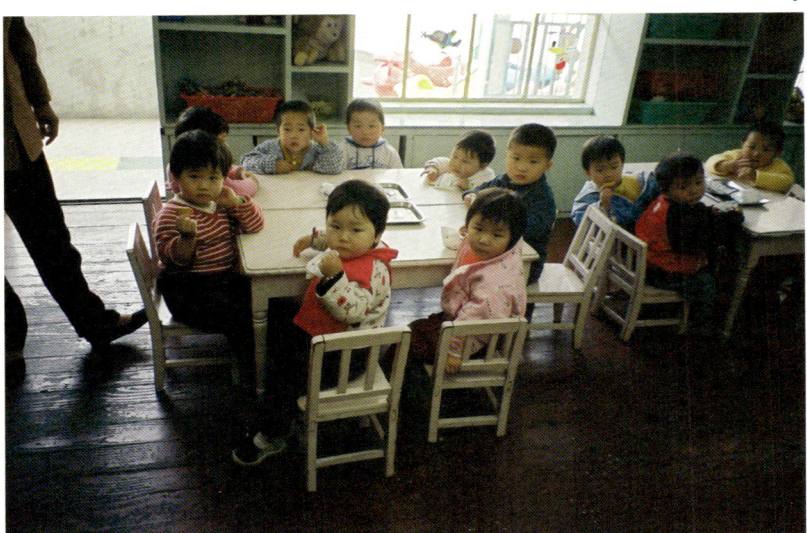

A kindergarten class. (Photo: Emiko Ochiai)

• CHINA •

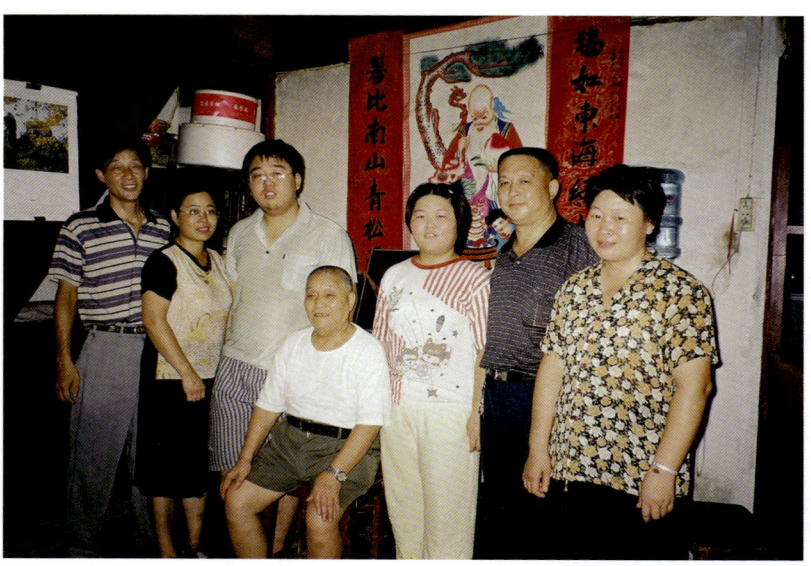

Separate households, but living like an extended family: The families of these brothers sub–divided their parents' house and raised their children living next to each other under one roof. (Photo: Emiko Ochiai)

11

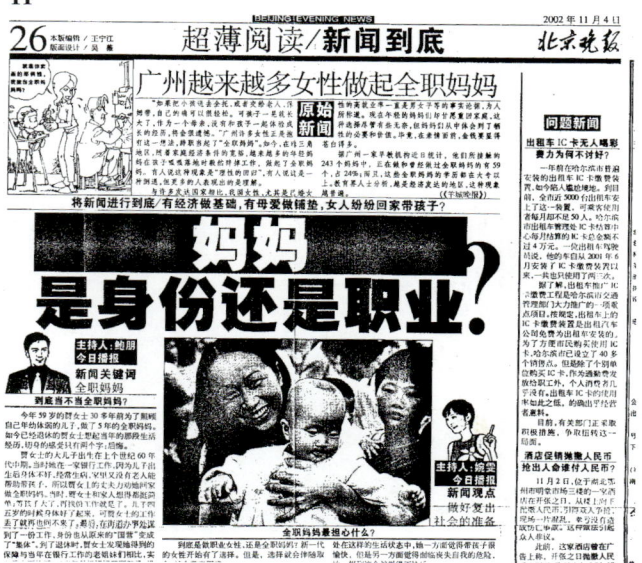

A newspaper article about the emergence of "full-time mothers" in Guangzhou (*Beijing Evening News*, November 4, 2002). Since that article appeared, full-time housewives have appeared in increasing numbers all over China. (See Ch.8)

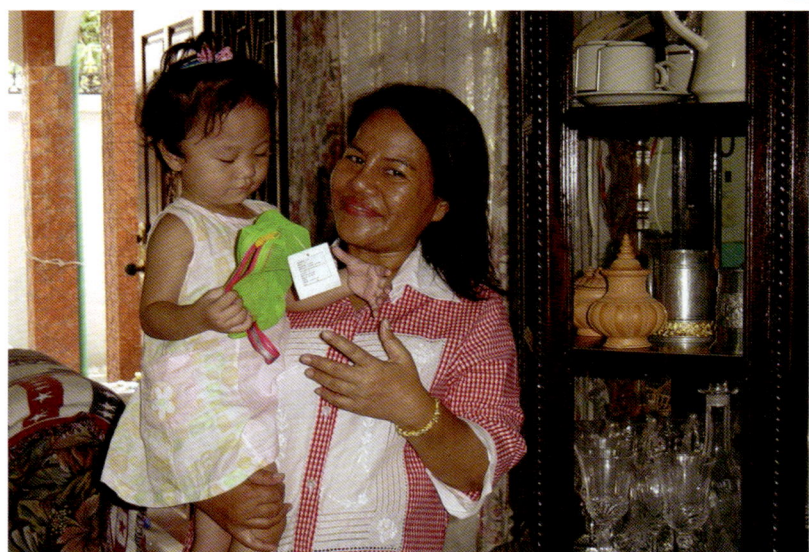

An aunt caring for her niece: She has custody of her niece, the daughter of her youngest brother, from Monday to Friday in her house in the suburbs of Bangkok. Her brother and his wife live and operate a shop in the city center. (Photo: Hashimoto Hiroko)

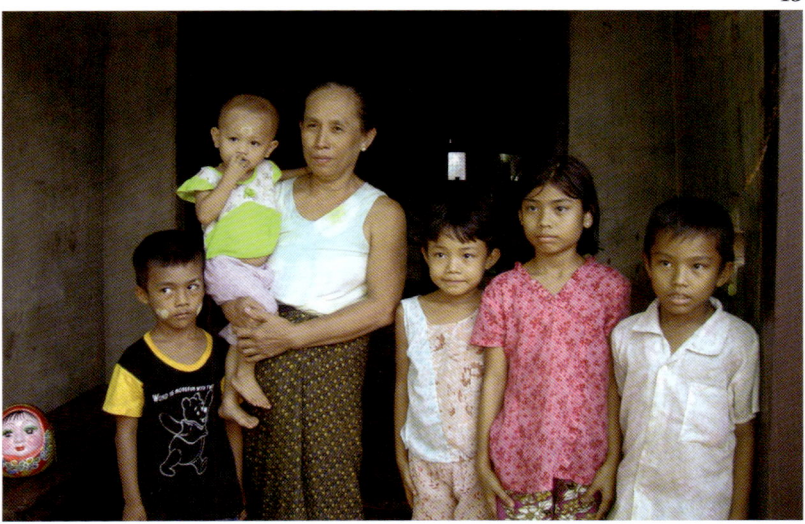

The family of a migrant worker from Myanmar: The grandmother cares for the children at home while the parents work in Thailand. Childrearing practices such as this are what make it possible for large numbers of workers, including domestic workers, to come to Thailand. The same practices occur in Thailand's rural villages. (Photo: Than Than Aung)

• THAILAND •

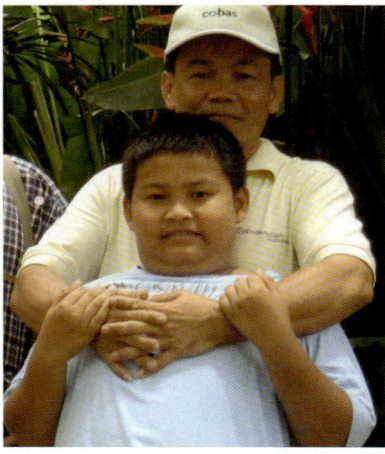

A father and his elementary-school-aged son: Because he has been involved in the childcare since his son was an infant, they have a close relationship. (Photo: Hashimoto Hiroko).

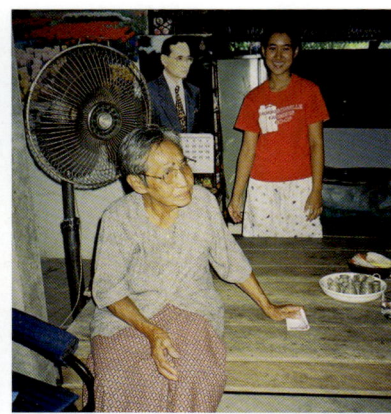

A granddaughter caring for her grandmother: The granddaughter lives with her 82-year-old grandmother and cares for her while attending high school. The girl was sent by her mother, the daughter of the old lady, who lived at another location. (Photo: Emiko Ochiai)

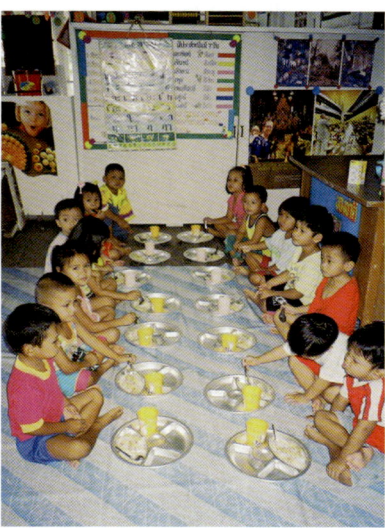

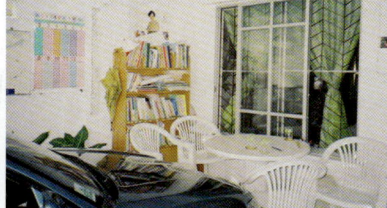

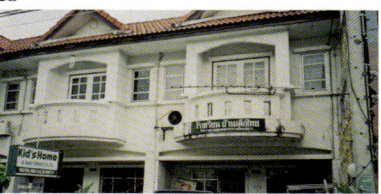

18 A private childcare facility that has been closed down: Public facilities for children aged 2 ½ and under are inadequate, while private ones are difficult to run profitably due to a lack of government funding. Nevertheless, the number of private childcare facilities in the metropolitan Bangkok area has been growing since this study was completed. (Photo: Hashimoto Hiroko)

16 A childcare facility constructed for children living in an impoverished district. (Photo: Emiko Ochiai)
17 A private supplementary cram school set up in the garage of a suburban home. (Photo: Emiko Ochiai)

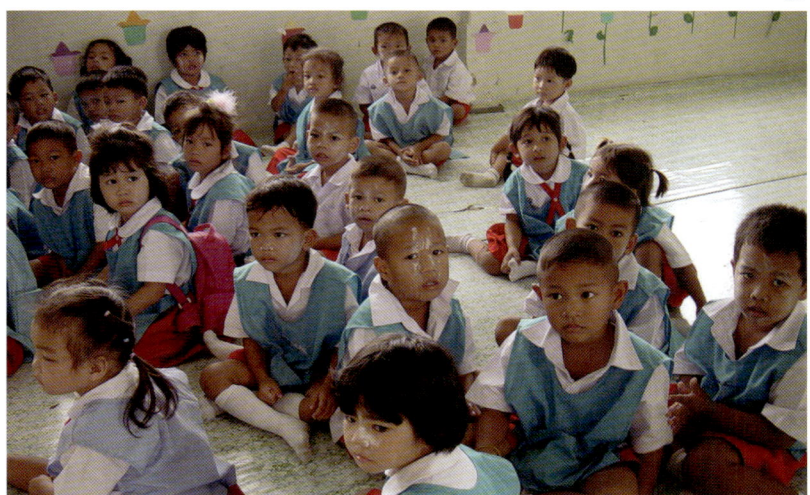

Children waiting for their caretakers to pick them up from their daycare center, which is affiliated with a public elementary school. (Photo: Hashimoto Hiroko)

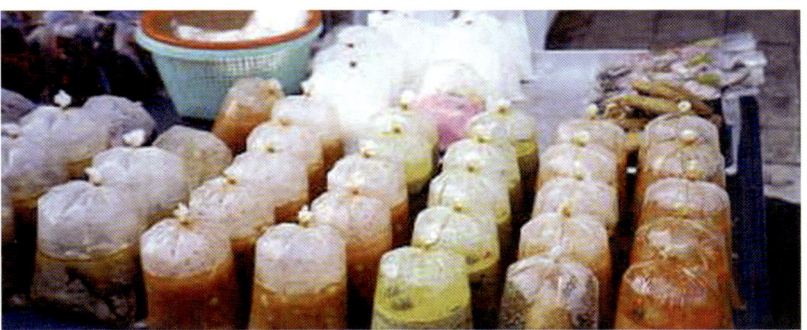

Prepared food packed in plastic bags: Many Thais purchase food at market stalls to use for the evening meal. (Photo: Emiko Ochiai)

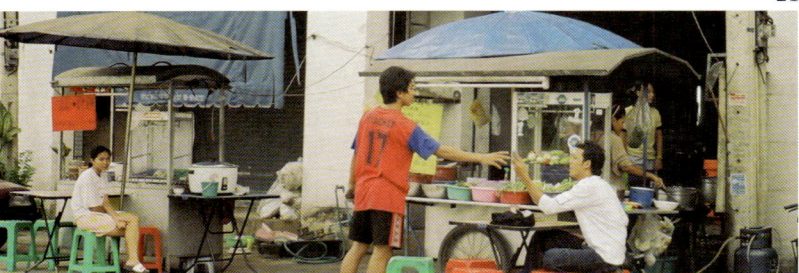

A cafeteria in a suburban residential district: There are many places where one can eat out. (Photo: Emiko Ochiai)

• THAILAND •

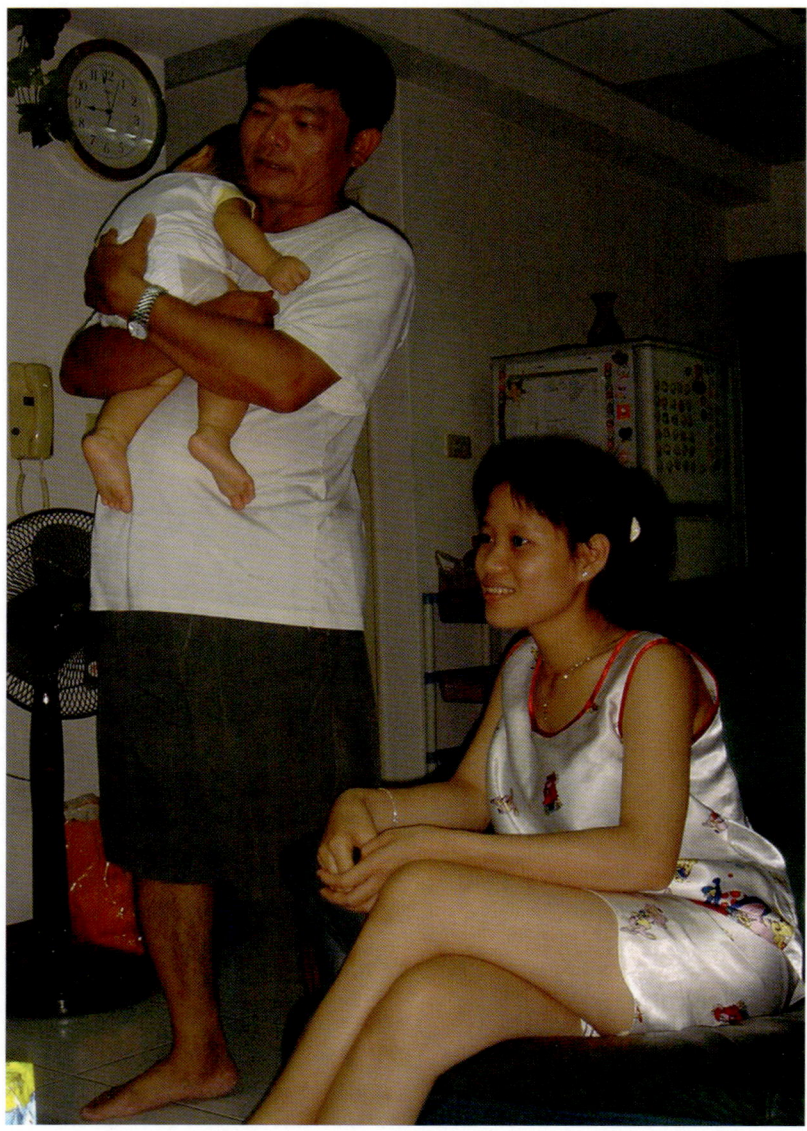

A father holding his baby, with his Vietnamese wife: In Taiwan, more than 20% of marriages are cross-border marriages, including cases where the wife is from Mainland China. (Photo: Emiko Ochiai)

• TAIWAN •

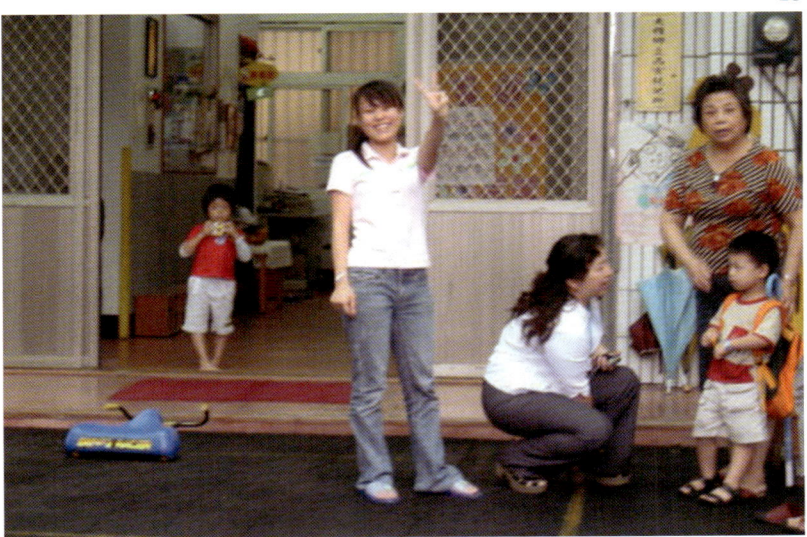

Picking up children at a daycare center: The woman on the right is the child's grandmother. Daycare centers accommodate children from age 2 to elementary school age. (Photo: Fujita Michiyo)

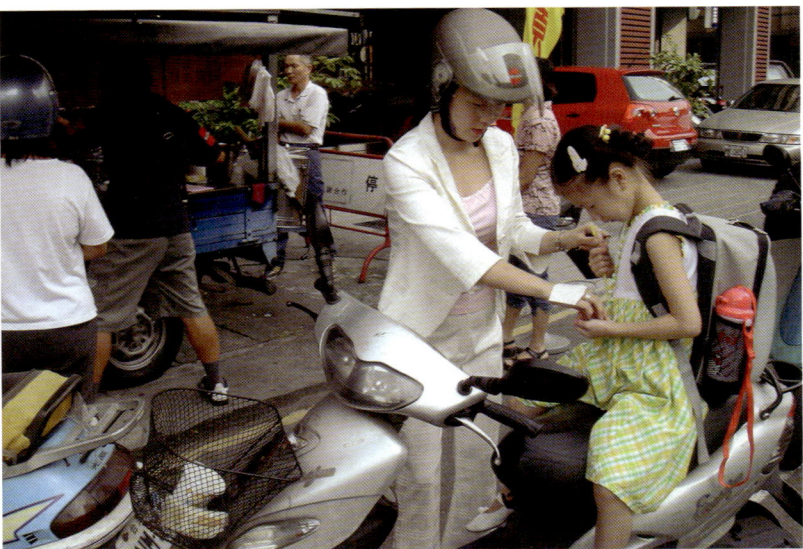

A mother taking her daughter to school on a motorbike: She has just bought breakfast for her daughter and herself at a "breakfast truck." Because commuting takes place at such an early hour, it is extremely common to buy breakfast and bring it to work or school. (Photo: Emiko Ochiai)

• TAIWAN •

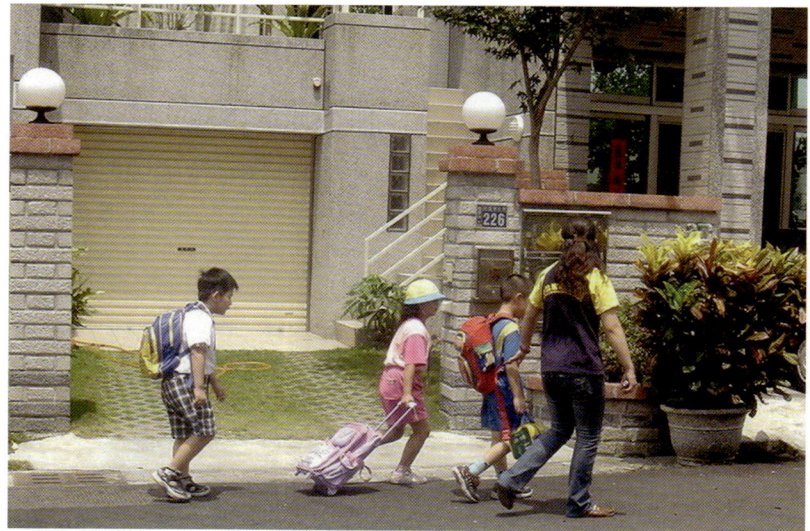

Elementary school students returning from school, escorted by a private cram-school teacher: It is common for cram schools to perform daycare functions for schoolchildren. (Photo: Emiko Ochiai)

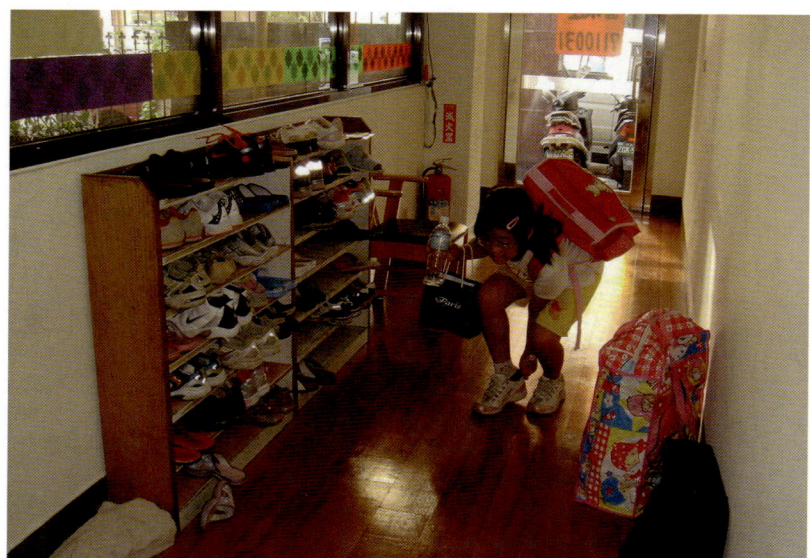

A daycare facility for school children that is attached to a kindergarten. (Photo: Emiko Ochiai)

• TAIWAN •

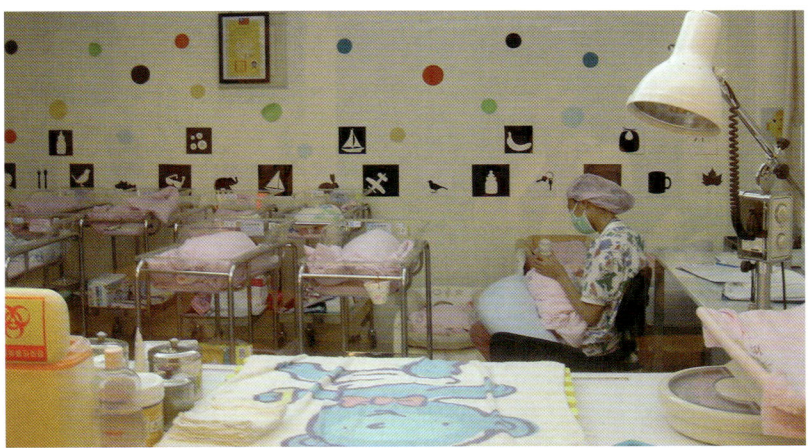

A state-of-the-art *zuo yuezi* center: *Zuo yuezi* centers are facilities that care for newborn children and their mothers. Through the glass door we can see a nurse, wearing a facemask, bottle-feeding an infant in the Infants' Room. In the foreground is a clean diaper-changing table. (Photo: Emiko Ochiai)

28

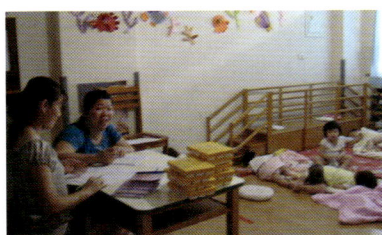

Nap time at a private infant care center: Infant care centers accept children from infancy to age 2. They are commonly found in downtown buildings. (Photo: Fujita Michiyo)

29

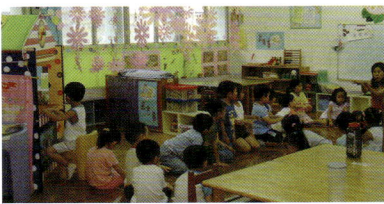

A class in a private kindergarten: Public kindergartens are intended for children from age 4 to just before entering elementary school, whereas private kindergartens accept children from about age 2 ½. (Photo: Fujita Michiyo)

30

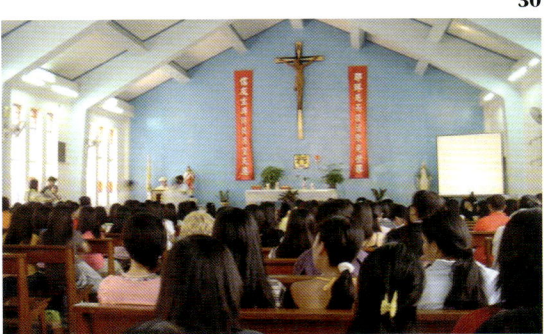

Many workers from the Philippines attend Catholic mass, conducted in English and Tagalog. (Photo: Emiko Ochiai)

• T A I W A N •

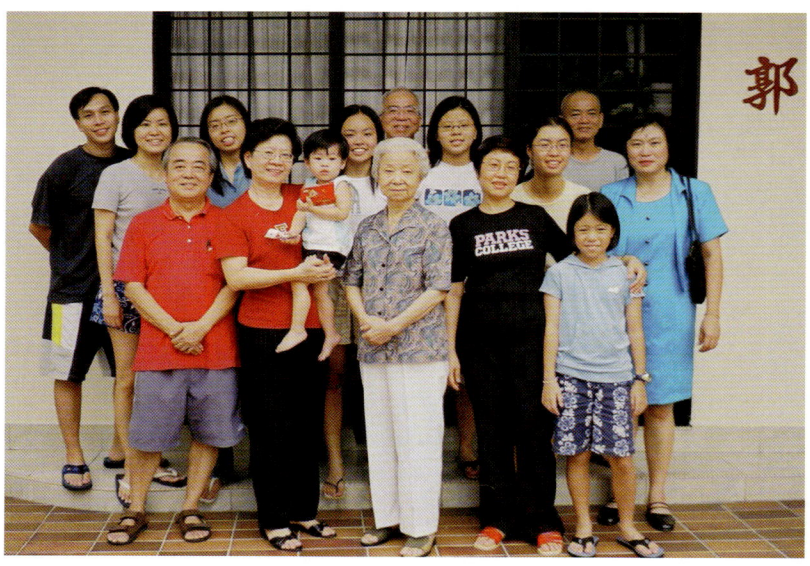

Weekend gathering of relatives (1): Every weekend, the families of this woman's five sons, her grandchildren, their spouses and children, and others meet to dine together. (Photo: Emiko Ochiai)

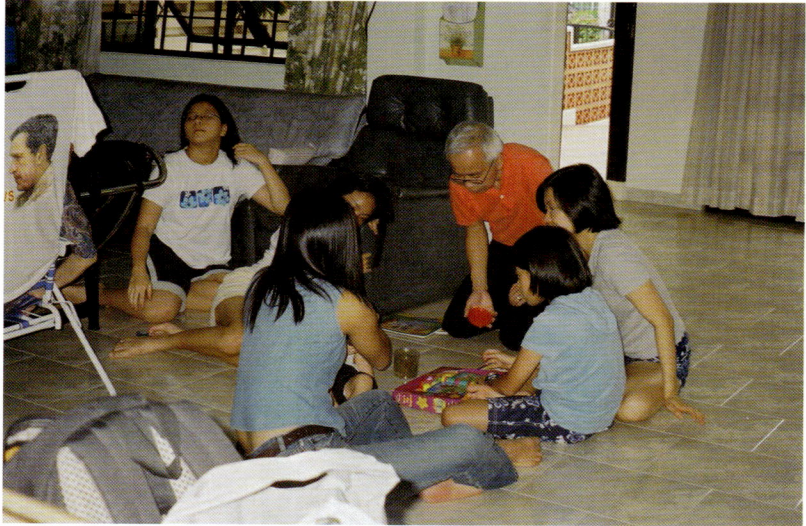

Weekend gathering of relatives (2): Cousins, aunts, uncles, nieces, nephews, grandfathers and great-uncles enjoy themselves together. (Photo: Emiko Ochiai)

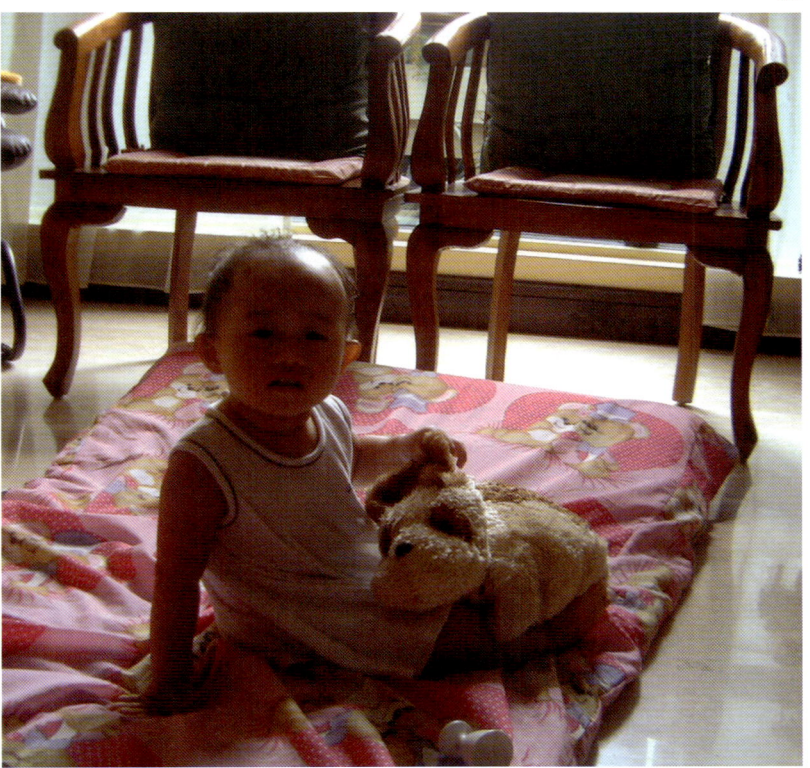

The 1-year-old daughter of a working couple: This girl is not sent to a daycare center, but cared for by her grandmother on her father's side, who lives with the family, and the maid. The maid does the physical work of babysitting while the grandmother supervises. (Photo: Kiwaki Nachiko)

• SINGAPORE •

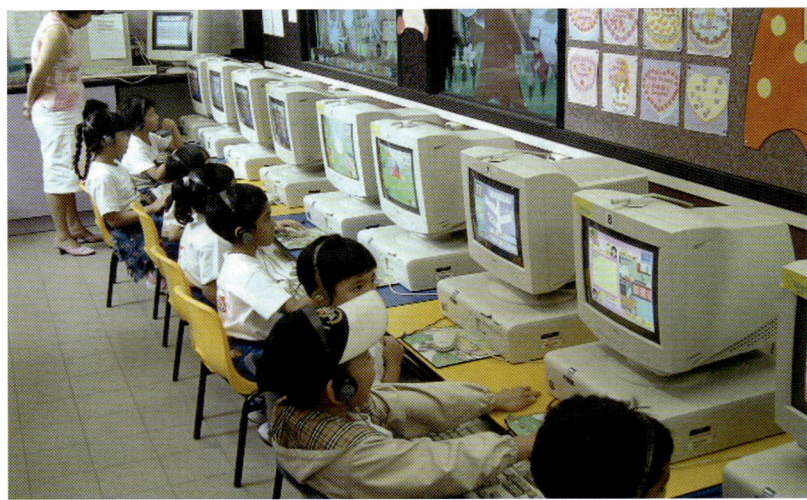

A computer classroom in a PCF kindergarten: A kindergarten established by the People's Action Party (PAP) Community Foundation (PCF). The PAP has worked to provide early childhood care and education since the 1960s. The kindergartens are primarily designed for children from 3 to 5 years old; there are also CCCs (Child Care Centres) for children from 18 months to 6 years. Recently the number of Infant Care Services for children 2 to 18 months old has also grown. (Photo and text: Ikeda Mitsuhiro)

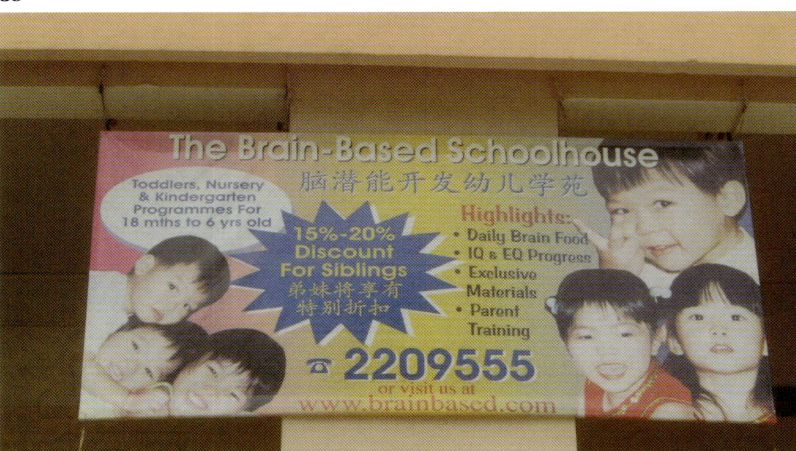

An advertisement for early education: In Singapore, with its zeal for education, classes offering academic training from early childhood are popular. Notices like this that advertise schools that combine childcare services with early childhood education can be found everywhere. (Photo: Kiwaki Nachiko)

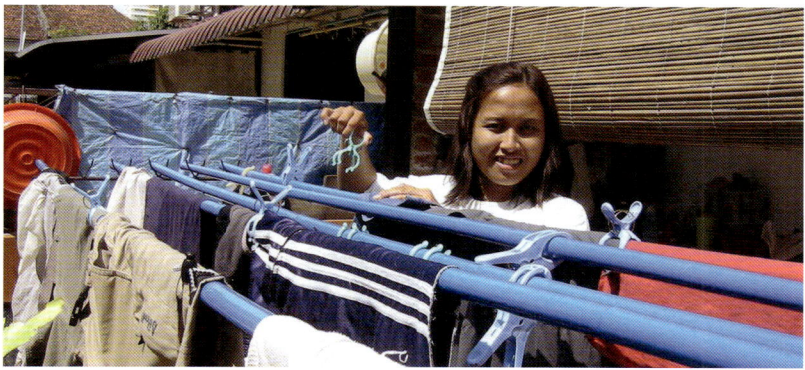

An Indonesian maid hanging up laundry for the family she works for: In Singapore, one out of 6 or 7 households employs a domestic worker from overseas. (Photo: Ueno Kayoko)

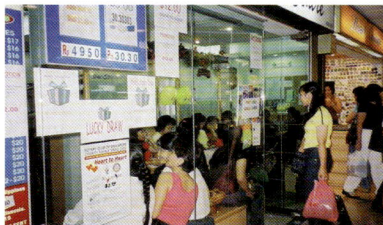

Domestic workers line up to send money home: On Sundays, the maids spend time at church, at shopping centers, and at overseas remittance offices. (Photo: Emiko Ochiai

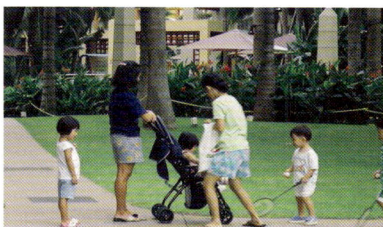

Maids watching over children at play: A number of maids gather in the courtyard of the condominium to watch over the children in their charge. (Photo: Emiko Ochiai)

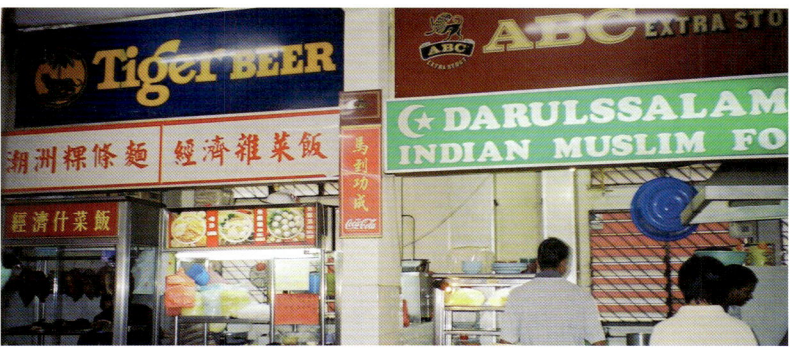

A food court on the first floor of a public housing facility built by the HDB (Housing Development Board): The variety of foods offered reflects the multi-ethnic composition of the population. (Photo: Emiko Ochiai)

• SINGAPORE •

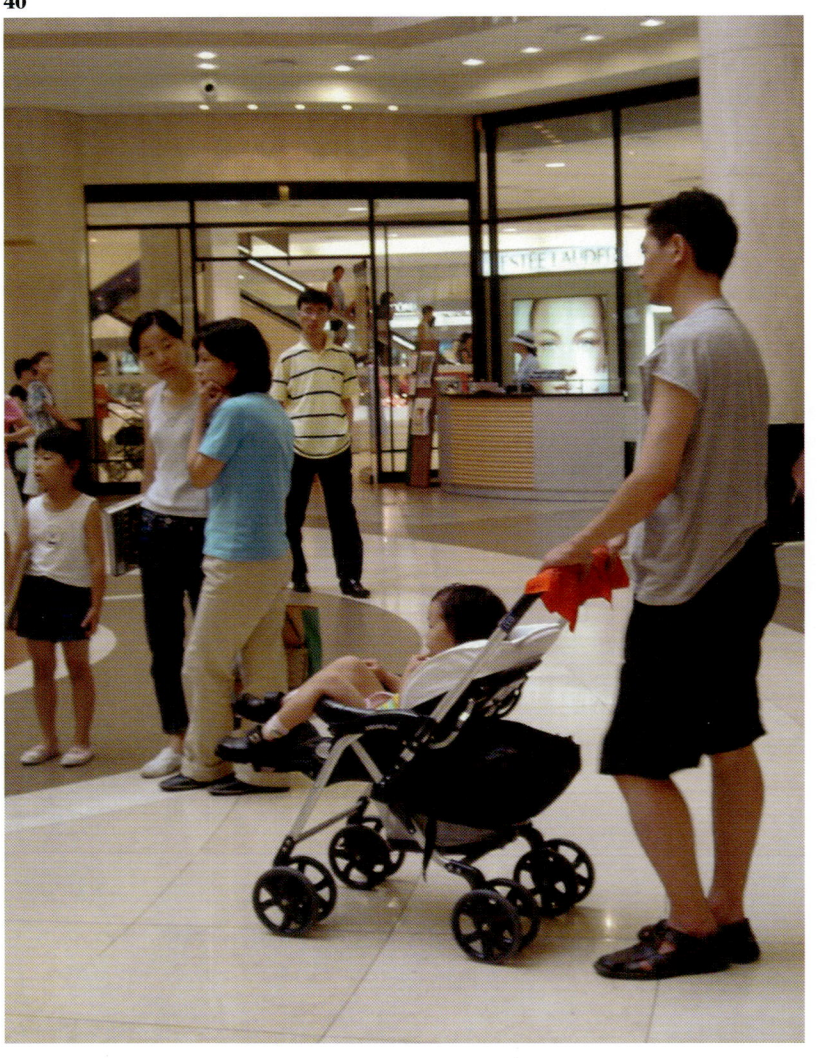

A father pushes a baby carriage at a shopping center. (Photo: Emiko Ochiai)

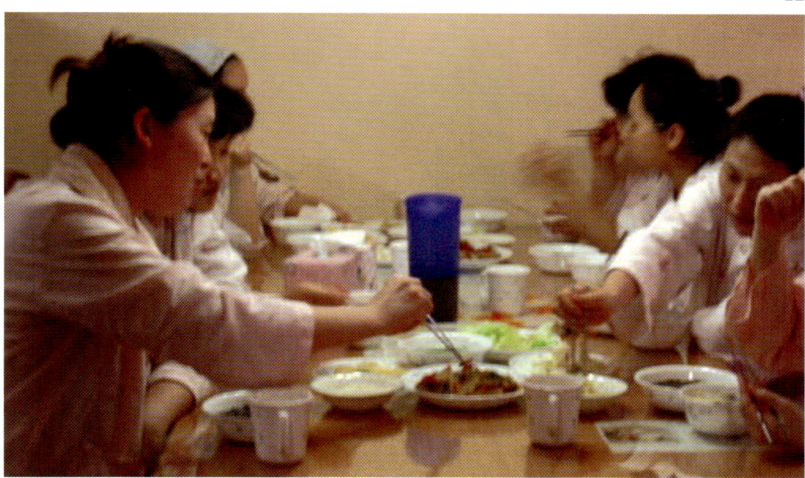

New mothers enjoying a meal at a Postpartum Recovery Center: Mothers and children can spend about two weeks at a Postpartum Recovery Center after the mother has been discharged from the hospital. These facilities have proliferated throughout the country since the late 1990s as the number of mothers with newborn children who lack someone to provide early infant care has increased. (Photo: Kobayashi Kazumi)

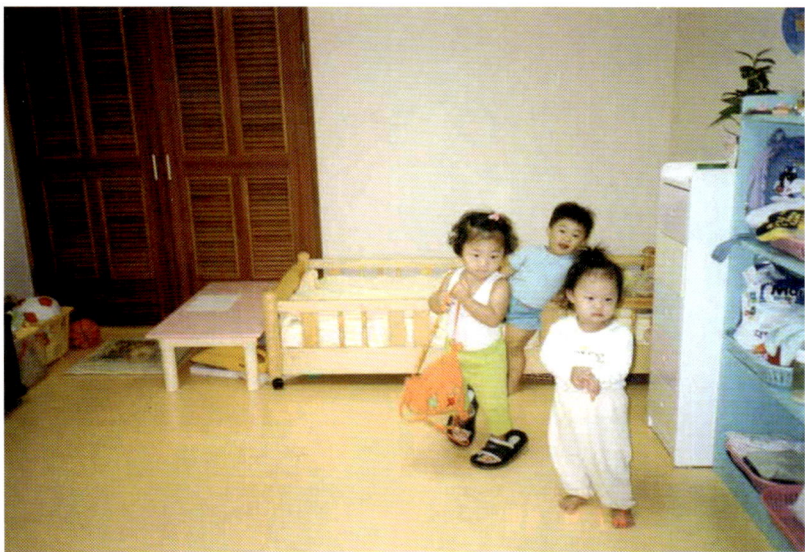

Eorini jip: *Eorini jip*, under jurisdiction of the Ministry of Health and Welfare, are for children aged 3 and over. (Photo: Yamane Mari)

• KOREA •

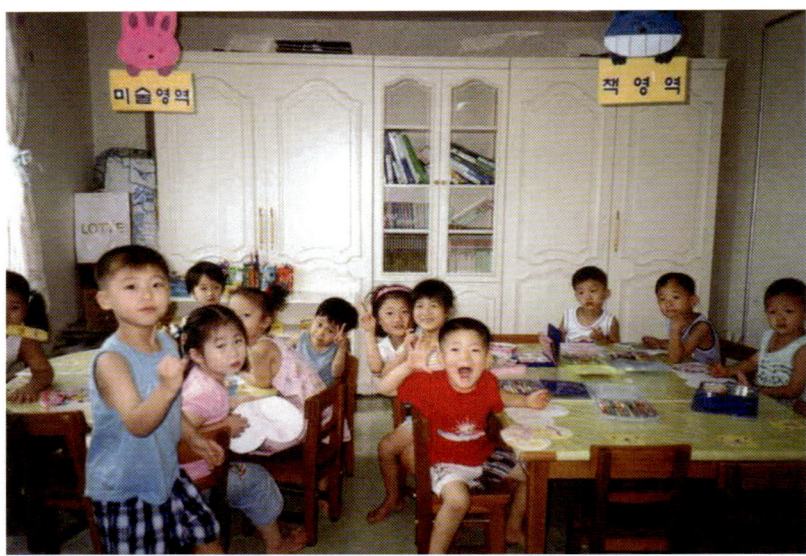

A kindergarten: Kindergartens are under the jurisdiction of the Ministry of Education, and accommodate children aged 3 and older. (Photo: Yamane Mari)

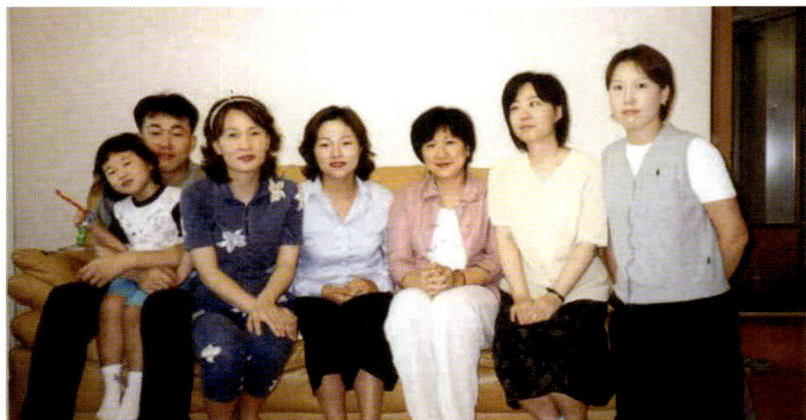

A network of kindergarten mothers: Kindergartens and *eorini jip* are available to families regardless of whether the mother is employed or not. This enables the formation of a network of mothers, both housewives and working mothers, who help each other with childcare. The investigators are 2nd and 3rd from the right. (Photo: Yamane Mari)

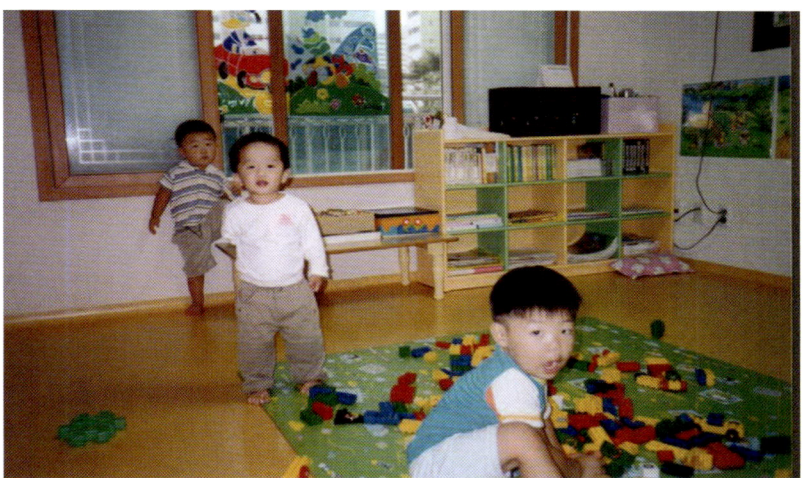

Nori bang: *Nori bang* are small-scale childcare facilities for children aged 1 to 3, often found in a room in a mass housing area. They are commonly used by working couples and single-parent families. (Photo: Yamane Mari)

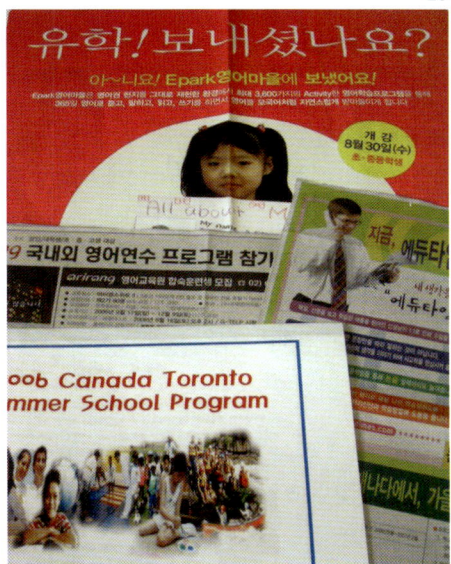

Advertisements for "English Villages," "English Internships," "Telephone English," and "Overseas Summer School": In Korea, cram schools are common, but there is a particular fervor for English-language education. "Educational migration," in which mothers live abroad with their children so the children can receive an English education, has become a common social phenomenon. The fathers, who remain in Korea to earn money for tuition and fees, are called "goose fathers" because they fly across the ocean to meet their wives and children. (Photo: Kobayashi Kazumi)

• KOREA •

Children playing in the water, watched by their grandfather. (Photo: Kiwaki Nachiko)

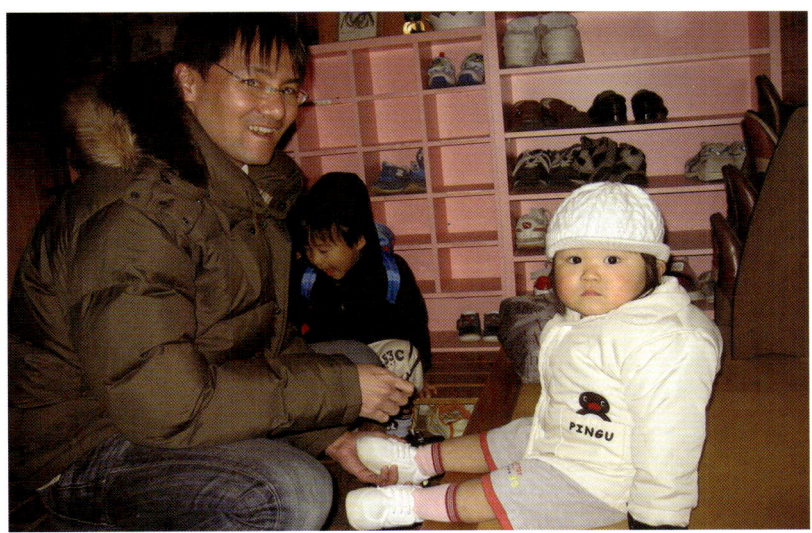

A father after picking up his children at a daycare center. (Photo: Kiwaki Nachiko)

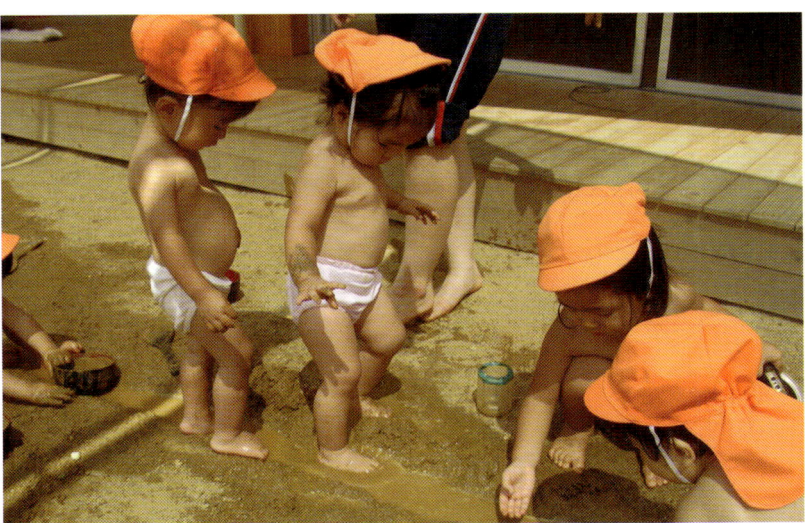

Children at a daycare facility (1): Because daycare centers are designed for the families of working mothers, some accept children from infancy onward. In contrast, kindergartens are considered educational facilities, and accept children from age 3 or 4 until elementary school age. The photograph shows small children playing in the mud out in the sunshine. (Photo: Takarazuka City Hiyoko Daycare Center)

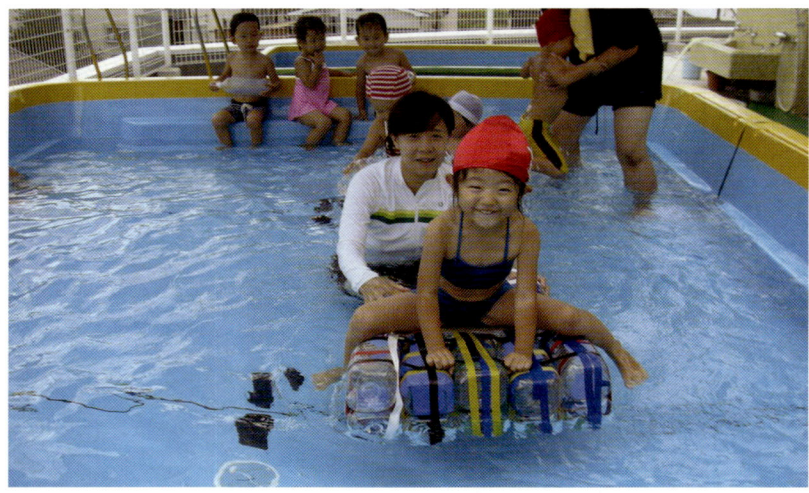

Children at a daycare facility (2): Children play in a pool on the roof of a daycare facility.
(Photo: Takarazuka City Hiyoko Daycare Center)

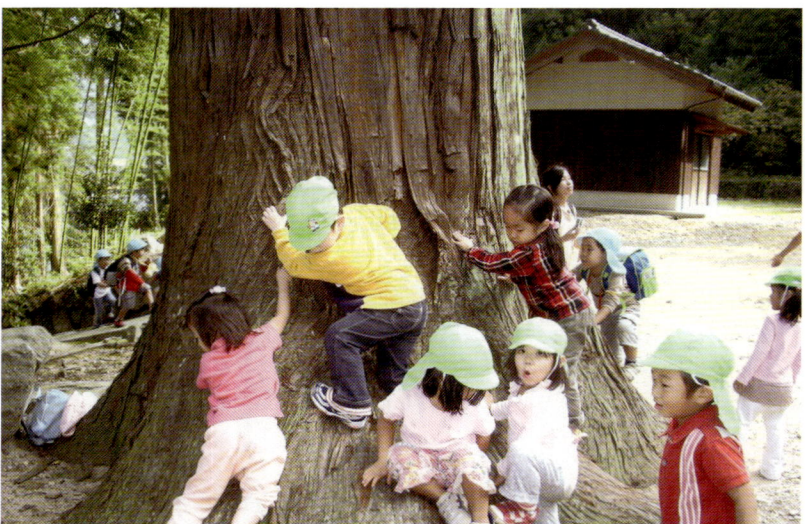

Children at a daycare facility (3): Children sometimes enjoy hiking at a nearby mountain.
(Photo: Takarazuka City Hiyoko Daycare Center)

• JAPAN •

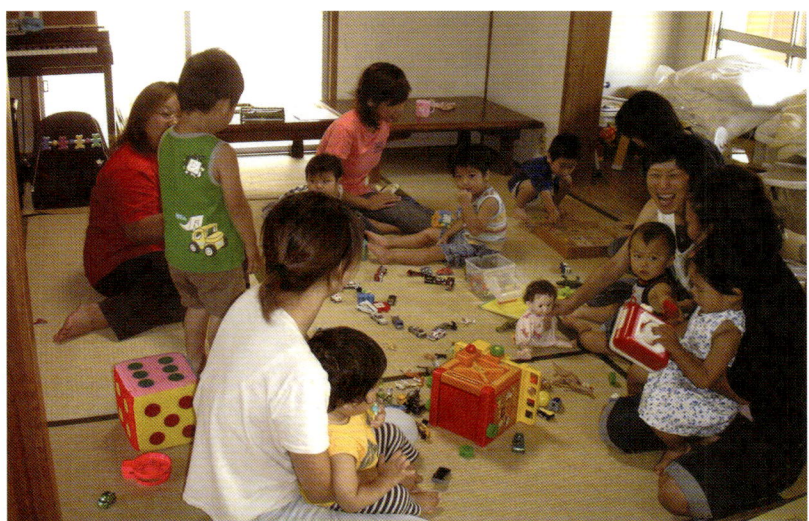

Activities of a non-profit childcare support organization (1): This organization provides regional childcare support, primarily run by childrearing mothers themselves. Its activities are geared toward creating a good childrearing environment by serving as a place where parents can meet other parents and drop in to get advice from experts. Mothers have brought their children and are sharing their experiences raising children with other mothers and with staff members. Support for "all families raising children," which is available to all mothers regardless of employment status, has been provided and developed since 2000 in order to address the problem of the isolation of unemployed mothers that has been identified as one of the causes of childcare anxiety and child abuse. (Photo: Furatto-Space Kongo)

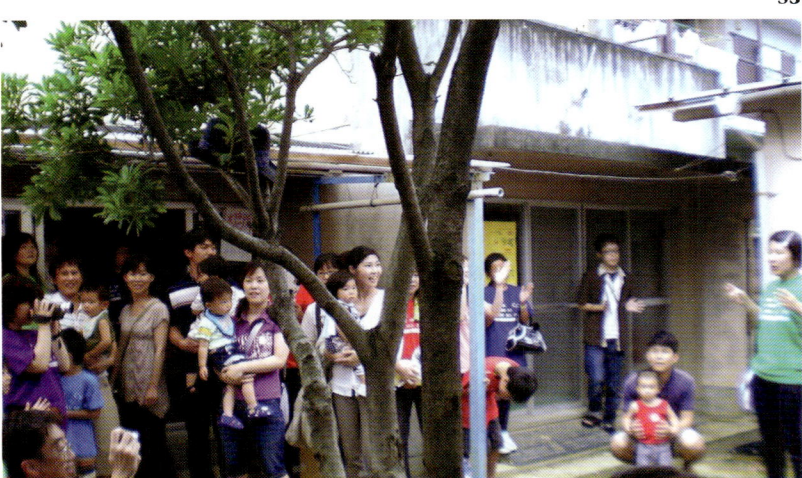

Activities of a non-profit childcare support organization (2): A festival held by a non-profit childcare support organization. The festival is held once a year on a public holiday. The staff set up booths, and fathers as well as mothers and children attend the festival. (Photo: Toe Tetsuri, Furatto-Space Kongo)

• JAPAN •

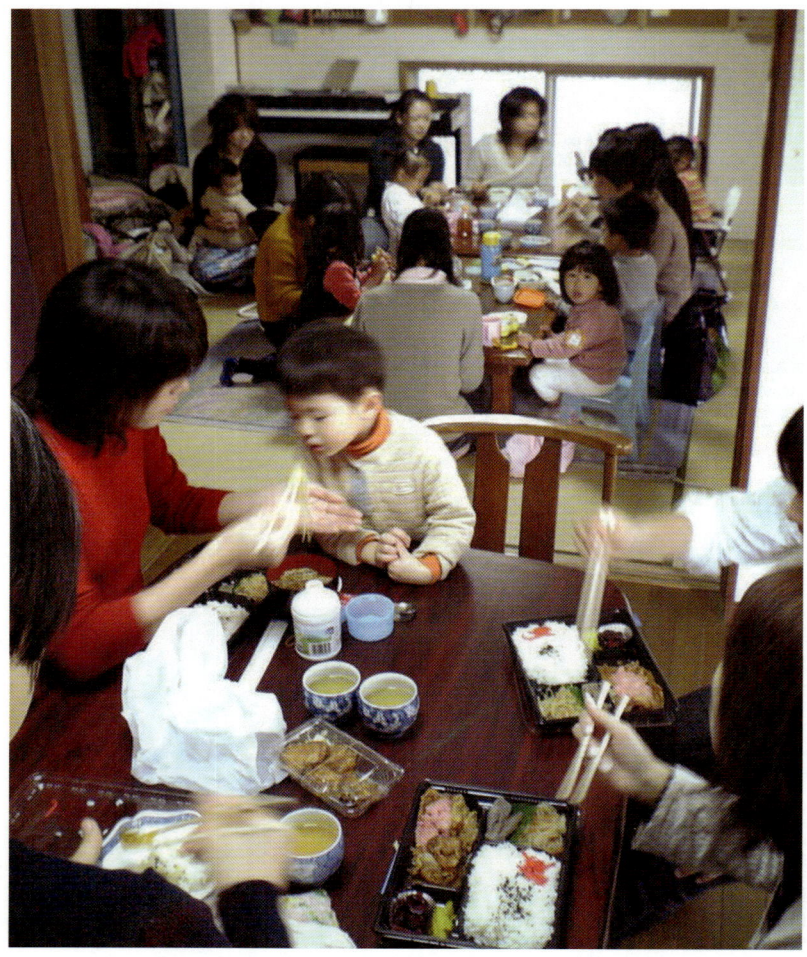

Activities of a non-profit childcare support organization (3): Parents and children who have been at the center since the morning are eating lunch, either brought from home or ordered from a shop. (Photo: Furatto-Space Kongo)

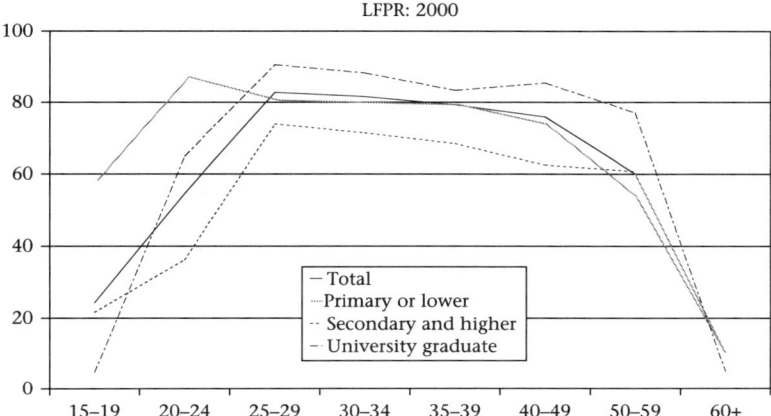

Figure 5.2   Female labor force participation rate (by level of education) in Bangkok Metropolitan Areas: 2000
Source: Wongboonsin, Kua, 2004b, "The Demographic Dividend and M-Curve Labor Participation in Thailand," *Applied Population and Policy*, 1(2):120.

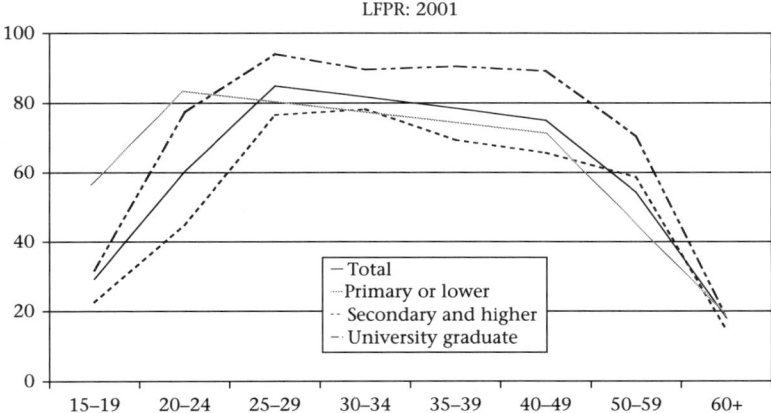

Figure 5.3   Female labor force participation rate (by level of education) in Bangkok Metropolitan Area: 2001
Source: Wongboonsin, Kua, 2004b, "The Demographic Dividend and M-Curve Labor Participation in Thailand," *Applied Population and Policy*, 1(2):120.

2002b: 42). A particularly serious problem is that there are almost no public facilities designed for the care of children younger than two-and-a-half years old. In Bangkok, for children three and older, apart from childcare facilities run directly by the city, each district (*Khet*) has childcare facilities run directly by that district ("children's centers"). At the time of the original study, in 2002, there were four children's centers in the research site, the Khlongsamwa district, but at the time of the supplementary study in August 2004, that number had grown to five. All of these facilities are in the old, traditional neighborhoods, not the more recent subdivided housing complexes. Furthermore, four of these five children's centers are small in size, designed to accommodate forty to eighty-five children; only one facility takes over 300 children. These facilities take care of children from approximately 7:30 a.m. to 5:30 p.m., and they are not used only by mothers who work outside the home. The children's centers located within the administrative districts are better described as preparatory educational institutions that provide standardized education to all children regardless of family circumstances rather than as childcare facilities. In Thailand, a society increasingly concerned with education, attention is shifting away from the development of childcare facilities for children and infants and towards early childhood education. Perhaps for this reason, there is a growing trend for early entrance to preschool (at age three). As a result, the childcare support system for children under three as well as other children not yet in elementary school is inadequate.

Meanwhile, in Bangkok it has become difficult to find live-in Thai maids, leading the wealthy classes to depend increasingly on foreign labor. In wealthy residential areas, many families now hire young women from Myanmar as live-in workers, despite differences in language and culture. Nevertheless, in education-centered Thailand there appear to be few cases of mothers leaving their children with foreign maids while they go out to work. The difficulty of securing hired labor and the change in attitudes about childcare appear to be leading to a decline in childcare practices dependent on hired labor. It is no longer believed that children will turn out well if simply left on their own. For highly educated working women, the choices seem to have narrowed to either arranging one's schedule to make it possible to send one's children to a "high quality" preschool or raising the children oneself.

OVERVIEW OF RESEARCH SITE AND METHOD OF INVESTIGATION

The research site was Residential Quarter B, a subdivided townhouse district in the Bangkok suburbs, located in *Khet* (district) Khlongsamwa. The Khlongsamwa district[1] is about 25 kilometers northeast of central Bangkok. Originally a farming region in the Bangkok suburbs, it was a part of the Minburi district until 1997, when the rapid population growth of the 1990s and the consequent transformation of the suburbs into residential districts led to its establishment as a separate district in 1998. The population of Khlongsamwa was 96,590 in 2001 (46,645 males and 49,945 females), and its population growth rate in 2000, at 7 percent, was the highest in Bangkok.[2]

The district is divided into five subdistricts or *Khwaeng*: Banchan, Saikongdin-tai, Samwatawan-tok, Samwatawan-ok, and Saikongdin.

Some subdistricts, like Banchan, are very urbanized, while others, like Samwatawan-ok, retain a very rural quality, with half or more of the land used for farming.

Residential Quarter B, the area where the research for this study was conducted, is a subdivided townhouse area that is typical of residential areas of the urban middle class. *Khwaeng* Samwatawan-tok, where Residential Quarter B is located, has a population of 23,110 (10,904 males and 12,106 females). In particular, Residential Quarter B is a huge housing project consisting of over 1,500 households that was built where there were once rice fields. On the other side of the canal lies a traditional agricultural village, and the land where Residential Quarter B is located was originally the villagers' land. According to basic data on Residential Quarter B published by the local government, in 2002 this quarter consisted of 700 households and 1,500 people (653 male, 847 female). Nearly half the residents (46 percent) of Residential Quarter B are civil servants; 20 percent are salaried workers or wage earners, and 7 percent are employed in a family business. Homes in Residential Quarter B were put on the market starting in 1996. The homes are townhouses, relatively inexpensive in comparison to detached houses. They are available in a variety of types and prices, with areas ranging from 16m^2 to 44m^2. They are thus affordable to young couples, and it may be assumed that many of the residents belong to the middle or lower range of the middle class.

The method of investigation was a questionnaire survey. Residences were visited in August of 2003, when responses were collected from 106 households. The data were classified according to type of household, the most common being nuclear households, which made up 60 percent of the total. Among these, there were seven cases of households consisting only of a husband and wife with no children or whose children had already grown up and had left the household, and six cases of households consisting of a widowed mother and her unmarried children. Stem households consisted of those households made up of a husband, wife, unmarried children, and one or more parents of the husband or wife, living together.[3] Single-member households included both unmarried persons and persons whose spouse had died or whose children had left home. Notably, even in the areas inhabited by the urban middle class in the Bangkok suburbs, the share of nuclear households was only about 60 percent. Also notable is the large number of households classified as "other." Households classified as "other" include cases where the couple lived with the parents of one or the other member, but the most common type in this category (twenty cases) were households that included siblings of the husband or wife, relatives, and other persons completely unrelated by blood to the family. In fact, even the stem households were simply households in which the parents of the husband or wife lived with the couple. This household structure is not informed by particular norms such as "one should live with the parents of the husband or wife" or "we invited the parents to live with us because this was the first (or second, etc.) child." In other words, these families were classified as stem households simply because the parents of the husband or wife were living with them; there is no qualitative difference between them and the families classified as "other." When the categories "other" and "stem" are combined they account for a considerable portion of the total; nuclear families by no means make up an overwhelming majority of households. In other words, it appears that the "network family" household structure is being maintained even in families of the urban middle class.

In this chapter, out of these 106 cases, we will take a closer look at the households that had school-age children (age fifteen and below), which we will call "parenting households."[4] In these seventy-five cases, the average age of the husband was forty and the average age of the wife thirty-six.[5] The average number of household members was 4.2. When divided according to the type of household, parenting households fell into the following categories: nuclear households (including three single-parent households), 62 percent; stem households, 15 percent; and other, 23 percent. There was great diversity in the home regions of both husbands and wives (the location where someone lived until age fifteen), but both husband and wife came from central Thailand in over 40 percent of households, with over half of these coming from Bangkok. The next most common region (for both husbands and wives) was northeast Thailand, with 21 percent of husbands and 25 percent of wives from that region.

As for professions, among the husbands, twenty-four were company workers (general office workers) and twenty-one worked for a family-run business, together accounting for a majority of the husbands. Only six men were civil servants. Among the wives, thirteen were office workers, and sixteen worked for a family-run business (including those who worked together with their husbands). Notable was the large number of women who were full-time housewives, thirty-four. We will discuss these housewives in detail later.

Concerning the highest level of education attained by the husbands and wives of parenting households, of seventy-five households, 48 percent of husbands and 44 percent of wives had graduated from a junior college or higher. Over 60 percent of both husbands and wives were high school graduates or higher. At the same time, however, it was found that a fairly large share (15 percent of husbands and 20 percent of wives) had only a primary school education. This is explained by two conditions that applied to several households. First, the questionnaire was directed at the head of household or the wife of the head of household, but in some cases it was filled out by one of the grandparents. Second, some households were headed by workers who had migrated from other regions and were living in townhouses rented out as company housing by employers.

The highest monthly income among the husbands was 100,000 *baht* (one U.S. dollar is equivalent to about 38 *baht*). The highest among the wives was 50,000 *baht*. There were twenty households in which the husband's income exceeded 30,000 *baht* and eight households in which it exceeded 40,000 *baht*. In the households in which the husband's income exceeded 30,000 *baht*, eleven of the wives were full-time housewives. On the other hand, there were six households in which the wife's monthly income was 30,000 *baht* or more; in all of these households, the husband also worked. Also, two-thirds of working women had monthly salaries of less than 20,000 *baht*. The most common response for wives regarding their income was "no income." These women classified as having "no income" were the very housewives we have mentioned above. In fact, about 40 percent of parenting households were households with full-time housewives, quite a departure from the traditional image of Thai women continuing to work after they have children. In the next section, we will turn our attention to these women who had become housewives, particularly those with university and junior college educations.

HOUSEWIVES WITH HIGH EDUCATIONAL ATTAINMENT IN RESIDENTIAL QUARTER B

Before looking in detail at full-time housewives raising children, it is necessary to adjust some of the data. This is because in some cases the respondents (couples) were the grandparents of those children. This was the case for five households out of thirty-four in which the wives were housewives. In the first case, the respondent (age forty-four) and her husband lived with her son's family. Both she and her daughter-in-law were housewives. Both her husband and son's work was classified as "general day labor," with monthly incomes of about 5,000 *baht*.

In the other four cases, the respondents were middle-aged and older women, all of whose children worked full-time. These women were looked after by their children while spending their time doing housekeeping and helping to raise their grandchildren and the children of nieces, nephews, and other family members. These households, then, were actually families with working couples.

To deal with this, in the first case we focused on the son's family (the son and his wife), while we disregarded the other four cases. We investigated in detail the remaining thirty cases as households with a housewife.

Among these thirty households, twenty-one were nuclear households (including one single-parent household), one was a stem household, and eight were classified as "other." The proportion of nuclear households among households with housewives was slightly higher than the proportion of nuclear households among all parenting households.

Turning to the husbands' occupations, the data indicate the following totals: general office workers, thirteen; family-owned business workers, six; retail sales, two; other skilled and unskilled workers, two. These professions account for over half of the total. The remainder belonged to the following categories, with one person in each: teacher, researcher, engineer, artisan, factory worker, public corporation employee, and unknown (a foreigner living abroad).[6]

Turning to the educational background of both husbands and wives, we note that two-thirds of both husbands and wives had high school or higher educations.[7] University graduates made up the largest group among the husbands, and the ratio of those with junior college education and higher to those with less education was about half and half. On the other hand, the background for wives was much more varied. Overall, the highest number, by a small degree, was of women who completed high school or higher, but eleven women had graduated from junior college or higher institutions. In sum, women who had completed high school, junior college, or university accounted for the majority.

In households with housewives, when the husband's yearly income was analyzed according to the wife's level of education, the following results were found. The monthly salaries of men whose wives had a primary school education or less were concentrated in the area of 20,000 *baht* or less.[8] Conversely, in households where the wife had a junior college education or higher, the monthly salary tended to be higher. In all five cases where the husband's income was 40,000 *baht* or more, the wife had a junior college education or higher. The lowest salary for the husband of a woman with a full university education (that is, not including junior college) was 20,000 *baht*, while the highest was 100,000 *baht*.

Below, we will focus on several cases of university-educated housewives.

CASE STUDIES: HIGHLY EDUCATED HOUSEWIVES

Case 1: Mar (age 37)
Mar is originally from the north. The townhouse is in her husband's name. She has been married for eight years. Her husband (age forty-three) is from the city and works as an engineer. Both she and her husband have university degrees. Her husband's monthly salary is 60,000 *baht*. They have a son (age seven) in elementary school and a daughter (age five) in preschool. She met her husband through her job. The key elements that influenced her in choosing her husband were educational background, personality, and appearance. She worked after graduating from college, but quit her job during the childcare period. She takes care of most of the housework and manages the household income. Both Mar and her husband want their children to get an education higher than university level. Although she herself is a housewife, she does not agree that "men should work outside and women should stay at home." She believes that a good life for a woman is "to get married, have children, temporarily quit working when you get married or give birth, and start working again after raising the children." However, she herself does not intend to seek employment again.

Case 2: Rat (age 35)
Rat is from a province that adjoins Bangkok. The townhouse is in her name. She moved to her present home when she married her husband, who is from the metropolitan Bangkok area. Her mother, age seventy-

one, lives in the same housing complex, and they spend most of their time together. Rat and her husband have a three-year-old son. Her husband, age thirty-five, has a Ph.D. and works in research. His monthly salary is 50,000 *baht*. In choosing her husband, the factors she considered were his ability, his kindness, and his love for his family. After graduating from university, she worked at a company for some time (she does not indicate when she quit). She and her husband both manage the family income. In her household, laundry is the wife's responsibility, but she, her husband, and her mother share the other chores. Childcare is shared among Rat, her husband, and her mother; her sister also comes from their family home to help out. They want their child to get as high an education as possible. She does not think that "men should work outside and women should stay at home." To her the ideal life for a woman is to "get married and have children, and to continue working all her life." It is not clear what she thinks about her own choice of a lifestyle different from her ideal, but she considers the most meaningful thing in her life right now to be "family."

Case 3: Chan (age 35)
Chan is from Bangkok; her husband is from a neighboring province. Both husband and wife are university graduates. The townhouse is in her husband's name. Her husband (age thirty-five) is a company worker and his monthly salary is 30,000 *baht*. The things she valued in deciding to marry her husband were his sense of responsibility and his good personality. Chan herself also worked for a company before marriage. They have two sons, ten and eight years old. When their sons were born, Chan's mother and her husband's mother came to help. Her parents live in Bangkok, and her father (age fifty-eight) is a civil servant. Her mother (also fifty-eight) is a housewife. They see her parents every week. She takes care of all housework and also manages the family income by herself. Normally, she cares for the children by herself, but when necessary, her mother helps; they also leave the children at her parents' home at times. Her sons were sent to a private preschool from the age of three-and-a-half. She hopes that her sons will get Ph.Ds. Although she is a housewife, she disagrees with the statement that "men should work outside and women should stay at home." The ideal life for a woman would be to successfully manage both work and marriage.

Case 4: Sao (age 35)
Sao is originally from a town neighboring Bangkok. Their townhouse is in the name of Sao and her husband. They moved there because they wanted to live in the suburbs, which had a good natural environment. She has a four-year-old son who goes to preschool. Both she and her husband are university graduates. They have known each other for a long time, ever since they were students, and they have been married for five years. Her husband, the same age as she, is from the south and operates his own business. His monthly income is 100,000 *baht*, the highest

income among all the parenting households. The key points in choosing her husband were his sense of responsibility, his earning ability, and the fact that he does not cheat on her. His sister (age forty-one and an office worker) is unmarried and lives with them. Sao worked for eight years after graduating from college. Because they sent their son to a private nursery school from age four months to eighteen months, it appears that she worked for some time after giving birth. After that, she stopped working to take care of her son herself, and sent him to a private preschool from the time he was thirty-two months old. Currently, she does most of the household chores, and she and her husband manage the household finances together. Although she is mainly in charge of childcare, her husband is responsible for taking their son to and from preschool. When they have to leave their son to go out, her husband's sister looks after him. She wants her son to receive an education higher than university level. She agrees somewhat with the idea that "men should work outside and women should stay at home." Her ideal for a woman's life is "to get married, have children, temporarily quit work when you get married or give birth, and start working again after raising the children." In everyday life, the most meaningful thing to her is "to see her son growing up."

Case 5: Mana (age 36)
Mana is from northeast Thailand. The townhouse is in her name. She has been married seven years. Both she and her husband are university graduates. Her husband is from central Thailand and is thirty-four years old. His monthly salary is 40,000 *baht*.[9] The factors she considered in choosing her husband were his earning ability, family assets, and sense of responsibility. They have a son in preschool (age three) and another son who is 3 months old. Also living with them are two maids from Mana's hometown, ages nineteen and twenty, who are paid 3,000 or 4,000 *baht*. Mana worked in various jobs, including civil service, sales, and working abroad, between her graduation from university and her marriage. Now she is a full-time housewife. She is responsible for handling the family finances, and does the shopping and cooking while leaving the rest of the housework to the maids. Either she or her husband takes their son to and from preschool, but they entrust a great deal of the childcare to the maids. The older son was sent to nursery school at the age of ten months. They also want to send the younger son to a private nursery school. She wants her sons to get an education higher than university level and to work as airline pilots or doctors. She does not really agree that "men should work outside and women should stay at home," but she does agree with "getting married, having children, temporarily quitting work when you get married or give birth, and starting working again after raising the children." At present, the most meaningful thing to her is "seeing her sons grow up."

Case 6: Wila (age 30)
Wila is from northeast Thailand. The townhouse is in her older brother's name. She has been married for five years. She and her husband moved

here three years ago. They have a two-year-old daughter. Both she and her husband are university graduates. They both come from farming families. Her husband (age thirty) is from the north. He works at a hotel for a monthly salary of 20,000 *baht*. She and her husband have known each other since they were in university. She based her decision to marry her husband on his sense of responsibility, his abilities in many areas, and his educational background. Wila, too, worked at a hotel after graduation. She does almost all of the housework. She and her husband manage the finances together, and both help in taking care of their daughter. They never leave their daughter at home to go out or leave her with relatives or their own parents and siblings. They want to send her to a private preschool when she turns three. She wants her daughter to get a Ph.D. She disagrees with the statement that "men should work outside and women should stay at home." She sees the ideal life for a woman as "not marrying and working throughout one's life."

We can see in the above six cases certain common elements. To summarize, these highly educated wives all are very interested in educating their children. They are all against the concept of division of gender roles, yet most of them support the woman's life course in which a woman leaves work during the childrearing period to become a housewife. We do not know, however, whether they will return to the workplace. In some cases a wish to return to work seems to be present, but there also are cases in which women continue to be housewives even when the support of relatives or live-in maids is available. This indicates that a lack of a place to leave their children is not the only reason they have become housewives. In addition, the fact that they are housewives does not necessarily mean that they are responsible for all of the housework. For what reasons did they quit their jobs to become housewives? What do they think are the most important roles for them to play as housewives? Questionnaires do not tell us enough to fully understand these questions; further investigation is needed.

CASE STUDIES: WORKING HOUSEWIVES AND CHILDREARING – ISSUES FOR EMPLOYED URBAN MIDDLE-CLASS WOMEN

Case 7: Yuw (age 38) (A typical case of the M-curve life course)
Yuw is from southern Thailand and is a graduate of a commercial college. The townhouse is in her husband's name. She has been married eleven years. The things that were important to her in choosing her husband were his sense of responsibility, personality, and appearance. Her husband (age forty-three) is from Bangkok. After graduating from a commercial high school he joined the military. After his discharge, he began working for a company providing employment introduction services, where he still works today. His monthly salary is 12,000 *baht*. They have a four-year-old daughter who is at preschool and a thirty-two-month-old son. After graduating from commercial college, Yuw worked in the management

department of a company before becoming a housewife. At present, she has gone back to work in the management section of a firm, but her monthly salary is only 5,000 *baht*. Although she and her husband are working, Yuw does most of the housework and also manages the family finances. She has three younger sisters in Bangkok, and meets them about once a week. Since the youngest sister, age twenty-three, is still single, Yuw asks her for help with the children when needed. A big factor in Yuw's return to work was her daughter's reaching the age of thirty-two months, when it became possible to send her to preschool. At present, this daughter is in a public preschool, while the younger child, the son, is at a private preschool. Yuw takes the children to and from preschool. She wants to give her children as much education as she can afford. She would like her son to become a policeman and her daughter a teacher. She disagrees with the statement that "men should work outside and women should stay at home," but she does agree with "getting married, having children, temporarily quitting work when you get married or give birth, and starting working again after raising the children."

Case 8: Ratna (age 40) (A typical case of managing both work and marriage)

Ratna is from northern Thailand and a university graduate. She works as a manager in a private firm. Her husband, forty-seven years old and from central Thailand, is a civil servant with a master's degree. Their responses do not indicate how many years they have been married, but based on the age of their oldest child, it has been at least fourteen years. Her husband's monthly salary is 40,000 *baht*. Her pay is 50,000 *baht*. They have two sons, one in junior high school (thirteen years old) and one in elementary school (ten years old). Her father, age seventy-seven, also lives with them. After graduating from university, Ratna continued working without interruption, and when her son was born her mother (age seventy-two) took care of him. (At present, her mother is living with her younger sister, and she sees her mother about every three months.) They are a high-income family but they do not hire maids or other help; the family takes care of all housekeeping. Ratna does the housecleaning and her husband does the cooking. They take turns with the shopping. After meals each person cleans up after himself or herself. The boys are responsible for taking out the trash. She and her husband each manage their own income separately. At present, the boys are able to take care of themselves, but when they were younger, she sometimes left them with her mother or siblings for short periods. They also used a variety of child-care services for bringing up their children. These included a childcare center at a hospital from age seven or eight months, and babysitters and private preschools from age two. They also made use of extended-hours childcare services at the preschool and childcare center. The sons are taking Tae Kwon Do. Ratna and her husband want their sons to get at least master's degrees, and hope to own their own business in the future. In this case the questionnaire was filled out not by the wife but by the husband, Pho. Pho disagrees with the statement that "men should work outside and women should stay at home," but does agree that a woman should "get married, have children, temporarily quit work when she gets married or gives birth, and start working again after raising the children."

Case 9: Saow (age 34)
Both Saow and her husband are originally from the south. They have known each other ever since they were students, and have been married for nine years. Her husband (thirty-four years old) graduated from college and is working for a company as a broker and sales representative. His monthly income is 10,000 *baht*. Saow graduated from a technical junior college, and is working for a computer company as a programmer. Her monthly income is 36,000 *baht*. They have a five-year-old daughter who goes to preschool and a two-year-old son. After Saow gave birth, her mother helped her with childcare. They employ a maid and entrust all of the housework to her. Saow manages the household finances, and her husband is in charge of taking their daughter to and from preschool. For childcare, they have hired maids and nannies to take care of their children, although they are the primary caregivers. She wants her children to receive an education higher than college level. She wants them to become people with a strong sense of responsibility. She disagrees with the idea that "men should work outside and women should stay at home." She sees "getting married, having children, temporarily quitting work when you get married or give birth, and starting working again after raising the children" as ideal for women.

It goes without saying that in order for the wife to work outside the home during the childrearing period, there must be places where and people with whom the children can be safely entrusted, including relatives and neighbors as well as private daycare centers. Interestingly, as in Case 9, some women who did not take a break from work after marrying still support the idea of taking at least a few years of maternity leave and later returning to work. In this study, we asked about their "ideal life course for a woman," and illustrated the responses from seventy-five parenting households (including those with working mothers) in Figure 5.4 and households with a housewife in Figure 5.5.

In parenting households, forty-five people, or 62 percent of respondents, agreed that the ideal life course for a woman is "to get married, have children, temporarily quit working when she gets married or gives birth, and start working again after childbearing" – that is, M-curve employment.[10] Only seventeen respondents (less than 40 percent) supported the idea of "getting married, having children, and continuing work for their whole life" – that is, evenly balancing work and family. Because these answers were collected household by household and some respondents were males, they do not necessarily reflect the wives' own opinions. However, they do show that opinions like this are held by a significant number of people in parenting households in Thailand.

Asia's New Mothers

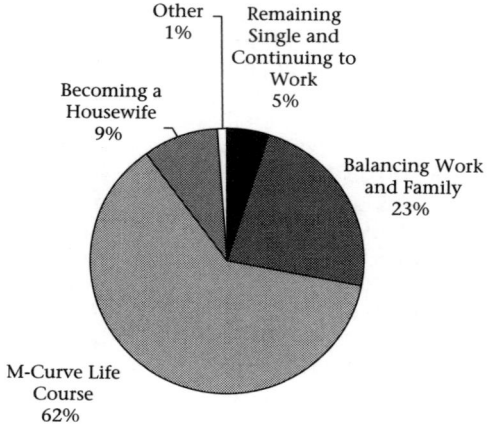

Figure 5.4 Ideal women's life course in parenting households (including those with working mothers)

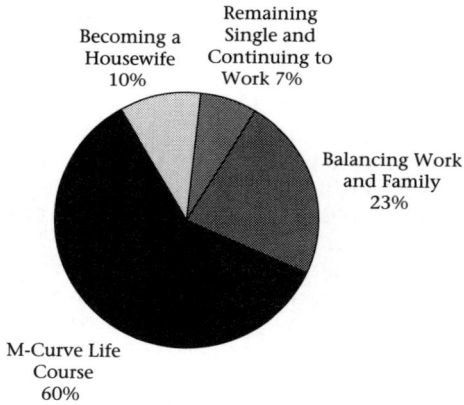

Figure 5.5 Ideal women's life course in parenting households with housewives

Moreover, when we limit our focus to households with a housewife, we find that 60 percent support M-curve employment and only seven people, or 23 percent, support "successfully balancing work and family." Seven respondents in parenting households supported "stopping working when one gets married or gives birth and remaining a housewife thereafter," and three of these were housewives.

These statistics show that a belief in M-curve employment as an ideal life course is found in a majority of the households surveyed, not only those with a housewife, but also in parenting households in general.

Why, then, do so many women believe life courses that are so different from their actual lives to be ideal? There are two possible reasons. First, in Thailand, and especially Bangkok, where there has been considerable growth in the importance attached to education, children are no longer seen as beings who "grow up on their own." For the urban middle-class population, a high level of education is the most useful device for moving upward in society. Thus, parents' primary gift to their children is a strong educational grounding. From the time their children are very small, parents think about how their children can survive in an education-based society. Another reason for women to leave the workplace despite their belief in gender equality may be the great difficulty for young couples to take care of their children while working. Unless couples employ a variety of networks of support, from parents living outside of Bangkok or siblings who have come to live there, as well as private childcare centers, babysitters, and maids, they will not be able to manage both raising children and working.

On the other hand, for middle-class families, it is possible to survive on the husband's income even if the wife stops working and becomes a housewife. Therefore, wives have the option of deciding which of two choices is best: to continue working or to focus on childcare. If there are no relatives, childcare facilities, or reliable childcare workers available, they may choose to become housewives.

Whether or not women return to the work force after raising children may depend on their educational background and career experiences. For women from rural areas without a high educational background, it is likely that once they stop working and become housewives to raise their children, they will remain housewives. But even for women with university degrees it is not at all easy to return to their original workplace, and it is as hard to find a suitable new position in Thailand as it is, for example, in Japan. In the city of Bangkok, along with the dramatic growth of the urban middle class, the importance of educational background for competing on the job market has grown greatly. The difference in salary and working conditions between those who have completed a university education and those who have not is growing rapidly. For this reason, increasing numbers of people are using their non-working hours to take courses in the Open University or to attend evening or weekend university courses in order to get a university degree. This increase in the number of university graduates has resulted in the phenomenon of "bachelor's degree inflation" in Bangkok. As a result, merely attaining the status of university graduate is no longer enough to guarantee a good job. As one resident said, "Nowadays, you can't get a good position even with a bachelor's degree. When childcare costs, transportation expenses, the cost of eating out, and the cost of work clothing are deducted there's hardly anything left of your salary. In such a case it makes more sense to stay home as a housewife." On the other hand, judging from the strong desire to give their children a high level of education, once the children get older, it is likely that to help pay for the growing costs of education, some of these wives will need to go to work again. Women who had quit their work "for the children" will find themselves going back to work "for the children" as well. This is the motive behind the "choice" of the M-curve life course.

Even if a woman does have the desire to work, the challenges faced by Bangkok women with university degrees in successfully managing both work and parenting are numerous. The inadequacy of the childcare support system, the decreasing number of good jobs, and the growing emphasis on high-level educational degrees for success in Thai society strongly influence not only the future of these women's children, but their choices about their own life course after having children.

FAMILY NETWORKS AND THE MODERN FAMILY

The author of this study has previously divided Bangkok housewives belonging to the urban middle class and living in suburban residential districts into two categories: "positive" and "passive" (Hashimoto 2003a: 67–72). "Passive" describes the women who, despite having the desire to work, decided to leave work during the childrearing period because it was difficult to continue to work. The passive type can be divided into those who wish to return to work and those who wish to remain housewives. "Positive" describes women who become housewives of their own accord, in order to raise their children. (Hashimoto 2003a: 67–71). However, an examination of the cases of the housewives living in Residential Quarter B gives one a sense that the boundary between "positive" and "passive" is unclear and ambiguous.

For instance, according to this classification, the M-curve life course would be an example of "passively" becoming a housewife. Yet if we look at the case studies of the housewives, we see that they did not necessarily make their decision passively. In every instance, these women had a strong desire for their children to achieve a high level of education, making it very possible that they will go to work in the future to help pay for their children's education.

With highly educated women no longer a rarity, with a higher degree becoming more and more essential to success, and with the permeation of the values and lifestyle of the "modern family" into Thai society, the traditional assumption that it is meaningful and important for educated women to continue working is certainly being shaken. Women who follow the M-curve pattern of "quitting work for their children and going back to work for their children" should probably be reclassified as "positive" housewives.

Despite this, the relatively high proportion of nuclear households among those with housewives suggests that some women become housewives precisely because other sources of childcare support are not available. In the cases of working couples in parenting households who are helped by people like grandmothers and relatives who take on "housewife" roles, we can see that the network of relatives characteristic of a "network family" society continues to function as an important source of childcare support.

The existence of highly educated housewives in the suburban areas of Bangkok appears to confirm Wongboonsin's hypothesis that the M-curve pattern is the result of women leaving work to care for children. Furthermore, when women's labor force participation rates are broken down according to level of education, the M-curve dip in the life course graph of university-educated women seems to indicate a discord in the lives of these highly educated urban women, who waver between traditional family culture and the newer modern family culture. The dip in the curve is quite small, and there is no indication at present that this M-curve labor pattern will become firmly established among urban middle-class women. However, it is certainly true that in our investigation, we encountered many more highly educated housewives than we had expected. There is no question that Thai women are facing numerous, unprecedented changes of various types in trying to successfully balance having children with continuing to work. These changes, which mainly do not appear on the graphs, continue their steady progress, raising many new questions for the future.

NOTES

1.   The Bangkok administrative unit known as *Khet*, here translated as "district," can also be translated as "special district." The latter term distinguishes it from the regional administrative units of *Muban* (the smallest administrative unit, meaning "settlement" or "village"), *Tambon* (the unit immediately above and larger than *Muban*), and *Amphur* which are also frequently translated as "districts." In this paper, unless indicated otherwise, "district" will be used to refer to *Khet*, that is, special districts of Bangkok.

2.   The figures for 2001 given below are taken from *Khomun chumchon* (Basic Data on the Communities), ed. and pub. Khlongsamwa District Department for Social Development, 2001.

3.   In this chapter, we will use the term "stem household" to mean not only those with both parents of the husband or wife present, but also those with only one such parent (mother or father).

4.   We selected households in which at the youngest child, at least, was fifteen or younger – the age of attending junior high school. We have also included one case in which the household consisted only of a husband and wife, but the wife was pregnant and already preparing for the birth of the child. This woman reported her concrete future plans for raising the child.

5.   This average omits the four men and three women whose age was unknown.

6.   The husband whose profession is not known was a Westerner living abroad. The respondent was his wife, a Thai woman. No response was given for the husband's profession. She was living as a housewife and raising their daughter, living on 30,000 *baht* sent monthly by her husband.

7.   In the case described at the beginning of this section of the chapter, in which the grandparents lived together with their son and his wife, both of the grandparents had only a primary school education. The son was a high school graduate, his wife a junior high school graduate.

8 The presence of extremely low-income households can be explained by cases in which parts of Residential Quarter B are rented by entities like construction companies to be used as company housing for workers, cases of home owners renting out their property, and so on.

9 On the response sheet, the husband's job was described as "hired labor paid with a daily wage," with the particular content of the job not specified. For purposes of this study, his job was classified under the heading "other skilled and unskilled labor."

10 It must be noted that because the questionnaires were directed at the household as a whole, the respondent was not always the wife herself. There were 21 such cases for parenting households (16 answered by the husband, 1 by the husband's aunt, 1 by the husband's mother, 1 by the wife's mother, 1 by the wife's younger sister) and 4 cases for full-time housewife households (3 by the husband and 1 by the wife's younger sister). Therefore, the opinions expressed were not necessarily those of the wife herself who was then involved in parenting. In the cases selected in this chapter, all questionnaires but one were answered by the wife. In any event it is very interesting that in Thai family culture, which encourages highly educated women to work outside the home, even family members other than the wife herself express opinions supporting the "M-curve life course."

Modern Population Trends, M-Curve Labor-Force Participation and the Family

KUA WONGBOONSIN
PATCHARAWALAI WONGBOONSIN

INTRODUCTION

Three major challenges characterize modern population trends: social complexity; transition from a demographic dividend to a demographic onus; and the strong impact on the family of the changing structure of labor-force participation. A "demographic dividend" is a beneficial feature of an age structure in which the working-age population, following a decline in fertility, is growing more rapidly than the overall population. A rising proportion of the population in the age range of labor-force participation relative to the population in the ages of dependency (children and the elderly) is considered a window of opportunity for accumulating economic benefits to individuals and society as a whole (Mason 2002). The demographic dividend normally takes place only once in the middle phase of a demographic transition and lasts just a few decades. Thereafter, an increase in the dependency ratio signals the fading away of the opportunity to capitalize on the conditions for a demographic dividend. Low fertility and stable mortality result in an increasing proportion of the population who are elderly (Wongboonsin and Guest, eds. 2005), potentially leading to a situation called a "demographic onus" that is associated with burdens to the society, the family, and individuals (Ogawa, Kondō and Matsukura 2004).

This study maintains that the demographic transition alone does not automatically result in a demographic dividend. If a state is not equipped with appropriate policies and supporting institutional mechanisms, it may face a burden rather than a dividend, or may lose the chance to maximize the benefits of a demographic dividend in time to provide resources for the future.

MODERN POPULATION TRENDS

Against the backdrop of globalization, modern societies are identified with increasing individualism, decreasing presence of intergenerational extended families, urbanization, tensions in the labor market, and advances in science and technology. These conditions affect the flows of labor migration and changes in reproductive behavior among women, which result in declining population growth and a complex population composition.

Migration has two aspects, internal and international. The latter includes three categories of persons: (a) regular migrants; (b) irregular or undocumented migrants; and (c) refugees, asylum seekers, and displaced persons. The influx of regular and irregular migrant workers into the Asia-Pacific region and the European Union has recently increased. In areas where population has stagnated, immigration may be considered a means of injection for demographic purposes. Of the three categories, irregular immigrants have become a very acute problem. Working conditions and social problems of migrant workers have become issues in most middle and high-income countries throughout the Asia-Pacific region and beyond. Migrants in those societies often cannot afford the higher costs of health, education, housing, and taxes. Meanwhile, a brain drain of scientists and skilled workers constitutes another serious factor affecting demographic trends (Patcharawalai and Kinnas 2005).

The natural population of a modern society is also marked by changes in age composition and growth. In Thailand, for example, anticipated changes in population growth, driven by changing fertility over the last four decades, are expected to have a profound impact on population composition. The proportion of the population below fifteen years of age is projected to decline from 24.65 percent in 2000 to 17.95 percent in 2025. This compares with an increasing proportion of those in the labor-force ages (fifteen to fifty-nine) from 65.92 percent in 2000 to 67.08 percent in 2009, followed by a decline to 62.05 percent in 2025. Thailand will also confront a substantial increase in the proportion of the population aged sixty and above, from 9.43 percent in 2000 to 19.99 percent in 2025 (Wongboonsin, Guest and Viphan 2004: 6, Fig. 3).

The data from the projection reveal that the proportion of population in the labor-force ages (fifteen to fifty-nine) will decline only slightly (around 3.87 percentage points) during the period 2000–2025. The decline in the proportion of children below fifteen is more pronounced, with a roll-back of around 6.70 percentage points. At the same time, the proportion of population above sixty years of age is anticipated to increase around 10.56 percentage points.

In contrast to the dwindling curve of the proportion of the population below fifteen and between fifteen and fifty-nine years of age, the

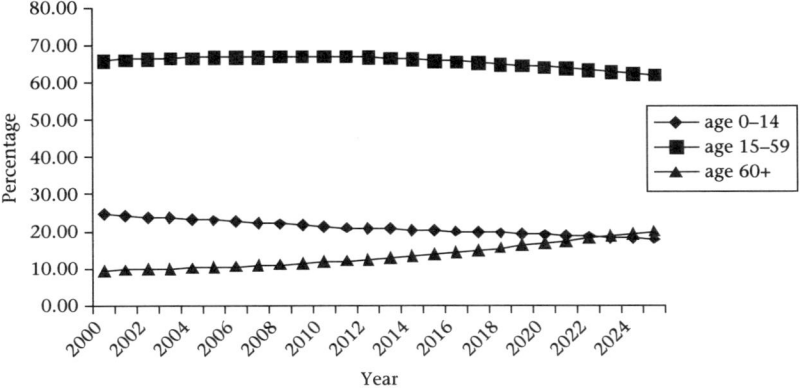

Figure 6.1 Percent of population below fifteen, fifteen to fifty-nine, and sixty and above (Medium Fertility Assumption)
Source: National Economic and Social Development Board (2005). *Population Projections for Thailand, 2005–2025*. NESDB, Bangkok.

proportional curve of the aging population (over sixty years of age) is rapidly increasing, doubling from 10 to 20 percentage points. This tsunami-like surge will have a negative impact on Thai society in the near future. This study designates such a situation a "tsunami aging-population phenomenon."

Southeast Asian countries, including Thailand, will experience a decline in the total fertility rate (TFR) in the period 2010–2015, with a continuing declining trend to 2025. Thailand is expected to experience a higher percentage decline in TFR (23.22%) than other Southeast Asian countries. The percentage decline in TFR will remain varied across the region during 2020–2025, ranging from an anticipated low of 1.46 births per woman in Singapore to a high of 2.91 in Cambodia. The UN medium projection adjusts the TFR of most Southeast Asian countries to 1.85 for the period of 2045–2050 (Patcharawalai 2003). At the same time, life expectancy is rising. Life expectancy at birth for women in Thailand is anticipated to increase from 74.08 years during 2000–2005 to 80.25 years in 2015–2020 (Wongboonsin, Guest and Prachuabmoh 2004). All other Southeast Asian countries will also experience an improvement in life expectancy in that period, ranging from 54.5 to 78.1 years. The trend is projected to continue in the decades after 2020, reaching a range between 69.8 and 83.0 years by 2050 (Patcharawalai 2003).

These demographic conditions indicate that most Southeast Asian countries are in transition from a demographic dividend to a demographic onus. Most developed countries in Europe and America, as well as in Asia, have benefited from a demographic dividend. The dividend's benefits are seen not only in the possibility of a more productive workforce leading to higher economic performance, but also an increase in the standard of living, high income for consumption, and high savings and investment.

Japan, South Korea, Taiwan, and Singapore are the pioneers in Asia in benefiting from a demographic dividend. According to Mason, one-third of the economic growth in South Korea, Taiwan, and Singapore between 1960 and 1990 can be attributed to such demographic shifts as two children per woman and an annual 2.7 percent increase in labor force growth (Mason 2002). Thailand and other Southeast Asian countries now have an opportunity to benefit from a demographic dividend as well. According to the Asian Development Bank (ADB 1997: 158; cited in Bloom et al. 2003: 53), the demographic dividend in Southeast Asia is currently approximately 0.7 percentage points of per capita annual income growth. That figure is expected to double by 2015 (Engardio 2002).

Yet a detailed comparative investigation of Southeast Asian countries suggests variations in pace and degree of attainable economic benefits. In Thailand, the proportion of the population in the age range for labor-force participation is projected to peak at 67.08 percent in 2009, and thereafter decline to 62.6 percent in 2025. Therefore, optimum conditions for a demographic dividend will last only until 2009 in Thailand (Wongboonsin 2004: 115). This compares with Vietnam where the labor-force peak of 66.2 percent in 2010 will decline to 66.0 percent of total population in 2015. Malaysia and Indonesia are following the trend and are anticipated to reach labor-force peaks of 63.0 percent and 65.0 percent, respectively, in 2020. In 2025, Malaysia and Indonesia will experience labor force declines to 62.4 and 64.9 percent of the total population, respectively (Patcharawalai 2003).

Most Asian countries have stimulated their demand for quality human development. That there was a big gap in human development within the ASEAN region was already evident in 1990, however, when the human development index (HDI) ranged from 0.186 in the case of Cambodia to 0.849 in the case of Singapore. (The Human Development Index is a comparative measure of life expectancy at birth, adult literacy rates, and standard of living as determined by per capita gross domestic product and purchasing power.)[1] Despite regional improvement in HDI to above 0.50 in all ASEAN member countries in 2001, the gap in human development within ASEAN has remained troubling. The Lao People's Democratic Republic had the lowest HDI (0.525) among ASEAN member countries in 2001, followed by Cambodia (0.556) and Myanmar (0.549). Singapore continued to experience the highest HDI (0.884) within ASEAN in 2001, followed by Brunei Darussalam (0.872), Malaysia (0.790), and Thailand (0.768) (UNDP 2003).

The gap in human development has been particularly evident in a number of Southeast Asian countries whose educational and training environments are inadequate for contemporary needs. As a result, a large part of their working population is unable to adapt to the demands of a flexible labor market (see Patcharawalai and Kinnas, 2005; Kojima 2005; and Jones 2005). Most of these countries lack appropriate policies and supporting institutional mechanisms to take full advantage of the current demographic dividend. That is, they are unable to enhance the productivity of their bulging workforce sufficiently before a rising old-age dependency ratio begins to hamper economic growth. In addition, alternative strategies in labor migration have not allowed these countries to fully optimize or to maximize the demographic dividend. Labor migration policies are self-defeating, subjecting migrants, employers, and national economies to a trap of insecure and unsustained socio-economic development. The socio-economic pressures on these societies will likely be exacerbated in the next few decades as the region's demographic dividend gives way to a demographic onus (Patcharawalai 2004).

IMPACTS ON THE M-CURVE LABOR-FORCE PARTICIPATION AND THE FAMILY

Changes in reproductive behavior among women and the increasing pressures of modern society have impacts on the family. This is particularly evident in policies concerning women – the main caregivers of children and the elderly – as well as in policies that might affect the dignity of the elderly themselves in an aging society. This section analyzes both elder care and childcare.

In the twenty-first century, the "tsunami aging-population phenomenon" – that is, the extremely rapid aging of societies – will progressively become a global phenomenon in a globalizing world. Realization of the potential of elderly workers is a recent phenomenon. Although employment of the elderly reduces their societal and household dependency and contributes to their well-being, their employment and employability continue to be topics of political debate in many societies. This is true even in Singapore, one of the Southeast Asian countries where preparations for addressing the aging of the population are most advanced. In addition to having a compulsory Central Provident Fund (CPF) for individuals' old-age security, Singapore has a mandatory delayed retirement age, currently set at sixty-two and anticipated to rise to sixty-seven years in the future. While some elderly persons wish to continue working if offered the opportunity to do so, many older workers and employers are less enthusiastic about such extended employment.[2] Maintaining their dignity may prove a considerable task for those elderly with low levels of education, poor health, and a lack of technological skills to carry out jobs in a knowledge-based society.[3] The problem may be exacerbated by employers who practice ageism.

Who supports the elderly is another important issue. Until the early 2000s, a decline in traditional family support was accompanied by a policy push to reverse that decline by encouraging continuing intergenerational support for the elderly in addition to state-based support. Maintaining a practice of traditional family support is increasingly difficult in China and Japan. The support ratio – that is, the ratio of working-age adults to retired elderly – decreased in China from 13.8 in 1950 to 10.0 in 2000; it is projected to fall to 2.7 in 2050. This compares to a decrease in Japan from 12.1 in 1950 to 4.0 in 2000, with a projection of 1.4 in 2050 (World Bank 1994, cited in Chan 2004; Demeney 2004). In Southeast Asia, most governments have adopted a policy push for continuing intergenerational support for the elderly in addition to state-based support (see Knodel and Debavalya 1997; Hermalin 1997; and Chan 2004). Nevertheless, the support ratios have declined in Southeast Asia as well. Between 2000 and 2050, the support ratio for the elderly is expected to decline from 15.3 to 4.2 in Malaysia, from 11.5 to 3.6 in Vietnam, and from 16.7 to 4.8 in Indonesia (Demeny 2004).

Families in societies with a declining number of dependents available to care for the elderly are in particular need of institutional and community supports to perform that care. Contemporary China, with its one-child per family policy since the late 1970s, may not be able to meet the future needs of elderly support through the family alone. Consequently, the government is expected to enhance its role in the system of elderly care as changes in the structure of the family make those enhancements necessary (Yuan 2004). The experience of Western welfare states as the dominant model of the institutionalized old-age economic support system proves that the system is not sustainable. The support ratio in the USA, for example, decreased from 7.8 in 1950 to 5.4 in 2000, and is projected to reach 3.1 in 2050. This compares to a decrease from 8.1 to 5.0 and 2.4 in the corresponding years in the Netherlands (Demeny 2004).

Support of dependents is, of course, not limited to the elderly, but embraces childcare as well. Without available community support, families confront dilemmas in societies that have inadequate childcare. Thailand, for example, has had insufficient childcare facilities since the late 1980s. The increasing shortfall since the mid-1990s has affected the structure of Thailand's female labor-force participation. From an age-group perspective, there are two basic patterns of female labor-force participation (Hanenberg and Wongboonsin 1991):

(1) An M-curve, or bimodal, pattern occurring when many women enter the labor force just after school, withdrawing from it when they have young children and later reentering the labor force after the young children enter school.
(2) A U-turn curve pattern, representing constant labor-force participation rates from age twenty to age fifty.

The M-curve pattern represents a trend in many modern societies. It is found in Japan, Singapore, Hong Kong, and South Korea. Thailand is undergoing a shift from the 1980s U-curve pattern to an M-curve one in urban areas where working mothers are withdrawing from the labor force. The Bangkok Metropolitan Area (BMA) started to experience an M-curve pattern of female labor-force participation in 1998 with a deepening M-curve in 1999 (Figure 6.2). This was followed by a shallow M-curve in 2000–2004 (Figure 6.3).[4]

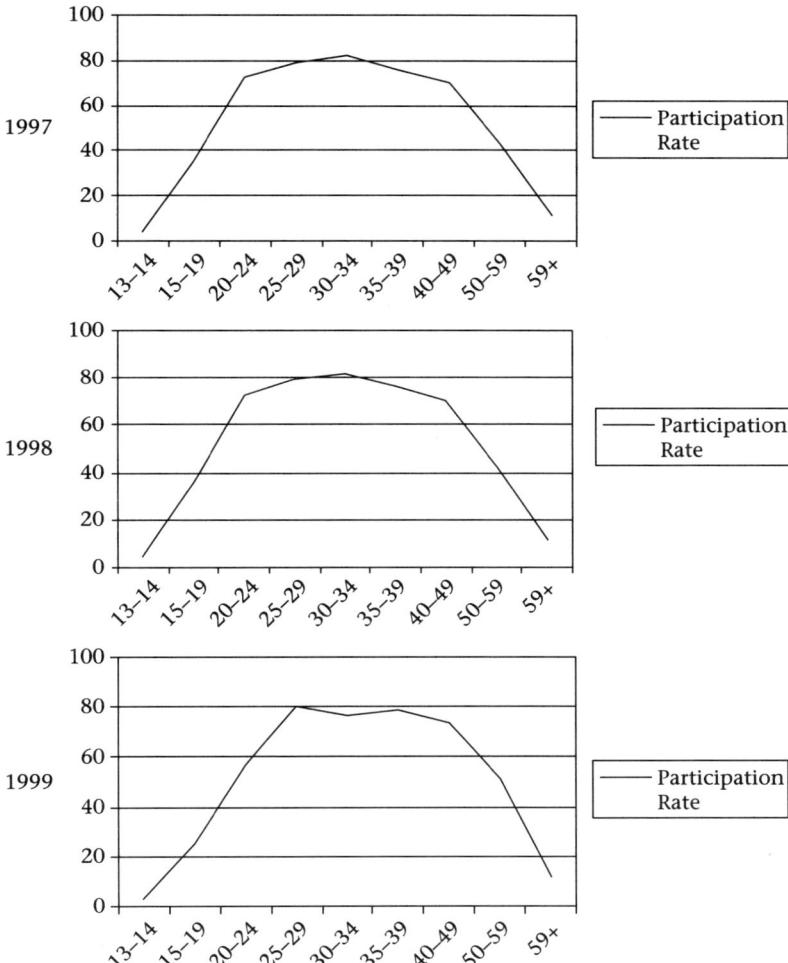

Figure 6.2 Female labor force participation rates in Bangkok Metropolitan Area, 1997–1999
Source: Wongboonsin, Kua (2004b), based on National Statistical Office: *Report of the Labor Force Survey Whole Kingdom Round 3 (various years: 1997–1999).*

The existence of the M-curve pattern of female labor-force participation in Thailand is confirmed by Hashimoto (2002b) and Ochiai (2003a). They found that most housewives between the ages of twenty and thirty in three districts of the Bangkok Metropolitan Area – Khlong Samwa, Lak Sii, and Din Daeng – were rearing children. Hashimoto and Ochiai

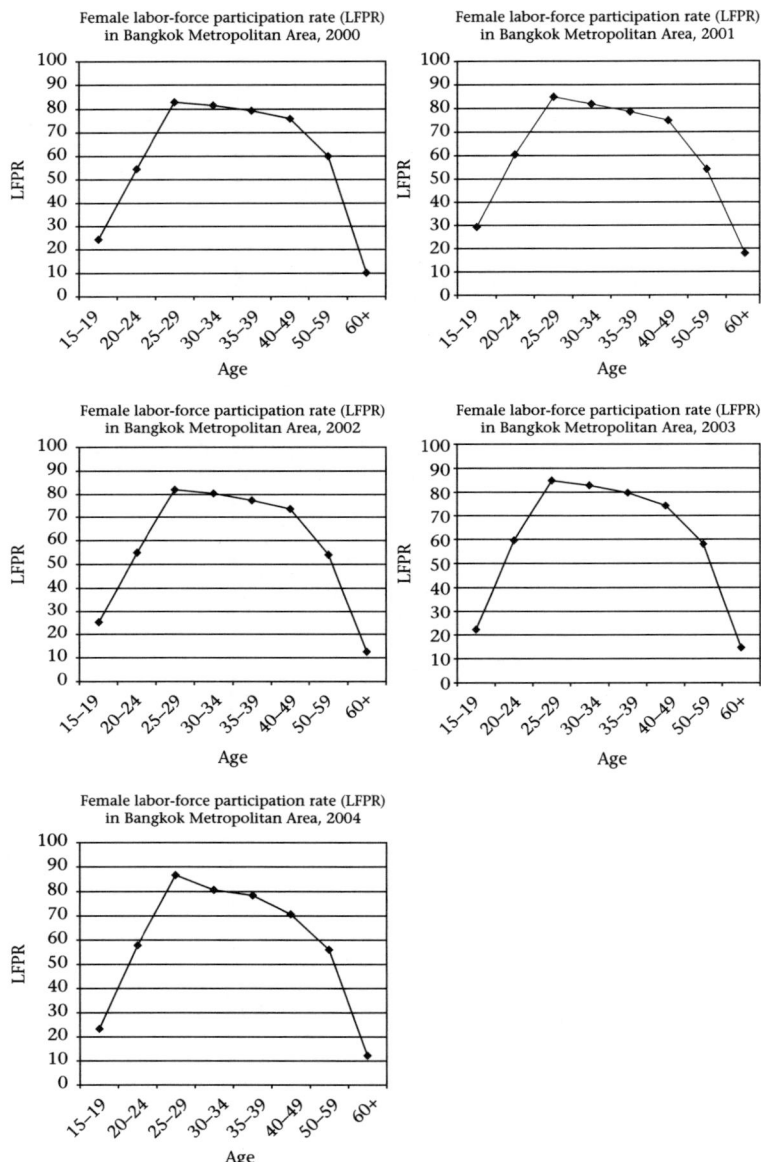

Figure 6.3 Female labor force participation rates in Bangkok Metropolitan Area, 2000–2004
Source: Based on data from the National Statistical Office: *Report of the Labor Force Survey Whole Kingdom Round 3 (various years: 2000–2004).*

established two categories of housewives in these three BMA districts, the "passive housewife" type and the "positive housewife" type (Hashimoto 2003b; Ochiai 2003b). The passive type were housewives with insufficient or no childcare facilities or kinship support. Quality childcare workers were also either not available or affordable by housewives in this category. The positive type were highly educated working mothers who stated that they were taking maternal leave in order to provide quality care for their children to help them survive in a competitive society. The positive type planned to return to the workforce once their children commenced schooling.

This study argues that the pattern of female labor-force participation is mostly explained by the conflicting roles of work and childrearing. If such conflicting roles are not resolved, one of the following phenomena can be expected in the Bangkok Metropolitan Area and other urban areas in Thailand:

(1) A deepening M-curve. This will be the case if an increasing proportion of the female labor force takes maternal leave to care for their children;

(2) A shallow M-curve. This will be the case if an increasing number of women decide to postpone their first childbirth to maintain or prolong their working life.[5]

Of these two scenarios, we assert that a shallow M-curve is more likely in a modern society like Bangkok, Thailand. This is based on the observation that Bangkok has been experiencing a decline in the total fertility rate (TFR). Having already declined from 1.25 in 1990 to 1.17 in 2000, the TFR in Bangkok is expected to decline further in the years to come. If even a shallow M-curve emerges, however, it will have negative consequences for Thailand, particularly if Thailand is trying to prolong the period of its current demographic dividend.

The trends described above stress the urgency of implementing appropriate childcare arrangements in Thailand and other modern societies. This study argues that an appropriate policy regime governing childcare arrangements is a prerequisite for Thailand and other modern societies to encourage female labor-force participation, which serves as a key factor for increasing the magnitude of the demographic dividend. A reevaluation of long-term fertility goals and policies is needed. A sociocultural approach to investigating fertility and family-formulation behavior, linking the trends in age at first marriage and the mother's age at first birth, both of which relate to the M-curve pattern of female labor-force participation, would serve as an effective tool for this reevaluation.

NEEDED POLICY REGIMES

Population trends in modern societies are more than ever determined by economic policies and visions designed to enhance a country's international competitiveness on a sustained basis. This is particularly the case in the new era of a dynamic, competitive, and knowledge-based world economy.

This study suggests that it will be too late to re-think policy avenues when the demographic dividend is over. Rather, comprehensive population and other supporting socio-economic policy regimes for risk management need to be in place while the demographic dividend is still in play. Such policy regimes serve to prolong the demographic dividend at the maximum level and to minimize setbacks for individuals, the family, and the society once the demographic dividend fades away.

Comprehensive population policy regimes refer here to those with both quantity and quality dimensions. This study maintains that a balance between the quantity and the quality of a population is the key to maximizing the demographic dividend. In other words, it is necessary to maintain fertility at a sustainable level and to develop a more productive population. Bloom et al. (2003) maintain that appropriate policy conditions for a more productive workforce include an open-market policy, a flexible labor market, human resource development policies for high-quality health care and high-quality education, and a financial system providing investment and saving incentives. This study very much agrees that those conditions are appropriate and necessary, but adds that policies supporting childcare and the health and dignity of the elderly are also required both before and after the demographic dividend fades away. A basic-need approach is part of the process. This includes human (individual) security and employment.[6] Policies concerning education, childcare, healthy aging with dignity, and female labor-force participation should be prioritized in countries with relatively poor development in those areas. Policy-making also needs to take into account the connections between human development and patterns of migration.

These policies should be supported by other public, economic, and financial policies to encourage increased productivity throughout the population. Strategies to minimize the risks of the coming demographic onus should encourage integration of individual resources and community networks for family care through mechanisms that promote horizontal coordination, policy supports, and ongoing study of effectiveness of these strategies. In all cases, intergenerational cooperation should be strengthened through adequate social protection of the elderly, taking into consideration societal trends, changes in family structures, economic changes in the labor market, and regional diversity. One may also need to consider the role of social developers in the formation of social capital as a basis for sustained dignity at the individual, family, and societal levels.

These recommendations are based on lessons learned from the experiences of East Asia's pioneers, countries viewed as having succeeded in capturing the demographic dividend. These pioneers were equipped with quality human resources, and they were able to benefit from policies for creating jobs and for encouraging workers to save and invest during the demographic dividend period (Bloom et al. 2003; Wongboonsin and Guest, ed. 2005). These countries are now, however, facing fiscal burdens.

To enhance the quality dimension of the population, Thailand's ninth Five-Year National Economic and Social Development Plan (2001–2006) established a population target in which the TFR was targeted at the replacement level. This represented a challenging task. The target was based on the notion that the longer Thailand maintained the TFR at or near the replacement level, the longer it could maintain a high proportion of the population in the labor-force age range. This was expected to help prolong the demographic dividend. Such a target was made despite the realization that no country in the world has managed to increase fertility after it has fallen below replacement level, even when pro-natalist policies have been implemented (Wongboonsin 2004).

Finally, risk management strategies require a better information base for public policy and cooperation. Information on mortality, morbidity, migration, gender, and regional and country differences on pension schemes, which need to become less sensitive to demographic changes, is particularly necessary.

The authors are grateful to the Thailand Research Fund and Chulalongkorn University for research financial support.

NOTES

[1] According to the United Nations' annual Human Development Reports, human development is concerned both with developing human capabilities and with using them productively; it stresses development for people and by people; and it is as concerned with the generation of economic growth as with its distribution, as concerned with basic needs as with the entire spectrum of human aspiration, as concerned with the human dilemmas of developed countries as with the human deprivation in developing countries. See United Nations Development Programme 1992.

[2] Among the current generation of elderly (aged fifty-nine and above), 16% are employed in Singapore. See Chan 2004.

[3] Most of the current generation of older Singaporeans (fifty-nine and over) who work are in sales or service occupations, production, or work as cleaners and laborers. See Chan (2004).

[4] There was a tendency for Thai women aged thirty to thirty-four years to participate in the labor force to a lesser extent than those aged twenty-five to twenty-nine years and thirty-five to thirty-nine years. See Kua 2004.

[5] There are women who want to work or to obtain advanced education or training so as to pursue a long-term career.

[6] The issue of basic needs plays a paramount role in the livelihoods of people and was first officially introduced internationally by ILO. "In all countries employment enters into a basic needs strategy both as a means and as an end." See International Labor Organization 1976.

7

Foreign Domestic Workers in Singapore

UENO KAYOKO

INTRODUCTION

According to the Singapore Ministry of Manpower (MOM), there are approximately 170,000 live-in foreign domestic workers currently in Singapore.[1] This is no insignificant number for a country with only 1,049,011 resident households (Singapore Department of Statistics 2006a). Singapore's ratio of one foreign domestic worker (FDW) for every six to seven households is much higher than those of Hong Kong and Taiwan, which have also been the subject of investigation in studies of transnational domestic workers in Southeast Asia (Asis 2002; Constable 1997; Lan 2006; Lin 1999; Palma-Beltran 1992; Tam 1999).

This chapter examines how Singapore has emerged as one of the top employers of FDWs, focusing on three aspects of the FDW issue: (1) government policies on labor, reproduction, and immigration, (2) the role played by employment agencies, and (3) the unique position of Singapore in relation to FDWs' career opportunities. The Singapore government's policies on FDWs are carefully engineered both to promote national economic development and to control the quality and quantity of the population. The policies are implemented by economic measures intended to encourage Singaporean women with higher educational and employment qualifications to stay in the workforce and, at the same time, to start their own families. The demand for FDWs in Singapore has also been buttressed by a proliferation of employment agencies. Agencies sustain the demand for FDWs by offering the employers of FDWs extremely attractive packages that are, at the same time, disadvantageous for the FDWs. Coupled with a lack of legislation to ensure the well-being of FDWs, those domestic workers, basically left in the hands of agencies and employers, are among the most vulnerable and exploited workers in Singapore.

Despite the adverse conditions, however, some of these women perceive a temporary migration to Singapore as a springboard to better, albeit often limited, career opportunities in other countries. This chapter highlights the complex double-edged realities of transnational mobility in multiple ways, noting its potential both for exploitation and for liberation.

Primary materials for this study were gathered in the course of my fieldwork from 2002 to 2006. During my four visits, I was basically attached to two Singaporean families for a total of three months. There I had the privilege of learning and observing the chores and activities and interviewing three live-in domestic workers who both acted as informants and helped me to contact their friends and relatives working in Singapore as FDWs. I also interviewed additional FDWs introduced to me by the relatives and friends of the families with whom I was staying. Although eight different nationalities are currently approved to work in Singapore as FDWs, all of the nineteen FDWs whom I interviewed were from the Philippines and Indonesia, the two largest sources of supply to Singapore (Human Rights Watch 2005). Their backgrounds seem to represent a typical profile of FDWs in Singapore; most are single and in their twenties. Filipina domestic workers tend to be college or high school graduates whereas Indonesian domestic workers tend to have junior secondary educations (see Table 7.1). All except three of those interviewed came to Singapore via employment agencies. In addition to FDWs, fifteen employers of FDWs were interviewed regarding their views on FDWs and their experience with hiring FDWs. Most employers are Chinese and have between two and twenty-two years of experience in hiring FDWs. Two employers allowed me to accompany them on their visits to over twenty employment agencies. This study also examined newspaper articles, employment agency advertisements, and the relevant materials and information issued by MOM.

THE ORIGIN OF FOREIGN DOMESTIC WORKERS AND DEVELOPMENT OF FDW POLICY

Paid domestic workers are not new in Singapore. Before Singapore gained independent status in 1965, wealthy families had "amahs" (servants) from China, India, or the regions of Malaya outside of Singapore (Kail 1980; Gaw 1988; Ooi 1992). There were no specific government policies regarding foreign domestic helpers, however, until the late 1970s, when the government first introduced policies concerning FDWs to encourage Singaporean women to enter the formal waged economy.

Historically, Singapore, separated from the Federation of Malaysia in 1965, was a small resource-poor state dependent on commerce. The partition exacerbated the effects in Singapore of high unemployment accompanied by rapid population growth. As the first Prime Minister put it, "surviving without the hinterland" became a matter of life and death (Lee 2000). Hence, the Singapore government strengthened its population control policy and implemented a comprehensive family planning

Table 7.1. Backgrounds of Filipina and Indonesian domestic workers in this study

Nationality	Age*	Marital Status*	Education	Previous Job before Singapore* Entry	First-time in Singapore*	Total Length of Stay in Singapore	Age at First Arrival	Monthly Salary (S$)**
Philippines	28	Single	University	Elementary school teacher	Second time	25 months	25	320
Philippines	25	Single	College	Midwife	Yes	24 months	23	320
Philippines	26	Single	University	Clerk	Yes	23 months	24	320
Indonesia	18	Single	Junior secondary school	Maid in homeland	Yes	8 months	18	240
Philippines	38	Divorced	High school	Housewife	Yes	13 years	25	400
Philippines	24	Single	College	FDW in Hong Kong	Second time	28 months	22	350
Indonesia	22	Single	Junior secondary school	Janitor in homeland	Third time	28 months	18	250
Indonesia	23	Single	Junior secondary school	Factory worker in Malaysia	Yes	11 months	22	250
Philippines	55	Widow	Unknown	Dressmaker	Yes	22 years	23	400
Indonesia	22	Single	Junior secondary school	Shop assistant	Yes	9 months	21	260
Indonesia	28	Single	Junior secondary school	Live-in baby sitter	Yes	71 months	23	280
Philippines	23	Single	High school	Service worker at Hotel	Yes	26 months	19	360
Philippines	Early thirties	Married	High school	FDW in Hong Kong	Third time	6 years	Late twenties	350

Indonesia	30	Single	Junior secondary school	Farmer	Third time	7 years	23	300
Indonesia	24	Single	Junior secondary school	Live-in baby sitter	Yes	13 months	23	280
Indonesia	29	Married	Junior secondary school	Housewife	Yes	18 months	27	280
Philippines	Late thirties	Single	Unknown	Unknown	Second time	13 years	Early twenties	Unknown
Philippines	Early thirties	Married	High school	Housewife	Yes	13 years	Early twenties	Unknown
Philippines	Late twenties	Single	High school	Clerk	Third time	6 years	Early twenties	340

* At the time of first interview

** One Singapore dollar is equivalent to about 0.6 U.S. dollar.

program to decrease family size. The crude birth rate (birth rate per thousand population) of 29.5 in 1965 declined to 17.8 in 1975, thus attaining the governmental target (Saw 1981). As for the economy, since the domestic market was small, the government launched a new economic strategy to promote labor intensive manufacturing industries targeting the export market in order to absorb the massive unemployment. This strategy resulted in solid success. Because the world economy was booming in the late 1960s and early 1970s, multinational firms began to look for low cost regions to assemble their products (Fong 1981).

Throughout the 1970s, the government's continuing commitment to creating an environment and infrastructure for business accelerated economic growth, producing a tight labor market. The labor shortage led to constant complaints from businesses. As a result, the government implemented various measures to encourage economically inactive women to enter or reenter the labor force. The female labor force participation rate rose from 19.3 in 1957 to 25.8 in 1970 (Lee et al. 1999). In light of the astounding speed of economic growth, however, female labor force participation was still insufficient. A series of progressive governmental measures was, therefore, undertaken to target married women. These measures included locating factories near potential workers' homes in housing complexes, providing transportation to and from work, establishing day-care centers for children, introducing part-time shift work, enhancing tax relief for dependent children of working female professionals with higher qualifications, and granting work permits to domestic workers from non-traditional sources (Saw 1984).

Specifically, the Foreign Domestic Workers Scheme was implemented in 1978. The government became actively involved in the process of obtaining FDWs throughout the 1980s with the introduction of regulatory measures that included requiring a two-year working contract, prohibiting marriage to a Singaporean, and mandating employers' payment of security bonds and monthly levies (taxes) (Wong 1996; 1997). The number of foreign domestic workers reached 20,000 in 1987; 40,000 in 1988; 50,000 in 1989; over 100,000 in 1999 (Yeoh et al. 1999), and, currently, 170,000.

Noteworthy among the features of Singapore government policy towards migrant workers in this context is its persistent "dual-track" policy (Teng 2000). Since the early 1970s, foreign workers have been largely categorized into two tracks: professional workers and low-skilled workers. Singapore has consistently welcomed the first category, encouraging professionals such as engineers, managers, and entrepreneurs to come, while placing restrictions and imposing levies on workers with low skill levels. In general, whereas those in the first category are eligible to receive an employment pass, those in the second category, including construction, manufacturing, and marine workers as well as FDWs, are eligible only for work permits (skilled workers have been able to apply for an S-Pass since 2004). Work permit holders are not allowed to bring dependents and are repatriated at the end of their work contracts.

In contrast, employment pass holders may bring dependents, employ FDWs themselves, and apply for permanent residence status. In fact, the Foreign Domestic Workers Scheme of 1978 was also intended to attract foreign professionals and entrepreneurs to stay for an extended time in Singapore by allowing them amenities like FDWs that would make their lives more convenient (Amarles 1990).

While transnational professionals with an employment pass or an S-pass are hired independent of their gender, the positions held by work permit holders tend to be gendered, with construction workers typically being male and domestic workers female. Domestic workers have no quota system, but all other unskilled and even skilled foreign laborers (S-pass holders) are bound by quotas; for example, one local worker must be allocated for every four foreign construction workers employed.[2] This implies that the government does not encourage Singaporeans to work as domestic helpers, unlike workers in other low-skilled types of work. The government's encouragement of Singaporean women's participation in the labor force has created a vacuum of care at home that must be filled by foreign women.

The purpose of the FDW policy is officially explained as follows: "By helping out with household chores and bearing part of the responsibility of caring for our children or elderly sick, these domestic workers often relieve Singaporean women for the workplace and help contribute to Singapore's economy and the well-being of families."[3] The Singapore government is attempting to ensure that Singaporean women are productive in the workplace and reproductive in the family. But there is more to it. By imposing a monthly levy on employers of FDWs, the government can adjust the quality and quantity of the Singaporean women in the workforce by adjusting the amount of the levy. In sluggish economic periods, the government may raise the levy to discourage married couples, especially married women, from relying on FDWs, thereby encouraging female workers with lower skills to leave the sluggish labor market. Indeed, the government's intention with its policies concerning FDWs is to encourage women with higher skills to remain in the workforce while also bearing and raising children (Yeoh et al. 1999; Yeoh and Huang 2004).

Singapore is known for implementing new, innovative policies and following up with testing, adjustment, and periodic quick revision of these policies to ensure success. The two most recent major revisions regarding FDW policy were enforced in 2004–2005. In August 2004, the monthly levy for FDWs was reduced from S$345 to S$250 for a Singaporean citizen with a child under twelve years of age or with an elderly person aged sixty-five and above. This levy reduction clearly indicates both the linkage of FDW policy and fertility and the continuing role of FDWs in Singapore as the proportion of the population aged sixty-five and above continues to grow.[4]

The second major revision was the government's implementation in January 2005 of regulations aimed at controlling the quality of FDWs in terms of maturity and education. Applicable only to first-time FDWs, the new regulations stipulate that a worker must be at least twenty-three (previously eighteen) years of age and have a minimum of eight years of formal education, with documented proof of that education. In addition, a prospective FDW is required to pass an entry test upon arrival in Singapore before she can be issued a work permit.

The requirements for hiring FDWs have become increasingly specific, but regulations of FDWs' working conditions in their place of employment have not. Since FDWs are housed in the private sphere of individual families, the government claims it is difficult to impose the terms of the Employment Act (Human Rights Watch 2005). The fact that FDWs are excluded from the Employment Act means that minimum wage, working hours, rest days, and sick leave are not regulated by law.

As an importer of temporary workers in East Asia, Singapore seeks to ensure that its policy for FDWs maximizes the advantages of migrant labor and minimizes the social and economic costs (Fong 1992). By allowing the majority of reproductive and care work to be privatized responsibilities, the FDW policy has made it possible for Singaporean families to utilize live-in domestic workers at their discretion. Importantly, this cheap domestic work is available not from Singapore's own nationals, but through international labor migration.

HIRING AN FDW

Typically, the employers of FDWs are middle- and upper-class working couples with at least one dependent family member. Although the criteria for eligibility to employ an FDW are not officially stipulated, MOM examines the employer's application in terms of the income tax of the applicant and the needs of the family.

There are two ways to employ an FDW – through a recruitment agency or directly. Direct hiring is usually initiated through an introduction by acquaintances. Filipina and Indonesian FDWs in Singapore may introduce friends and relatives who are either in Singapore or still resident in their home countries. The former include FDWs who are about to complete the two-year working contract and are looking for their next employer. Since the direct hiring method benefits the FDW more than the employer because it eliminates some of the fees the FDW would have to pay an agency, employers do not have a strong incentive to use this method and more commonly go through an agency.

There are purportedly more than 600 employment agencies in Singapore through which FDWs enter the country (Human Rights Watch 2005). Advertisements for FDWs put forward by agencies can be found in newspapers, under the heading "Domestic Help Available." Apart from the usual information about agency fees and services, newspaper advertisements sometimes indicate monthly salaries for FDWs by nationality. Many of these agencies are prominently located in downtown areas like the busy shopping area of Orchard Road. Some are Singaporean offices that work closely with overseas recruitment companies, while others may be branch offices of employment agencies in the Philippines or Indonesia.

Agencies handle FDWs in two ways – as "CV maids" or as "transfer maids." Applicants who are still in their home countries fall into the former category. Employers examine the qualifications of potential FDWs based on the information in their CVs (curriculum vitae or résumés), the standardized questionnaire filled in by applicants, and the agency's standardized evaluation check list regarding personality, appearance, color of skin, neatness, dress, complexion, and facial expression. CVs are often accompanied by comments by the agency staff. A letter to the prospective employer and even a self-introductory video can be attached. Upon selection of a potential employee based on this data, the agency arranges for the employer an overseas phone interview with the FDW applicant. "Transfer maids," on the other hand, are already in Singapore and available for personal interviews immediately or at agreed-upon times. They are FDWs who have either been fired within the contract period or are about to complete the two-year contract and are looking for their next employer. While the number of applicants who submit their CVs is enormous, transfer FDWs, who are often "displayed" in an agency's room waiting to be selected for an interview, are much fewer in number.

Employers choose FDWs based on the criteria of nationality, language, religion, age, education, and prior employment. Impressions from photos, in the case of "CV maids," or from interviews, in the case of transfer FDWs, also play a role. Among these criteria, nationality comes first since it largely defines the range of salary, language, and religion. Standard monthly salaries for Filipina FDWs are S\$320–380, Indonesian FDWs S\$220–280, and Sri Lankan FDWs S\$200–220.

Employers of Chinese origin generally prefer Filipina FDWs who speak good English. Moreover, Filipina FDW applicants, most of whom are Catholic, are particularly attractive to Christian employers. Most Filipina applicants have high school or college educations. In addition, it is believed that the Philippines' historical background of Spanish and American colonization allows Filipina FDWs to adjust well to life in modern Singapore. In contrast, FDW applicants from Indonesia, a predominantly Muslim country, often have only junior secondary education and have weaker English skills, placing them at a disadvantage in terms of communicating in Singapore. In most cases, Indonesian FDWs will have to make extra efforts to adapt to the culture of the employer, which often requires such things as handling pork, eating Chinese food, or looking after a dog, which almost all of the Indonesian women in my study hesitated to do in the beginning. Unless the employer is of Malay origin[5] – where there are similarities in culture, language, and food – difficulties may arise between the employer and the Indonesian FDW.

In addition to nationality, language, and religion, potential employers take into consideration an applicant's character and experience with housework. In terms of housework, some employers emphasize cooking skills, preferring a woman who has previously worked as a domestic helper for a family of similar ethnicity. If there is a school-age child in the family, the employer may choose a Filipina woman with a college degree in education or, preferably, a former school teacher who can look after the child's homework. As far as character is concerned, recruitment agencies usually stress that Filipina women are outspoken, responsible, and determined, whereas Indonesian women are deemed to be obedient, patient, caring, and hard working women who display womanly characteristics. In other words, the employment agencies construct the images of nationalities as suited to certain types of domestic work.

Employers commonly attach importance to the FDW's character and value diligence, honesty, and reliability. Also, employers with small children or elderly parents claim they prefer FDWs with a "smart and strong" character, the ability to send the family's children to the nursery or school, and the intelligence to give medication to their aged parents and small children. However, it is noteworthy that some interviewees (employers) express contrary views, such as "We don't want a clever maid" or "I don't like a graduate." Given the choice, FDWs prefer to work for expatriates. Similarly, Singaporean employers often avoid FDWs who have previous experiences working for Japanese and Western families. They express such views as: "They are spoiled;" "We never employ them;" "It is the same type of household work, but it's wrong to think their families and our families are the same;" and "They will slack off in their duties due to an easy experience." Indeed, the FDWs' wishes and employers' expectations are asymmetrical.

The costs of hiring an FDW include the agency fee, insurance fee, monthly salary, security bond and monthly levy payable to the government, medical examination fee, and airfare. The type and range of the necessities the employer provides to the FDW vary from one employer to another. In addition to a bed or mattress, most of the employers provide the FDW with basic necessities such as soap, shampoo, towels, and toothbrush. In some cases, the FDW may be required to sleep on a floor mattress in the living room, in the children's room, or next to an elderly family member. It is also common for employers to provide underwear, simple daily clothes, and sanitary napkins. And some employers may provide FDWs with bonuses on Christmas and/or upon completion of the contract. Working conditions all depend on the "good will" of the employers.

Agency fees for the potential employers range from S$88 to several hundred Singapore dollars. The fee is largely determined by the FDW's country of origin. The agency fee for a Filipina who has received no advanced payments in the form of loans from the agency and who has more than two years working experience in Singapore is the highest, while that for the Indonesian woman who has received more than six months of prepayment in the form of loans and without previous working experience in Singapore is much lower – and sometimes there is no fee at all. These variations in fees allow the agency to profit from lending money to FDWs while promoting the least desirable FDWs to employers.

The prospective employer is required by law to deposit with the government a S$5,000 security bond, to be forfeited should the FDW violate the Immigration Act by committing a crime, running away, or getting pregnant. The bond, with the government's approval, is integrated into the FDW's insurance to be purchased by the employer. The type of insurance varies from basic to comprehensive (S$50 to S$100), covering the security bond and personal accidents of at least S$10,000. Applications for work permits require this insurance in order to receive government approval. The agency documentation will at least include insurance and the application for the work permit. An agency may also be hired by an employer to help prepare all the necessary documents if the employer chooses to hire an FDW he or she has found independently.

BECOMING AN FDW

Technically, any woman from an approved country of origin above the age of twenty-three who is medically fit for employment and has met required educational standards is eligible to work as an FDW in Singapore. Currently countries approved to supply FDWs are the Philippines, Indonesia, Sri Lanka, Malaysia, Thailand, Myanmar, India, and Bangladesh. Usually all the expenses of the FDW's preparation for work in Singapore – including airfare to Singapore, medical examination, application for a passport, vocational training, and food and shelter in the agency (if necessary) – are initially borne by the agency. FDWs generally do not pay any money in advance. The debt money will then be deducted from the monthly salary of the FDW. The FDW may get only S$10–40 from the employer for the first four to ten months in the course of work, due to deductions to repay the debt.

Interviews with nineteen FDWs and examination of fifty-five CVs of FDW applicants in employment agencies offer a general profile of applicants prior to becoming FDWs in Singapore. This profile can be summarized as follows: Filipina women tend to be clerks, elementary school teachers, domestic helpers, nurses, housewives, college students, or unemployed, whereas Indonesian women tend to be unemployed, domestic workers, or helpers in their families' small businesses prior to employment as FDWs.

The time required for Filipinas to become FDWs in Singapore is usually shorter than that for Indonesian women. Filipinas enroll themselves with a recruiting agency and fill out all the necessary documents under the instruction of the agency's staff while still in the Philippines. They leave their country when the agency matches them with an employer. In the case of Indonesian women, this process usually takes longer. The prospective FDWs make their way from their hometowns to training centers in big cities like Jakarta, where they are registered and given training. They remain there while their CVs are selected prior to flying into Singapore. In the training center, they study basic English using a textbook designed for FDWs. The English vocabulary and phrases consist of indispensable words and phrases, simple everyday greetings, and English expressions for showing the FDW's honesty, ability to apologize, and obedience, which supposedly will help prevent future troubles and misunderstandings with a new employer. As part of their basic housework training, the FDWs are introduced to the use of electric appliances, including washing machines, vacuum cleaners, ovens, toasters, and blenders. The basics of childcare are also taught in the center. Furthermore, both Filipina and Indonesian women respond to questionnaires distributed by the agency. The following questions are typical of this type of questionnaire:

> Are you prepared to work for employers of any race?
> Are you prepared to work with a family of more than six members?
> Are you prepared to cook any type of food your employer wishes?
> Are you willing to work with a family where the mother-in-law or any older relative lives with the family?
> Are you willing to work with no days off?
> Are you willing to finish your morning chores before you leave the house on your days off?
> Can you promise not to use the telephone without permission or invite friends and relatives without the permission of your employer?
> Can you promise not to put on make-up but to dress properly while at work?
> Can you promise not to ask for advance salary from your employer under any circumstances?

Questionnaires of this type are attached to the cv application, and very few applicants answer "no" to any of the questions. While detailed information about the FDW is given to the employer, information about the employer is limited to the family's race and size, and even that information is, at times, inaccurate. In cases where the employer's family turns out to be larger than reported, the FDW is hardly in a position to decline a job offer, as she often has accumulated debt from the hiring process and faces apparent competition from other applicants for her job. This is especially the case for Indonesian women who come to Singapore via Indonesian training centers. These women are told that there are literally thousands waiting for the next job in the training centers. Filipina and Indonesian women in my study were approximately S$800–2,700 in debt when they arrived in Singapore, the equivalent of four to ten times an FDW's monthly pay. In cases where nominal agency fees were charged to the employer, the FDW ultimately bore more cost, as the cost was transferred to her by the agency.

THE PLIGHT OF FDWS

Studies of the lives of foreign domestic workers in Southeast Asia have often addressed restrictive and oppressive government policies to regulate migrant domestic workers, with the accompanying problem of "exploitation" in employment agencies as well as individual work environments (Cheng 1996; Constable 1997; Lin 1999; Tyner 1994). In this section, I first touch upon the difficulties facing the FDWs by focusing on the Singapore Immigration Regulations that allow employers to exercise discretionary power to the point of abusing FDWs. Second, I discuss the employment agencies' free FDW exchange plan that has become a standard practice and that forces the FDW to incur economic as well as psychological damage.

First, Singapore's Immigration Act stipulates that it is the employer's responsibility to supervise the FDW. If the FDW works in a location other than the employer's house, becomes pregnant, disturbs the order of society, or stays too long in Singapore without proper authorization following termination of her work permit or visit pass, the security bond (S$5,000) is forfeited and the FDW is repatriated at once. The Immigration Act encourages the employer to keep the FDW's passport. This practice derives from the belief that without her passport in her hands, an FDW who had committed theft in her employer's house would not be able to leave the island easily. In addition to holding her passport, some employers do not allow their domestic worker to have even one day off per month, to use the house phone, to talk to anyone other than family members, or to step out the front door. The social behavior pattern of the FWD can be tightly controlled by the employer. Employers who control their FDWs in this way explain that they take all these precautions to minimize the risk of the FDW becoming pregnant and to protect her from associating with male foreign workers, being cheated, or losing money by gambling. Such employers assert that if they control her, their FDW will be better able to stick to her original purpose for coming to Singapore – that is, sending money home.

To be sure, many employers have high opinions of their FDW's character. In addition, letters from readers sometimes appear in newspapers elaborating their trusting relationships with their FDWs. The means through which employers obtain their workers' "trust," however, often betrays the meaning of that trust.

One employer explained, during an interview, how he had confirmed his belief that "our maid is a good one." Coming home a day earlier than expected from a vacation to Australia, this employer and his family found the FDW in the house sweeping the floor. He added that money and jewelry had never been lost or stolen. A sudden change of schedule or an unexpected check is regarded as a chance to test the worker's honesty and diligence in carrying out her daily chores. This kind of testing goes on quite often. If the test result is positive, it reinforces the employer's trust, but a single negative experience can cause immediate change in the employer's estimation of the FDW.

The surveillance of the FDW is not limited to her primary employer; it is omnipresent. Family members observe the worker and comment on such things as the negative impact of the FDW on the children's English language skills. Visitors may compare another family's FDW with their own, observing her every move and gesture. They often become severe critics, speculating on every conceivable possibility relating to her character: Does she have thievish habits; Is she a compulsive liar; Does she have bad manners; Is she filthy; Does she litter in public places; Are her morals loose? FDWs are often portrayed as lacking in good character in newspapers as well (Ponnampalam 2000). One employer noted that "a thousand eyes are fixed on her." The Immigration Act has forced the FDWs to be exposed to patriarchal relationships with their employers and local society who then become the meddlesome guardians of the FDWs.

FDWs are also constrained by the free exchange plan practiced by the agencies. This plan allows the employer to return the FDW to the agency within a certain period of time with little or no financial penalty to the employer should he or she find the FDW unsuitable. (The number of times a worker can be exchanged varies by agency.) For instance, some agencies stipulate a free-exchange period of one year, while other agencies allow six months for Filipina FDWs and ten months for Indonesian FDWs. This gives the employer a certain amount of power to threaten the FDW. With this plan, the FDW risks being returned to the agency where she will have to incur additional financial expenses and possible scoldings from the agency. When an FDW is returned to the agency, she must pay a placement fee to the agent (one or two months' salary) and a lodging fee (S$ 10 per day), despite the fact that she will be sleeping with other FDWs on the floor of the agency owner's apartment or a rented house and will be helping with the household chores without any salary. Before being scheduled for interviews with prospective employers, the returned FDW will be strictly trained to provide a "correct" explanation for the premature termination of contract with her previous employer. Psychologically and financially, FDWs are not in a position to negotiate their working conditions or to state their desire not to work for abusive and unreasonable employers or under difficult conditions (such as a family with a huge house or several cars needing to be washed daily). That FDWs, like the employers, are customers of the agency is ignored. The FDWs' vulnerability in the regulatory system allows the agencies to treat these two categories of customers – employees and employers – very differently.

In an interview, one FDW, an Indonesian, who had recently been returned twice to her agency, recollected the fragments of what she had gone through in the previous ten months. She stated sorrowfully that the "training center is crazy, agency is crazy, employer is crazy, and this government is crazy." She added that if her parents and brothers had understood the system, they would not have pestered her for money.

TWO YEARS' WORKING EXPERIENCE IN SINGAPORE: A PORTAL FOR WHAT?

Just as "disposable domestics" are an indispensable feature of the global economy (Chang 2000), FDWs, treated as expendable or refundable commodities, are the linchpin of middle- and upper-class families in Singapore. At the same time, it should be noted that despite the adverse conditions of their employment, FDWs often view their temporary migration to Singapore as one of a limited set of alternatives that could make a difference in their lives. As one Indonesian woman said, "I thought, I've got to do something about [my life]."

Some FDWs contend that their decision to work in Singapore was motivated by their wish to improve the economic status of their families. Filipina women with high school or college educations can earn salaries in Singapore that are two to four times higher than what they can command in their home country. Indonesians with junior secondary school education may make four to six times as much in Singapore as in their homeland. Both migrate to Singapore to support their family or kin in varying degrees.

At the same time, many also recognize that working abroad can be a way to gain their independence. Upon completion of their two-year stint, some wish to leave Singapore for good and return to their own countries to start their families. One twenty-four-year old Indonesian FDW said, "My boyfriend didn't want me to leave him, but I want to save enough money to build our house. There is nothing good to live with his parents." For others, a stint in Singapore may serve as a springboard to better career opportunities in other countries. Life scenarios for FDWs can be classified in terms of the following types of migration after their employment in Singapore.

The first is the "shuttle traffic" type. After completion of her two-year contract, this type of FDW returns to her country but makes repeated trips back to Singapore. This practice is possible because of geographic proximity and because the FDW has friends and relatives in Singapore, a small country with a well developed traffic system. Using their networks, FDWs can either select an agency that best serves their needs or save money by finding a new employer without going through an agency at all. Recently, some FDWs, with the consent of their employers, have started attending various part-time courses to develop skills in computers, crafts, international cooking, nursing aid, haircutting, advanced English, and the like through classes conducted and sponsored by the Philippine and Indonesian embassies and other organizations. Obtaining skills may help current FDWs prepare for their return in the future.

The second type of migration is a regional move among the country of origin, Singapore, Hong Kong, Taiwan, and sometimes Malaysia or Brunei, and the oil-rich Middle East. Hong Kong is often perceived as a better place to work due to higher wages and legally secured days off on Sunday and public holidays. Taiwan also provides workers with the highest wages in the region. However, the agencies charge the FDWs higher fees, and there is a longer wait for work in Hong Kong and Taiwan. Indonesian women without experience, spoken English ability, and money find it nearly impossible to obtain employment in Hong Kong. It is believed and often asserted by the employment agency staff that employers in Hong Kong prefer FDWs with two years' working experience in Singapore. Also Taiwan limits the working period to six years and has a unique policy that periodically chooses the sending countries.[6] To many, Singapore continues to be a reliable place to secure a job.

The third type of migration – least common among FDWs – is migration to the West, typically Canada, using Southeast Asia as a transit point. This is applicable to Filipina women with college degrees, but might be the least likely scenario. Stories are repeatedly told about the success of some Filipina women who have moved to Canada. These success stories undoubtedly function as an ideological device to keep migration going (Cohen 1987). The exploitation of foreign domestic workers is likely to be repeated in Western countries (Anderson 2000; Chang 2000; England and Stiell 1997; Pratt and Philippine Women's Center 1999; Stiell and England 1999; Zarembka 2004). And yet, it is also true that for Filipino college graduates permanent settlement after two years of work is an option in Canada. Once they are settled, most intend to change jobs, probably to one that is not heavily gendered. Planning to work in Canada is one example of the choices individuals make to overcome difficult circumstances.

Two things highlight the unique position of Singapore in the trajectories of foreign domestic workers in this region. First, as an entry point for FDWs, Singapore functions as an information center to newcomers. Among the FDWs working in Singapore, there is a rich exchange of information through short messaging services (SMSs), personal meetings and group gatherings in churches, and weekend enclaves. FDWs convey job prospects to their kin and neighborhood friends in their home countries by letters, phone calls, and SMSs. Often they act as referral persons for those coming to Singapore. Matchmaking on their own, without using an employment agency, may reduce not only the cost due to the agency but also the risks of employment by weeding out undesirable employers.

Second, in light of the transnationalization of domestic workers, in addition to the training centers in the workers' countries of origin and skill improvement courses coordinated by the Philippine and Indonesian Embassies in Singapore, it can be argued that Singapore itself has become a training ground for FDWs. While unrealistically high expectations from employers' families, restrictive immigration policies marginalizing FDWs, and distrustful public opinion towards these foreign women might serve to discipline them, these practices also force FDWs to develop various means of negotiation (Yeoh and Huang 2000), bargaining, and personal (if not collective) forms of resistance.

It must be noted that the massive transfer of women has led to a "care drain" from the countries of origin where the young, the old, and the sick could have been otherwise attended by these women (Hochschild

2004; Parrenas 2004). In addition, transnational domestic work reproduces males and females as gendered subjects at the global level (Yeoh and Willis 1999). At the same time, however, the discussion of transnational mobility needs to be dealt with as a double-edged reality operating on multiple levels. This mobility simultaneously opens up possibilities of exploitation and of liberation (Yeoh and Huang 2004), reveals both structural constraints and personal and collective resistance (Lin 1999; Ogaya 2004), and exemplifies more complex forms of power, i.e. self-discipline coexisting with docility (Constable 1997). FDWs are not necessarily victims, and, more importantly, do not view themselves as entirely passive beings.

In relation to the resistance of FDWs, this chapter ends with an incident that highlights the strength and agency of FDWs. Although Filipina and Indonesian domestic workers in Singapore are called "FDWs" by the government and "maids" by employers, agencies, and the public, Filipina domestic workers address themselves differently. A conversation I had with one worker exemplifies this choice:

> A (author): "How would you address yourself in terms of your job? I mean, shall I call you a maid?"
> B (Filipina domestic worker with eight years working experience in Singapore):"No, DH is the one."
> A: "What is DH ?"
> B: "It means domestic helper."
> A: "So then, I will use the phrase 'domestic helper' from now on."
> B: "Don't. DH."
> A: "Domestic helper, right?"
> B: "No, no, DH, Madame."
> A: "Why?"
> B: "Because it's cool."

The difference between the category of "maid" or even "FDW" and the category of "DH" is neither nominal nor trivial. For these workers, "maid" is perceived to denote a degraded position, and "FDW," a term used by Singapore society, may indicate loyalty to the government. Neither designation enhances the self-esteem of these women. In contrast, "DH" is defined by the workers themselves. Those who dare call themselves "DH" can be regarded as positive actors of a self-enforcing category (Sacks 1979). Such women claim a voice and agency when they expand the circle of people for whom "DH" is an accepted term.

NOTES

[1] Although the Singapore government seldom refers to the number of foreign domestic workers, various sources estimate there were around 170,000 in 2007.

2   MOM homepage, Foreign Worker Levy Rates 2007. http://www.mom.gov.sg/
    publish/momportal/en/communities/work_pass/work_permit/during_emplo
    yment/foreign_worker_levy.html

3   MOM homepage, A General Guide on Employing Foreign Domestic Workers
    2004.   http://www.mom.gov.sg/MOM/WPD/Others/General_Guide_FDW_
    Employment(4Apr03).pdf

4   The proportion of those aged 65 and above increased from 3.4% in 1970, to
    7.2% in 2000, and to 8.2% in 2005 (Singapore Department of Statistics 2006b).

5   Malay employers are much fewer in number than Chinese employers. Malays
    constitute just 13.6% of Singapore residents (Ministry of Information,
    Communications and the Arts 2006) and have relatively lower average
    incomes (Singapore Department of Statistics 2001).

6   This is from an interview with government officials in the Council of Labor
    Affairs, Taichung, Taiwan.

8

The Birth of the Housewife in Contemporary Asia: New Mothers in the Era of Globalization

EMIKO OCHIAI

EMERGENCE OF HOUSEWIVES

The goal of our research was to illuminate the transformation of gender roles in East and Southeast Asia, areas of strong economic development. Of central concern to us was the question of whether a pattern of gender division of labor, with the husband as the "breadwinner" or money-earner and the wife as the homemaker, would emerge in these societies, as it has in other modern societies. In Europe, the United States, Japan, and elsewhere, the process of modernization was accompanied by the birth of the "modern family." The modern family has as its precondition the division between a public sphere and a domestic sphere, and is characterized by mutual affection between family members, the gender division of labor, and strong concern and attention paid to a small number of children (Ochiai 1997 and Chapter 5).

Our research showed that, in contemporary East and Southeast Asia, there are indeed many societies in which mothers continue to work during their childrearing years, and that enough support exists in such societies to enable both parents to work while raising children. An unexpected discovery of this investigation, however, was the significant number of "housewives" we encountered in societies of Types 1 and 2 where mothers of small children continue to work. In some of these societies, there is indeed a trend for childrearing support to become less and less adequate, but a movement towards "housewifization" could be found even in societies where there is no obvious inadequacy in childrearing support. Why did women become housewives and will they remain situated in the role of housewife in the future? In this chapter, we will consider "housewifization" in the three Type 1 and 2 societies by paying fresh attention to the cases of housewives we encountered in these regions.

HOUSEWIVES IN ASIAN SOCIETIES

(1) Housewives in China

China, like Thailand, is a Type 1 society in terms of patterns of labor-force participation rates for women. (For a detailed description of Types 1, 2, and 3, see Chapter 1 of this volume.) Like the United States and Sweden, those rates form a reversed U-shaped pattern when graphed against age. However, the causes for this are different in China and Thailand. Presumably, China took on this pattern following the socialist revolution in the 1950s. As Sechiyama has stated (Sechiyama 1996), women had long taken part in agricultural labor in Southern China but usually had not done so in Northern China. While the definition of "housework" and hence women's work differs (from that in modern Europe) in that it included caring for domestic animals like pigs and chickens and the cultivation of vegetables to be consumed by the family,[1] the fact remains that the gender division of labor, with "men working outside and women working inside," existed in certain regions before the advent of the modern family. We thus need to modify the preconditions in the theory of the modern family as it was developed in Europe, which had relatively high labor-force participation rates for women before modernization started. It was socialism that uniformly "de-housewived" women in China regardless of regional differences. While some feel that taking on a double burden was excessively hard on women, one woman, ninety-one-years old when interviewed in 2004, described her first experience of leaving home to work at a daycare center as very fulfilling.[2] The subjects in Lisa Rofel's study on the gendered experience of socialist revolution in China cite similar experiences (Rofel 1994). In a survey of attitudes taken for our study, conducted in Wuxi City in 2002, 88 percent of women and 84 percent of men indicated a preference for women to follow the "dual roles" pattern balancing marriage, childbirth, and childcare with work, while only 9 percent and 10 percent, respectively, preferred the pattern of temporary retirement from work followed by reemployment (Miyasaka 2007: 105).

China is distinguished by the ample presence of three types of childcare agents other than the mother. Childcare may be described as more the role of the grandparents than of the mother, and quite a few children live in their grandparents' house during their infant years. The reversed U-shaped pattern of women's labor-force participation is due to the continuing intergenerational division of labor in the traditional extended family, with older individuals leaving the workforce early to take care of their grandchildren. China's official retirement age is currently fifty-five for women and sixty for men. With aunts, uncles, and others also commonly helping with childcare, the contribution by relatives is extremely effective. Daycare centers established by socialist policy play a substantial role, while maids and babysitters called *ayi* and *baomu* are also employed. Above all, men who are skilled at housework, including cooking, provide considerable support.

In such a society, with all the necessary prerequisites for both parents to work, and with high labor-force participation rates, what kinds of women become housewives? Let us consider some particular cases.

Case 1
R (AGE 44, WUXI CITY, INTERVIEWED IN 2002)
R was born in 1957 and married her huband (born in 1958) in 1984. Her three-member household contained her husband and a daughter (nineteen) who studied at a professional school. Following their marriage, her husband worked at a chemical plant, while R worked at a textile factory. In accordance with national policies of the time, she received a fifty-six-day maternity leave. Because the factory's daycare facilities did not accept children under one-year old, and both her husband's and her own parents were working, R hired a retired woman in the neighborhood to take care of her daughter during the day until she was four years old. This cost 60 *yuan* per month, one-third to two-fifths of her salary, but there was no other choice. When R worked the night shift, her husband and mother-in-law watched their daughter.

In 1998, R quit her job at the textile factory and became a staff member at an institutional dormitory/hotel (*zhaodaisuo*). She quit the job at the textile factory because its three-shift system forced her to work the night shift twice a week; in addition, she asserted, working on her feet was particularly hard for her as a woman. The pay at her new workplace was lower, but she gained free time.

In 1998, R was laid off from the new job (*xiagang*) when her workplace was closed down for urban development. Thus, she became a full-time housewife, but since she was not considered retired but merely temporarily unemployed, her pension was taken care of by her former workplace. In 2002, she received about 200 *yuan* each month from the *zhaodaisuo*.

Her daily life consisted of doing housecleaning in the morning, after which she went to a securities firm.[3] Over ten years, she made 70,000 *yuan* in stock trading. When she lived with her parents and had some money to spare, she and her husband managed their savings separately; her husband also bought stocks. By 2002, R handled their combined savings. She used her husband's stocks to buy their home. There was no sense that she could not use money earned by her husband.

Regarding the possibility of working again, R stated that she would be interested if she could find suitable employment, such as a comfortable job working on the staff of a hotel or shop. She was not, however, looking for work. At her age (forty-four), it was difficult to look for employment.

She estimated that in her housing complex about one out of five women in her age group was a full-time housewife.

Here her husband interjected that "I, personally, would like her to work to improve the economic status of our household." R responded that "If possible, I would like the type of job where I could still pay attention to the household."

Case 2
L (AGE 33, LIVING IN A FORMER "FARMING VILLAGE" ON THE OUTSKIRTS OF WUXI CITY NOT INCLUDED IN CITY AREA, INTERVIEWED IN 2002)

L was born in a provincial farming village. Sixteen years earlier, at age seventeen, L moved to her mother's hometown, not far from her present-day area of residence, and took a job. Two or three years later her parents followed her there, and a few years after that her younger sister moved there as well. L's household consisted of five members: L, her husband, their eight-year-old daughter, and L's parents.

L was working at a textile factory when she gave birth to her daughter. Four months after her maternity leave, her daughter contracted an illness of unknown cause, so she left work for a year to care for her. L brought her parents from their hometown to help care for her daughter,[4] and they have lived together ever since. The daughter recovered from her illness after ten months without the cause ever being known. L then quit her job at the factory and began working at a supermarket.

In 2002, her husband's salary was raised to 1,000 *yuan* per month, but L lost her job when the supermarket was sold.

She expressed no interest in becoming a *quanzhi taitai* (full-time housewife).[5] It was difficult for her husband to support her and their daughter on his salary alone. Temporary work was available but she was interested only in a permanent, full-time position. At first, she was unable to seek employment because she did not have residency in the city. In June, 2002, she gained residency, but her age then made finding work difficult. Getting a job in the village was difficult, as her city residency made potential employers reluctant to hire someone to whom, they believed, they would have to pay a high salary and whose insurance they would have to cover. Employers in the village were private companies that prefered to hire people at low salaries who did not need insurance. L considered seeking work in the city.

The above cases both involve a woman becoming a full-time housewife due to loss of employment. However, while R had little desire to return to work, and preferred an easy, comfortable job if she did, L wanted to find a long-term, established job. R tended to think of herself as a housewife, but L was clearly only temporarily unemployed. The difference between their attitudes can be explained first by the difference in their ages, second by their economic conditions, and third by their attitudes towards work. R was much older than L and her chance of finding a job in an early retirement society was small. Furthermore, not only was R able to live on her husband's salary, she also had the financial resources to make money from trading stocks. L, by contrast, stated that her husband's salary was not enough to support her family. The different attitudes towards work between someone from a farming village, who had to struggle to find work, and someone from the city are also significant. For L, who came to Wuxi from the countryside looking for work and suffered employment discrimination due to her lack of city residency, finding a stable position in the city was one of her primary goals in life. R, on the other hand, had come to see work as a troublesome burden. While there is effective public support in China for women to continue working (see Chapter 2), R's case shows that in individual situations, this public support may not reach the persons who need it. For R, balancing childrearing and work was a hardship; the lack of support for women in the supposedly "equal" conditions of the workplace were intolerable. For her, becoming a housewife was partly occasioned by her unemployment, but it was also the fulfillment of a long-held dream of living a household- and family-centered life different from that experienced by men.

Also of interest is the remark by R's husband, who earned what may be considered an adequate income, that he would like R to work to improve the family finances. In addition to anxiety about supporting the family on the husband's salary alone, we see that he did not believe that it was the husband's responsibility alone to support the family. If anything, it was R who did not want to work. It is not necessarily true that "housewifization" always takes place because of its benefits for men.

Also very surprising was R's estimate that one in five women of her age in her housing complex was a full-time housewife. Women were particularly vulnerable to the widespread unemployment resulting from China's opening of the economy. There was also a growing gap between men's and women's salaries (Yang and Shen 2004). A fundamental principle of socialism thus appeared to be collapsing. Immediately prior to the Tiananmen Square suppression in 1989, when free-market reforms were being rapidly implemented, it was argued that women should return to the home in order to reduce surplus labor (the *funü huijia* debate) (Ochiai 1988). This argument became a reality later, when economic growth accelerated.

The next case, that of H, is arguably the polar opposite of the previous two.

Case 3

H (AGE 36, BEIJING, INTERVIEWED IN 2004)

From Tianjin, H graduated from a prestigious national university in 1990. After taking a job at a Japan/U.S./China joint venture company, she took part in the establishment of a Chinese-funded industrial-academic joint venture company. She achieved the high-level position of executive vice manager. She married in 1992. Her husband works for a U.S.-based corporation. In 1998 her son was born. After a one-year leave, she returned to work.

She brought her parents to Beijing to help care for her child, and they shared an apartment. She also relied on a non-live-in domestic worker (*ayi*). When their son turned three, they placed him in a city daycare facility, where he stayed overnight except on Wednesday nights and weekends. They chose this option because they believed an overnight facility was better for studying. Although he was only six years old at the time of the interview, he had already finished the classes for the first year of elementary school. He also played sports. The boy entered an elementary school affiliated with a famous university. The entrance examination for the school was easy; the school is for the children of professors of that university, but is also open to outsiders who make a donation.

H quit her job at the beginning of 2004. She said she left because personnel changes associated with a merger the previous year made the job no longer enjoyable. She had sufficient savings to support herself for the rest of her life. For the last seven years, her husband's salary has been the higher of the two.

At the time of the interview, she worked as a housewife, taking care of her child. She had also begun studying simultaneous translation, but had not decided how long she would remain at home.

While she left work for home mainly for work-related reasons, another clearly important reason was to be able to take care of her child. Since her child was about to enter elementary school, he needed to learn such things as computers, music, and sports, but the grandparents were no longer able to help. In contrast to Japan's "three-year-old myth" – the idea that only a mother is suited to care for her child personally during the first three years of his or her life – we might call this the "seven-year-old myth."

"I think a woman should be at home. No matter how successful you are at work, if your home is a failure, you don't have a thing," H noted. Her husband concurred that H's decision to stay at home was a good thing.

H can be described as belonging to the highest economic stratum of Chinese society. By her mid-thirties, she had saved sufficient money to support herself for life. The young generation in China is producing more and more young people like her, with talent and education. It has been observed that in contemporary China, the phenomenon of women voluntarily becoming housewives is limited to the urban upper class in Guangzhou, Shanghai, and Beijing.

Upper-class housewives can be further divided into two types. One type is women like H who deliberately become housewives even though they have both the ability and opportunity to get high-level jobs. The other type is women who are commonly called "merely pretty" women who become the wives of men with economic power. A variation of the latter is the well-known recent phenomenon of so-called "second women" or "kept women" of rich men.

While H's primary reason for becoming a housewife was due to conditions at work, an additional major motive was the wish to raise and educate her child. Her zeal for education can be seen even in her selection of a kindergarten for her child. With urban families normally limited to one child by Chinese law, there is a passionate concern with childrearing and education, especially in the urban sector.

Especially noteworthy is the expression "seven-year-old myth." These were H's words in response to the inteviewer's allusion to Japan's "three-year-old myth." According to H, in China the crucial age is not three, but seven – that is, the year the child starts school. Professor Zhou Weihong of the Beijing Japan Research Center calls this the "elementary school myth" (Miyasaka 2007: 114). As in H's case, it is common for very small children to be completely entrusted to the grandparents or left to fend for themselves in kindergarten classes, but there is a common belief in China that if the child is not returned to the care of the parents by the time he or she enters elementary school, the child's education may suffer. There is a strong view that one cannot entrust the child to uneducated grandparents. Zhou Weihong cites newspaper articles that ask, "How can we get rid of the grandparents whom we brought here to take care of the child?"[6]

Is the idea of becoming a housewife to support one's child's education gaining ground outside the top classes in the major cities? For a comparison, we interviewed a woman in her thirties in Fushun, a regional city in northeastern China. This woman was at the time working at a construction company while bringing up her seven-year-old child. She was intensely devoted to her child's education, and said that she bought textbooks and taught her child at home subjects like English, traditional Chinese poetry, and arithmetic. She was strongly concerned not only with her own child's education, but that of her younger brother's child as well. She said that when her child reached the age of being intensely involved with studies – that is, the period from the end of the first year of middle school to graduation from high school, when an exhausting amount of time is spent studying – she would consider whether to quit her job and devote herself to helping her child. At that time, she said, it would be important for the child to eat a balanced diet and be healthy in order to get good grades. She sometimes discussed the education of children with her colleagues at work, and said that 60 percent of them had similar ideas.[7] It seemed apparent that this way of thinking was no longer unusual even outside of the highest classes among women under forty.

The housewife has also become a popular topic in the media. There are frequent reports about the increasing number of women who become full-time housewives (*quanzhi taiti, quanzhi zhufu, quanzhi mama*) of their own volition in cities like Guangzhou, Shanghai, and Beijing.[8] One Internet newspaper, the *Sohu News*, put out a special issue in 2004 called "From Half of the Sky to Full-Time Housewife" that discussed how women, who under socialism were said to "hold up half of the sky," were wavering between home and the workplace.[9] This issue featured Pan Yunkang, a researcher of marriage and family in China, who argued that the reasons women become full-time housewives were mainly passive ones, such as raising small children, supporting the husband's work, and their own unemployment.

The special issue of *Sohu News* centered on the psychological damage suffered by women who became full-time housewives. One example cited was of a thirty-five-year-old Beijing woman, a specialist in overseas trade and finance, who left work at the urging of her husband when she became pregnant. In an interview she commented: "Sometimes I went from morning to evening without combing my hair or washing my face . . . When I spent long hours with old people and children, we had the same conversations over and over, and I thought about the same things . . . What I needed was not so much to work, as it was a certain atmosphere and colleagues to interact with . . . My husband is always supportive of me as a housewife – "Dear, I'll earn the money. Your only obligation is to enjoy your life." But I was at a complete loss as to how to enjoy my life." The "nameless distress" which Betty Friedan found in the United States in the 1950s and 1960s seems to be emerging in contemporary China (Friedan 1963). However, the *Sohu News* did not go so far as to criticize the practice of becoming a housewife, instead recommending that women enrich their lives through charitable work and social activities, citing examples from the United States and Taiwan.

(2) Housewives in Singapore
Singapore falls under Type 2 of labor-force participation rates. In this pattern, a high level of labor-force participation is maintained not only before marriage but throughout a woman's early thirties, followed by a steady decline (see Figure 2.3 in Chapter 2). In this pattern, women continue working during the childbearing and early childrearing years, beginning to leave work when the children have reached a certain grade in school. Since the pattern in Singapore is very similar to that in Hong Kong and Taiwan, this may be considered a manifestation of a common Southern Chinese pattern.

Viewed historically, the labor-force participation rates for women in Singapore have risen (see Figure 2.3 in Chapter 2). Singapore separated from Malaysia to become an independent republic in 1965 and, as part of a national policy that viewed economic development as necessary for survival, instituted a policy of economic mobilization of women through emphasis on education and family planning. At the end of the 1970s, with a reduction in birthrates having been successfully achieved, government policy was changed to encourage childbirth, and efforts were made to expand daycare and related facilities (Tamura 1999b). Ample after-school care is provided even after children have entered elementary school. The hiring of domestic workers from foreign countries like the Philippines and Indonesia has steadily increased since the 1990s, with between 100,000 and 170,000 such workers presently in the country; between 11 and 15 percent of all households employ such workers. The delegation of household work to outsiders, including eating in food courts instead of cooking at home, is a distinct feature of Singapore's encouragement of working couples. Support from relatives with childrearing, housework, and health-care may be even more extensive than in China.

Singapore stands with China as one of the two leading nations for supporting working couples, but here, too, some women have become housewives. In particular, many women leave their jobs in their late thirties. How can this be explained? Let us consider some cases.

Case 1
G (AGE 41, INTERVIEWED IN 2002)
G, an ethnic Chinese, was born in 1961. She lived in an expensive condominium with her husband, three children (one daughter, thirteen; twin sons, eleven), and one maid.

G's mother died when she was nine and her father when she was twenty-one. She had a diploma in accounting from a "pre-university" (a "centralized institute" or three-year school between junior high school and university). This path was chosen because her father did not have the economic means to send his daughter to a university, but she was satisfied with her diploma. She became a Christian (Protestant) during her student years.

G worked as an accountant for a private business from 1981 to 1990 and married in 1986. Her husband, who had a diploma in mechanical engineering, used to help with his brother's work, but in 1988 he became the project manager for a private company, where he was later promoted to the rank of director. They lived in an "HDB," a high-rise public housing complex built by the Housing Development Bureau.

G had her first child, a daughter, in 1989. She quit her job four months after giving birth, since both her parents and her husband's parents were dead, and there was no household helper. Her husband did almost no housework. They hired a maid in 1991 when she learned she was going to have twins. From 1993 to 1999, they lived in Hong Kong for her husband's work, and brought the maid back to Singapore with them in 1999. That year they bought the condominium in which they lived at the time of the interview. They had to let the maid go, however, because G's husband did not receive the extra salary he had in Hong Kong. The maid moved to Canada where she was employed as a maid.

G was a "homemaker" (her expression) from 1990 to 2001, but after doing catch-up study, started working again as an insurance advisor in 2001. She thought it was better for her to stay at home until the children were twelve years old, but since school hours were longer in middle school, she and her husband agreed that she would start working again. She wanted to keep working at her present job. She did not want to hold a regular office job because she wanted work with flexible hours.

The maid did almost all the housework. When the maid was not there they ate at the neighboring HDB restaurant across the street. The maid's main task was the housework, and she only helped with the childcare from time to time. Having the maid do the housework enabled G to focus on childcare.

She responded to statements about attitudes toward the family as follows: "It is better for the mother not to work while the children are small" – agreed; "It is better for the mother to stay at home even after the children have gotten bigger" – did not particularly agree; "Women, like men, should work throughout their lives" – did not particularly agree.

Case 2

N (ABOUT 40 YEARS OLD, INTERVIEWED IN 2002)

N's father was a professional driver, and her mother was a full-time housewife. She convinced her parents to let her go to university even though she was female, and worked during school holidays. She graduated from university in 1985 with a major in management. In February of 1985, a time of economic recession, she finally found a job as personnel manager for an American-funded enterprise in the communications industry.

She married the son of a very wealthy family in 1987. Feeling that having married young she could have children later, after their honeymoon N began working during the day and studying personnel management until 10 p.m. three nights a week, finally receiving a diploma in personnel management.

After marriage, N and her husband lived with her parents-in-law in their home in a wealthy residential district, along with an aunt (her father-in-law's younger sister), and her older brother-in-law and his wife. They moved out in 1989 after buying a condominium. Her first child was born in 1992, and because she did not want her child to go to childcare (caretaking for children for their first eighteen months, prior to entering a regular daycare center), they decided to return to her mother-in-law's home. Her second child was born two years later. Having lived with her in-laws for nine years, and with the children now older, she felt that they needed to establish an independent household, so they again moved out. Living with her mother-in-law was convenient, she said, but she felt like a tenant, not a female head of household.

After eleven years working as a personnel manager for the American-financed enterprise, she quit that job in 1996. Her reason was that the job made it impossible for her to live a "human" life. Exhausted from work, she had very little energy to spend on her family. She developed allergies on a business trip to America and took this as a sign that she should quit. She did like her job and found it meaningful, and she was fortunate to have an understanding boss. The boss initially allowed her to reduce her work to four days a week on a trial basis, something commonly done in America. However, having tried this she realized that although her salary could be cut it was impossible to reduce her job responsibilities, so she left the job completely after six months. After quitting her job, she continued working as an external consultant for her old company and other companies.

When working, she made a big economic contribution to her family – in fact she brought in 60 percent of the household budget – but she is not sure if she managed to make an emotional contribution. One day she realized that she did not know her own children. She thought about her priorities in life.

N used her personnel skills to plan her children's schedules, and thought about time management and how to help her children prepare for their examinations. Some mothers quit their jobs to study the same subjects as their children, but she did not agree with this. One needs to "teach them how to catch a fish rather than giving them a fish."

Her children's daily routine was as follows: wake up at 6:00 (because of the maid, N did not need to get up). Go to school at 7:00. Return home at 1:30 for lunch and rest time. From 2:30 onward, study with a tutor of Chinese, play piano, go to swim school, and do homework both from school and the tutor. N spent $1000 each month on the children's lessons and tutoring. Dinner was from 7:30 to 8:00. From 8:00, study continued if there was more to do, but sometimes the children played. If the children were tired she told them to go play outside, but because everyone was studying, there would be no one in the courtyard of the condominium.

To get into good schools, she noted, the fifth and sixth years were essential. A parent who was not at home would not be able to manage this period successfully. At the time of the interview, she read books on education. She was glad that she was not working full-time. She thought parenting was a difficult job.

If children are constantly forced to study, she concluded, their childhood would become impoverished, and they would develop an impoverished view of themselves. Academic achievement is not the most important thing. The important thing is to be healthy morally. One must instill correct values in their minds, she contended; childhood was the only time. When they were older she would let them be free, and entrust them to the hands of God. This was why she was raising them under her strict authority. Things like sports and music were also important.

G and her husband were Christians. For G, the most important thing was God, the second was family; then came other things. Since marriage was at the center of the family, one's spouse was most important, then children, then work.

G responded thus to statements about attitudes toward the family: "It is better for the mother not to work while the children are small" – did not strongly agree; "It is better for the mother to stay at home even after the children have gotten bigger" – did not particularly agree; "Women, like men, should work throughout their lives" – did not particularly agree.

Neither of these women came from a wealthy family, but both worked hard to get good educations and jobs and achieve an affluent lifestyle. N's level of education and employment can be considered particularly high. Each woman gave up a highly desirable position, became a full-time housewife for some time, and was doing work that had flexible hours and allowed her to use her specialized knowledge. G left work at twenty-eight, N at thirty-three (estimated). Both encountered troubles balancing work and home, and chose the home.

Why did they run into difficulty balancing work and home in Singapore, where support for balancing work and home is extensive? For G, a major factor was the lack of support from relatives due to the death of both her parents and those of her husband. Because of Singapore's historically high mortality rates through the present older generation, there are many middle-aged people today who lost their parents at a young age. For N, the harsh demands of her job may have been too great.

Beyond specific hardship reasons, in the background the notion that a mother should be directly involved with her own child appears to be spreading. While one often observes maids watching the children, statements that the maid's main job is housework and that child care cannot be left to the maid were heard from G as well as others. In Singapore, where delegation of tasks has been carried almost to an extreme, the first realm that the family is trying to reclaim is childcare. There is no indication of any similar trend for food preparation, housework, or elder care. In the past, a foster-parent system was common, in which it was common to leave children with the foster parent on weekdays, but this system is currently in decline.

We should also note that even though they both declared the importance of the mother caring for her child personally, G and N emphasized different periods of the child's life as requiring more intense maternal care. G returned to the home immediately after giving birth and returned to work after her child entered middle school, which had longer school hours. Her attitude about family was that the time when the mother should not have a job was when the child was small – not when the child was older. By contrast, N saw supervising the child's education as more important when the child was older, namely, the fifth and sixth years of school. For her, it was better for the mother not to work when the child was older.

Kiwaki (2007) divides childrearing in Singapore into an early and a late period, with maternal age thirty-five marking the boundary between the two. Kiwaki writes: "The early period is the 'upbringing' period, and the number of women who leave work during this period is small compared with Japan. This is because the job of bringing up the child has been delegated to relatives, foster parents, maids, and the like. The later period is the 'educational' period and the role of the mother as the supervisor of the child's education is thought to be essential." G's case demonstrates that during the "upbringing" period, when support from relatives is not available, becoming a housewife is an option. But N's approach, becoming a housewife for the purpose of education, probably represents the majority at present. In Singapore, with a child's educational path being decided by examinations during such times as the fourth year of elementary school, graduation from elementary school, and the last year of middle school, parents' competition for their children's education can become desperately intense.

I would like to draw attention here to how the nature of education is being discussed. N described her philosophy of education using the Christian expression "moral values," but her emphasis on education developing total character through activities like sports and music was shared by H in China. This is, in fact, the traditional Chinese foundation of education, summed up in the expression *zuoren* (develop character; literally "make a person") used by the elderly woman in Fushun who was so devoted to her grandchild's education.[10] Even in Singapore, where the competition for academic achievement has become so intense, one perceives the humane influence that traditional Chinese culture, with its emphasis on educating the whole person, continues to have, sometimes mixed with Western influences through Christianity.

(3) Housewives in Thailand
Labor-force participation rates for women in Thailand, also a Type 1 country, have traditionally followed this pattern. Europeans in the age of exploration remarked that women in Southeast Asia frequently worked and had strong property rights (Reid 1993). At the beginning of the twentieth century, efforts were made to introduce the ideology of *ryōsai kenbo* (good wife, wise mother), a gender ideal created in modern Japan under the influence of the modern Western gender norm, to Southeast Asia, but this apparently did not manage to change actual practices (Hashimoto 2005). In short, we can call Thailand a "prehousewifization" society. Furthermore, according to the calculations of Umemura Mataji et al., the labor-force participation rates for women in Japan around 1880 followed a similar pattern to that of present-day Thailand (Umemura, ed. 1988; also see Chapter 1, Figure 1.4). The traditional Japanese gender system was somewhat similar to that in Southeast Asia. Since Japan is now a Type 3 society, we cannot assume that Thailand will remain as it is.

As had been expected, Thailand showed the greatest change of any society in this investigation. The target locale studied in Thailand was a new residential development in a farming village on the outskirts of Bangkok, populated by new middle-class families living in townhouses and detached houses. This new middle class itself is a new social group which has been the subject of little research to date. Hashimoto (2004b) has made the startling discovery that the wives in thirty out of seventy-five households in townhouse developments with children under fifteen years old – that is, 40 percent – are full-time housewives. In addition, among the respondents for these seventy-five households (including both men and women), 62 percent describe the ideal life course for a woman as: "get married, have children, leave work either when marrying or having children, and work again after the children grow up," showing preference for an M-curve type of employment pattern.

Since there were no full-time housewives among the subjects I interviewed, I will cite cases taken from Hashimoto (2003a; 2004a).

Case 1

T (AGE 45, INTERVIEWED IN 2002)

Her husband (self-employed) was thirty-eight years old at the time of the interview. They had one son, aged thirteen.

T was a full-time housewife and did all the household work herself. Her reason for becoming a housewife was that her husband's income was more than enough to support the family, and since he was a responsible and reliable person, she thought it would be best for her to run the household herself. She thought about getting a job, but her husband did not help with the housework at all, and it would be hard on their child if no one were there when he got home. She would worry about letting a stranger in their home as a caregiver, and it would be expensive to pay one, so she decided it would be more economical to quit her job. Her husband told her to stay at home. So she decided to do so. She enjoyed housework, and by the time she cleaned the house and straightened up, her child returned home.

Case 2

S (AGE 42, MALE INTERVIEWED IN 2002, SPEAKING ABOUT HIS WIFE)

S worked as a police officer. His wife had been a nurse, but became a full-time housewife after they had two children. The reason was that they considered it unsafe to hire a person they did not know as a caregiver. They would worry about leaving childcare to a babysitter. Since the husband had to move frequently for his job, his wife quit her job to become a full-time housewife. However, they planned for her to become a nurse again when the children became a bit older and she had more time.

Hashimoto (2004a) distinguishes two patterns by which women in their childrearing years leave work to become housewives: "passive," in which the woman wants to work but decides to quit her job to care for her children for some external reason, and "positive," in which the woman chooses to become a housewife to care for her children and family.

The above two cases are both treated by Hashimoto as "passive." In both cases the women decided on their own to become housewives because there was no one to whom they could entrust childcare. Determining whether or not there is someone with whom the children can be entrusted depends on one's assessment of what type of person the children can be entrusted with. The dividing line between passive and positive is not necessarily clear.

Traditionally, childcare in Thailand has been provided by relatives and babysitters, but since it is rare for couples with children in the new housing developments to live near their relatives, they would have to leave their children with relatives in provincial areas for years at a time if they took advantage of this type of family assistance.

Another former pattern in Thailand was for parents to hire a young girl as a maid. This girl could be either the daughter of relatives or a stranger. An eighty-year-old Mon[11] woman living in a village adjacent to the townhouse area that we surveyed reported that she raised eight children, relying on babysitters during busy farming periods. "I had to prepare meals for the people who came to help with the farm work [temporary laborers from the northeast], and I left the children with a babysitter at that time. The babysitter would come in the morning, stay all day, and go home in the evening. It was easy to find babysitters since there were poor people in our village. A babysitter would be fifteen or sixteen years old; when they are older than that they're not trustworthy. A babysitter would watch the children when I was sick or had to go somewhere" (Ochiai 2006).

However, today the situation is different. Economic growth has led to skyrocketing increases in the cost of babysitters and maids, so it is difficult for the average middle-class family to hire one. In recent years some families have begun hiring maids from Myanmar, whose labor is relatively cheap, but even this is limited to the upper end of the middle class (Hashimoto 2004a). Furthermore, some families have developed a new sense of unease about bringing strangers into the home as maids or babysitters. This feeling played a part in the two cases described above, where the wife herself decided to become a housewife in order to take care of the children. This choice was arguably made "positively." The resulting trend to "take back" childcare, which had been delegated to others, resembles the situation in Singapore.

Daycare facilities, which are supposed to be the new providers of childcare, are clearly inadequate in Thailand. In particular, there are no public facilities at all for babies and infants under the age of two-and-a-half, and private facilities are extremely expensive. One survey found that only 3.5 percent of respondents reported using institutional daycare for two-year-olds.[12] Even after the children started kindergarten, they needed to be picked up at 3:00 and taken to the workplace to play until 5:00, which turned the workplace into a daycare center (Ochiai 2003b). Although it is commonly stated that there is little support for public assistance because of the belief that childcare is the job of parents or relatives, there is a strong public demand for the construction of daycare facilities; in the 2004 elections for governor of Bangkok, most of the candidates made this a part of their platform.

Kua Wongboonsin, professor at Chulalongkorn University and one of the authors of this volume, found a dip in labor-force participation rates for women in Bangkok between the ages of thirty and thirty-four in 1998 and 1999, constituting a shallow M-curve pattern (Wongboonsin 2002: 97–101). However, this dip disappeared in 2000. Kua interprets this as women's reacting to difficulties in getting jobs by choosing not to have children rather than to leave work. The birthrate in Bangkok was a record low of 1.17 in 2000 (Wongboonsin 2004a: 202).

Not only childcare but loss of employment can lead to the "passive" decision to become a housewife. Since the economic recession of 1997, Thai society has become even more preoccupied with educational achievement, so that it has become difficult for women with only a high school degree to find work (Hashimoto 2004b).

Also noteworthy is T's explanation that "her husband's income was more than enough to support the family, and he is a responsible and reliable person." Since it is normal for husbands and wives both to work in Thailand, a sense that the man is responsible for "supporting the family" has traditionally been lacking. However, the notion of male responsibility to provide for the family has emerged in tandem with the idea of the woman's role as housewife.

Next, we will look at a case of a woman clearly making a positive choice to become a housewife.

Case 3
P (APPROXIMATELY IN HER 40S, INTERVIEWED IN 2002)
P lives in a district of detached houses. She and her husband are both graduates of prestigious universities.

She formerly had a job, but became a full-time housewife after her child was born. She stated that she became a housewife because raising children was a specialized job, difficult to do correctly. Their two children attended a prestigious elementary school in the capital. Classes were tracked according to ability, and their children were in the top class. P supported the children's schoolwork by taking them to school and picking them up, as well as helping them with their studies. She said that there was an increasing trend for the parents of children in the top class in school to be heavily involved with their children's education, no matter how good their jobs were. Highly educated mothers sent their children to school for themselves.

The "positive" decision to be a housewife to give one's children a better education is often found in the highly-educated population with university degrees, as in Case 3. P was a resident of a detached-house district, where the income and education levels were higher than those in the townhouse districts.

There were few respondents whose concern with education matched P's in intensity, but a case analysis of eight university-educated housewives revealed that all of them wanted their children to earn higher degrees, with two respondents wanting their children to obtain Ph.Ds. They deliberately chose to become housewives despite having access to childcare support from relatives and maids and the financial resources to use private daycare facilities (Hashimoto 2004b).

GLOBALIZATION AND ASIAN HOUSEWIVES

(1) Diversity in Social Background
The societies studied in this chapter are diverse both ethnically and in terms of their social systems. China is a multi-ethnic society with a Han Chinese majority. Singapore describes itself as a multi-ethnic and multi-

lingual nation that is ethnically 77 percent Chinese, 14 percent Malay, and 8 percent Indian; but it, too, is primarily a Chinese society (all of the subjects for this study were ethnic Chinese). Thailand is made up of ethnic Thais and a variety of non-Thai minority groups.

In surveying our results, the distinctive and transnational quality of Chinese culture stands out. The pattern of a decline in labor-force participation rates for women in their thirties was distinctive of the Southern Chinese societies of Singapore, Hong Kong, and Taiwan. Behind this pattern is a childrearing culture involving a tight network of relatives which could be called a modified extended family, in which childcare in the childrearing period is supported by relatives and in the educational period returns to the parents who work to educate the "whole person." While expressions like "the elementary school myth" and the "seven-year-old myth" may be neologisms in the People's Republic of China, the practices they describe are increasingly common. It is very possible that common cultural factors may lead to the development of a Type 2 pattern in China as well, if the income of the middle class rises and women in their thirties, like those in Fushun, are able to realize their hopes of helping their children.

The traditional culture of Thailand has unique characteristics. With a bilateral kinship system and residence in the wife's parental house, Thai women have strong inheritance rights and it is the norm for both husband and wife to work; if anything, women may be said to work more than men. Despite these cultural characteristics, in this study it was Thailand that showed the strongest tendency towards "housewifization." Thai society makes great use of kinship ties, but if relatives in China amount to an organization, perhaps in Thailand they are more of a "network," lacking the ability to persist through change as much as in China. Housewifization in Thailand is suggestive in many ways of Japan's transformation from Type 1 to Type 3 in the past.

From the perspective of social systems, China is a formerly socialist country currently moving towards a market economy through the government's openness policy, while the other two societies are capitalist. However, the strong function of the state in Singapore has sometimes had results similar to systems under socialism. In the context of this chapter, both China and Singapore are societies that have pursued "de-housewifization" for the purpose of mobilizing women economically. Whether those societies will move from there to "re-housewifization" remains in question.

In contrast, it seems highly possible that Thailand, as a capitalist culture, will follow a pattern similar to that of Europe and Japan, in which modernization was accompanied by housewifization. Perhaps as a result of the tradition that both husband and wife work, "housewifization" has yet to take place even in the urban areas. However, the economic growth of recent years is causing many changes.

(2) Similarity in Patterns of Change
Despite the diverse social backgrounds in these three societies, there is a surprising amount of commonality in the changes currently taking

place. First, "housewifization" can be observed in all of these societies, although to differing degrees. Since researchers in these countries see this as a minor phenomenon and have done almost no research on it,[13] it is difficult to make quantitative comparisons. A more precise definition is needed for the difference between a housewife and someone who is merely unemployed, and more attention must be paid to differences in class. However, the broad phenomena can be described as follows: in China, housewifization remains a limited phenomenon; in Thailand, it is limited but proceeding to an unexpected degree; in Singapore, a general rise in women's labor-force participation rates for all age groups is countered by a decline starting in mid-life.

Regarding the causes of "housewifization," we can see in a cross-section of societies:

(1) Housewifization due to unemployment;
(2) Housewifization for the purpose of childcare;
(3) Housewifizaton for the purpose of the children's education.

Among the interviewed cases, R and L in China belonged to the first category.

The economic crisis that gripped Southeast Asia and East Asia in 1997 led to large-scale unemployment of previously employed women. Furthermore, the increasing importance of educational background brought about by economic development led to housewifization among older and less-educated individuals. This phenomenon was confirmed in Thailand and China and probably occurred elsewhere.

Housewifization for the purpose of childcare involves both the external factor of a lack of support for childcare and the internal factor of the idea that a mother should be directly involved in caring for her children. An example of the former is the case of women in Thailand leaving work due to a lack of daycare facilities; the conscious choice of G from Singapore and T and S from Thailand to become housewives instead of employing maids and babysitters belongs to the latter category. No cases of housewifization for the purpose of childcare were observed in China, where there is ample support for childcare.

In those cases in which housewifization took place for internal reasons for childcare (that is, a mother's choice), mothers avoided employing non-family members like maids, babysitters, and foster parents for childcare. On the other hand, in the three societies studied, and particularly in the ethnically Chinese societies, childcare support from grandparents and relatives outside the nuclear familiy was taken for granted. The recognition of and standards for an appropriate giver of childcare were such that some previous options were no longer available. Internal and external causes were thus interrelated with one another.

Significant cases of housewifizaton for the purpose of the children's education include H from China, N from Singapore, and P from Thailand. Each of these women was zealously performing the role of an "educator mother," a role clearly distinguished from simple childcare. At present, this practice appears as a general social phenomenon only in Singapore, where it has become a normal pattern for women to leave work during the child's "education period." There are also indications of a similar trend in the highest tier of Chinese society, and the spread of the "elementary school myth" suggests that this trend will be adopted by the next level of Chinese society if economic conditions permit. In the wealthier segments of Thai society, a similar inclination is increasing.

The timing of mothers' withdrawal from their jobs varies according to the causes of their housewifization. Those who leave work to perform childcare quit earlier, while those who leave to support their children's education quit later. However, the "elementary school myth," with its implication that the grandparents cannot be trusted with the child's education, suggests the possibility that concern with education at increasingly younger ages could lead to an acceleration in housewifization in China. Other conditions are necessary if education and housewifization are to become linked. The mother herself needs to have a certain level of education if she is to become an "educator mother." It is also possible that educational support could be delegated to private after-hours schools, as in Japan and Korea, and that, in turn, could lead more mothers to get jobs to pay for tuition fees.

Housewifization can also be divided into "passive" and "positive" types according to the presence or absence of personal agency (Hashimoto 2004a). Of the three causes listed above, unemployment is passive, desire to be involved in children's education is positive, and desire to be involved in childcare can be either passive or positive.

(3) The Globalization of Human Reproduction

In this chapter we have examined the continuing transformation of the contemporary Asian family using housewifization as a gauge. Our identification of housewifization as a common trend transcending ethnic and political differences – though varying in degree – represents a major factual discovery.

While common characteristics can be found across national boundaries, there is, at the same time, considerable variation within a single country. Voluntarily choosing to become a housewife for the purpose of educating one's children is done by women in the top tier of Chinese society, the upper tier in Thailand, and probably the middle-upper tier in Singapore. The intense devotion to education goes well beyond the level of the "education mama" (*kyōiku unama*) seen in Japan in the 1960s (Hirota 1999; Honda 2000), reminding one of the elite social tier of the United States. Many women return to more flexible jobs so they can use their specialized knowledge while still caring for their families. By contrast, women in the lower middle class with relatively poor educations may become housewives through loss of employment, in some cases accepting this outcome and in other cases seeking re-employment.

Looking at each of the three societies in cross-section, the various social strata in each society show commonalities with their counterparts in other countries. What are the factors that determine the character of each social stratum? In the globalized world, social strata are involved not only in the division of labor, but in the division of human reproduction. When the upper social tiers choose housewifization for the purpose of children's education, their goal is not simply university education but the production of individuals whose skills are valued everywhere in the world. With the parents' generation already experienced in living in foreign countries, they are likely to be thinking seriously about sending their children to study in foreign universities. Studying in foreign universities for undergraduate or graduate education is no longer rare in these three societies. The size of this sector of the population in each society, however, still differs greatly.

For the next-lower levels of society, the goal is to produce a university-educated worker to be employed mostly within the country. We can call this stratum a typical or traditional modern middle class. This white-collar class, which until recently was concentrated in advanced economies in Europe, America, and Japan, has grown considerably in Asia. The zeal for education in members of this class reflects the social reality that a university degree is a passport to higher social status. The majority of mothers in this class continue to be in the workforce in most parts of East and Southeast Asia, but many have become housewives due to unemployment and lack of adequate childcare support. At the same time, the hollowing out of this class, shown in increasing numbers of non-career jobs, is becoming the reality in the world today.

It is not only the parents of the global elite and the university-educated white-collar groups that have become global in terms of human reproduction. Domestic workers (maids) have also become an established global class of reproductive workers. Families in Singapore could not get along without domestic workers from the Philippines and Indonesia. In Thailand, domestic workers are brought in both from rural areas within the country and from Myanmar. China, fittingly for a giant country, provides for this need internally by employing women from rural villages.[14]

Thus, the globalization of reproduction has two facets. One is the international division of labor in childrearing and education in order to create a particular type of worker for the global economy; the other is the international migration of reproductive workers. A "housewife" is defined primarily as a type of reproductive worker, with the production of goods or services as secondary. In European and American history, housewives have been a phenomenon of families that produced educated white-collar workers. The phenomenon observed in contemporary Asia has indeed similarities with the emergence of the modern family in nineteenth-century Europe. Both cases were characterized by a strong concern with children's education and the use of domestic workers. The nationality of domestic workers has changed, however, and the goal of parents is no longer limited to the production of a national middle class but now includes the production of a global elite.

It is not easy to predict the future trends of housewifization in this region of Asia. The paths toward housewifization appear similar but are not identical to those taken in other societies decades ago. The future of Asian women is now tied up with the process of global reconfiguration of human reproduction.

(4) Ideology and women's agency
Globalization can be discussed not only in the context of production and reproduction, but also ideology. While not discussed in this chapter, a brief mention should be made of the ideologies of "Asian values" and "the value of the family." The debate over "Asian values" appeared in the 1993 Human Rights Conference of the United Nations, in which the countries of Europe and the United States faced off against the countries of Asia, especially China and Singapore, with the former arguing for the universality of human rights and democracy, and the latter arguing that Asian culture is based on collectivism and consensus, which give priority to order and stability, and that this is the necessary prerequisite for Asia's economic success (Tamura 1999b). "The value of the family" is deemed central to "Asian values," according to Lee Kwan Yew, the former Prime Minister of Singapore, in his speech in 1994 entitled "Family Ties: The Foundation of Asia's Success" (Tamura 1999b).

Both of these concepts were the "reverse-Orientalist" (Sakai 1996) constructions of international political dynamics. The idea of "the value of the family" was a synthesis of the "modern-family" component emphasizing the housewife's role of caretaker for children and the "traditional" component emphasizing the family's duty to care for the elderly. In Singapore and China, the Confucian idea of filial piety has been reified in law with the "Maintenance of Parents Act" and the "Protection of the Rights and Interests of Elderly People Law" (Shinozaki 1999).

Overlooking the fact that female labor-force participation rates were high prior to modernization in many parts of Asia and the fact that men at times made considerable contributions to housework, the "modern family" and its housewife have been extolled as the symbol of "traditional" culture, providing a good excuse for the government to cut the cost of social security. Ideology thus paved the way for the actual progress of housewifization due to the insufficiency of public childcare.

Having considered the ways that housewifization in Asia has progressed in the context of globalization, let us consider the ways in which women act as subjects or agents in their decision to become a housewife. Putting aside the question of whether the decision to become a housewife was voluntary, of the eight women in the three societies discussed in this study, only L from a farming village in China had a negative view of being a housewife and planned to change her situation. By contrast, R from China, who also became a housewife due to unemployment, says that she quit her previous steady job "because it was too hard for a woman," and that now she would want to work "provided that there was a comfortable job available" and would prefer "a job which would still leave time to care for my family." G from Singapore and T and S from Thailand, all of whom became housewives due to the lack of someone to help care for the children, accept and affirm a life centering on their children.

H from China, who said "I think a woman should be at home. No matter how successful you are at work, if your home is a failure, you have nothing," and N from Singapore, who complained bitterly that "I quit because the job made it impossible to live a human life. I had no energy left to spend on my family," both arrived at these feelings after battling it out in the harsh competition of global capitalism. Both of them see their children's education as their central task at present, in order to develop academic ability as well as good character in their children.

While there may be some self-justification involved, these cases do show women choosing to become housewives – or accepting the role – of their own volition. Since a survey of attitudes is important in assessing changing trends, we should consider that 40 percent of Thai respondents cited the M-pattern life course as ideal, while in China the rate was only 10 percent. Some Thai respondents expressed a strong preference for and envy of the M-curve pattern of labor-force participation as found in Japan.

The central hypothesis of our study was that the crucial factor behind a gender role change was a change in childcare practices. This is true, but the structure of the childcare network, despite what our original framework may suggest, is not the only determining factor. More important in this process are the strategies of the family or the mother herself. The most important reason for a contemporary Asian mother to decide to become a housewife voluntarily is her children's education. Nowadays, producing a university-educated white-collar worker is not a sufficient goal for an upper middle-class family. Their goal is to produce members of a global elite who can survive and succeed in any place in the world. For that purpose, even a highly-educated woman may quit her job to concentrate on her children's education even when support from domestic workers and relatives is available. The reason explicitly cited by them is generally their children's future happiness, but probably their decision is also a rational strategy for helping the family to attain a higher status in the next generation.

As we have seen, a common reason for becoming a domestic worker is to earn money for sending children to high school. A Vietnamese woman, aged thirty-six, working as a domestic worker in a Taiwanese household commented that "I came to Taiwan to send my two daughters to high school. Otherwise, they could not go to high school because the income from farming is very small" (Ochiai 2007). Again, education is key to a mother's decision. Women of this class are struggling to attain middle-class status through their children's education. Domestic workers are also Asia's new mothers.

The interviews of Asian housewives, especially those with a high level of education, do not merely reveal a strong concern about their children's education. They also show in many ways the importance for them of family life in general. For some of them, the family seems to be a shelter from the competition of global capitalism. For others, the family is a platform for a middle-class life style. As noted elsewhere, family ties are stronger among those who have attained middle-class status than among those remaining in lower statuses (Ochiai 2003a). Among the latter, divorce is more frequent, and the relationships of mutual support with relatives do not function as well. In the case of Thailand, it seems that the people who succeeded in building a stable family were able to get out of the slums and achieve middle-class status (Ochiai 2003a). In the background of the emergence of housewives in Asia, the formation of the modern family is also occurring as part of the formation of the civil society. This is similar to what was called the birth of the "modern family" that occurred in Europe, America, and Japan. The links between family, education, and social status seem to be the key to a deeper understanding of gender role changes. The ideology of the "value of the family" extolled by governments matches the mentality of the people.

It is certainly desirable to have a stable basis for personal life and a shelter from the hardship and competition of global capitalism. The M-curve pattern of the female life course that Thai women see as ideal could be a valid option for a decent human life under global capitalism, if a system could be created which properly valued both reproductive and productive labor and made them available to both men and women.

However, a gender-free view that would apply equally to men and women was, notably, nearly absent in the responses of the subjects of this study. From a Japanese point of view, these three societies seem to have a smaller gender gap due to the large number of working couples, but for this very reason there has been relatively little discussion of issues of gender. Furthermore, there was no doubt expressed about the "value of the family." Considering the experience and discussions regarding gender and family issues that have taken place in Europe, America, and elsewhere since the 1960s, we cannot be optimistic about the outcome of housewifization and international migration of reproductive workers now in progress in Asian countries. For example, in China, the "nameless distress" noted by Friedan forty-five years ago in the American case is already being reported, and the gap between men's and women's salaries is becoming wider. The M-curve pattern of labor-force participation of women, considered to be ideal by Thai women, has, in Japan, proved to be a poor system that has unfairly devalued both reproductive and productive labor of women. In spite of the fact that the international migration of domestic workers is becoming a necessity for family life in both sending and receiving countries, no region in the world has found a good solution to the issues of their working conditions and citizenship. Happiness of family life should not be built on the marginalization of women's individual lives. The trends of housewifization of women require both individuals and governments in Asia to reconsider their views of family and gender in order to construct a better modernity in the era of globalization.

* I would like to express my special thanks to Professor Hashimoto Hiroko for giving me a chance to do follow-up research with support from her project "Comparative Research on the Transformation of the Asian Family and the Construction of Tradition" (Grants-in-Aid for Scientific Research B1) conducted in 2003-2005 and to Professor Shutō Toshikazu for arranging a field research trip in Fushun, China. I am also grateful for Dr. Sakabe Akiko, who helped manage the Chinese-language materials.

NOTES

1. From December 2004 interview done by Shuto and Ochiai of elderly informant in Fushun City in the northeastern region of China. She also stated that poor women sometimes did engage in farm work.
2. From December 2004 interview of elderly informant in Fushun City.
3. Going to a securities firm is not considered a job, but a kind of hobby and source of a small amount of pocket money, by others and even by women themselves who stay at home in this society. The case is the same in Japan. To undervalue women's economic activity and not recognize them as working is a typical tendency in "housewifization" defined by Mies (1986) and Mies et al. (1988).
4. L and H in China brought their parents to live with them in order to help with childcare. The family of N in Singapore, by contrast, went to live with her parents-in-law. In China we see the actual application of Rajkai's hypothesis about the linking of a child-centered attitude of the modern family to the form of the traditional extended family (Rajkai 2002).
5. A new word invented quite recently. There are more new words with similar meaning such as *quanzhi mama* (full-time mother) and *quanzhi zhufu* (full-time housewife).
6. The author is grateful to Professor Zhou Weihong, Beijing Foreign Languages University, Japan Research Center, for kindly sending this information.
7. Interview, Fushun City, December 2004.
8. "More women are becoming full-time housewives in Guangzhou," *Beijing Wanbao*, November 4, 2002, and "One-Child Policy at a Fork in the Road," *Asahi Shinbun*, November 29, 2003.
9. *Sohu Shinwen*, December 6, 2004 (<http://news.sohu.com>). The author is grateful for Professor Zhou Weihong for kindly sending this information.
10. Interview, Fushun City, December 2004.
11. An ethnic minority in Thailand and Myanmar.
12. From a 1991-1992 study by the Mahidol University Demographic and Social Research Center. See Onode (2007).
13. Regarding China, I have benefited from the opinions of Professor Lu Xueyi of the Institute of Sociology, Chinese Academy of Social Sciences, one of the foremost researchers of social class, and Professor Wang Zhenyu, a family sociologist at the same institute. Dr. Bhasso Limanonda of the Institute of Population Studies, Chulalongkorn University offered advice about Thailand.
14. The regions enumerated here are major sources for the world's domestic workers. Vietnam is also growing as a sending country of domestic workers. For the cases of Vietnamese domestic workers in Taiwan, see Ochiai (2007).

9

Afterword

BARBARA MOLONY

The studies in this volume offer a pathbreaking approach to understanding gender, maternalism, and childcare in a globalizing world. All of them make extensive use of the economic and employment data common to studies of gender and work, but unlike most longitudinal studies by historians and other social scientists, these chapters expand the materialist "housewifization" paradigm implicit in many of those studies by introducing the affective role of maternalism. In a nutshell, the concept of housewifization, a neologism created by Maria Mies in her influential work, *Lace Makers of Narsapur: Indian Housewives Produce for the World Market*, can be defined as "the process by which women are socially defined as housewives, dependent for their sustenance on the income of a husband, irrespective of whether they are de facto housewives or not" (Mies 1982: 180n2). Although Mies had first applied the term to women doing home-based income-producing work in a rural postcolonial setting, stressing that these women lace makers were seen as economically expendable because, as "housewives," the income they produced was not "counted," the category of the housewife Mies applied to these late-twentieth century Indian women was, in fact, a pre-existing category. Mies drew on that category, developed as a means of understanding the roles of middle-class married women following the industrial revolution in the United States and Western Europe, to describe the social and ideological construction of married women as non-working and economically dependent in a setting quite different from the term's original context.

Mies's application of the term in a universalizing way – to a society and time distinct from its historical frame – was not, however, inappropriate. That is, if those who interact with married women treat them as if they were housewives, constructing them socially as housewives, then these women are, indeed, housewifized. Thus, the discourse of "housewifization" can potentially create its reality, "housewifizing" labor, especially that of women in the developing world, as both necessary and invisible. As the chapters in this book indicate, however, no single, universal pattern of housewifization necessarily emerges in societies evolving a middle class under conditions of capitalist development and globalization. Each of the chapters addresses housewifization in varying degrees, and each modifies Mies's construction of the term.

MATERNALISM AND HOUSEWIFIZATION

One reason for those modifications of Mies's primarily materialist definition is that the chapters in this study focus on care networks, primarily childcare networks. Mies's housewifization focuses on the smaller unit of the family rather than networks (of which the family is one) and stresses the economic role of the wife more than the affective relationship of the child with its mother or other caregivers. The primary binary relationship embedded in the Miesian concept of housewifization is the husband/wife relationship, as it foregrounds the gendered nature of work that counts as income. Although later applications expanded its scope, Mies's original definition was historically contingent. Following the industrial revolution in Western nations, husbands became the breadwinners, and children and wives, at least among the rich or middle-class, were pushed from the workplace by new discourses of modern wifehood, motherhood, and childhood.

Mothers had long played a significant role in childrearing in the United States and Western Europe before the industrial revolution and the rise of the modern middle-class family. In the late eighteenth century, mothers as well as fathers had been seen as responsible for molding their children for adult duties, in particular developing their sons' self-sufficiency, the basis for citizenship (Norton 1980; Kerber 1980; Ryan 1981). By the mid- to late nineteenth century, middle-class mothers in the United States and Western Europe came to be deemed uniquely suited to childrearing, as they alone were viewed as able to maintain the purity of the home and its newly innocent children (the notion of childhood as a time of innocence and freedom from income-earning labor also developed at the same time). Housewifization, which had originally defined separate economic spheres for husbands and wives, came to be linked with maternalism, a focus on the affective and educational aspects of the mother-child relationship and, by extension, the extolling of mothers' socially valued virtues of care and morality (Yalom 2002; Coontz 2005). To be sure, not all children were raised by mothers. Children of the wealthy had always been cared for by servants, and children of working-class families without helpful relatives often raised themselves while roaming in the streets as their parents toiled for income. Despite its initial application to middle-class members of society, the concept of the housewife whose responsibilities were closely tied to childrearing soon became normative in the United States and Western Europe. As the concept spread in those countries, the percentage of women employed as income-earners dropped, and the process of housewifization expanded.

In Chapter 1, Emiko Ochiai describes the historiographical shift in the linkage of modernity with economic, political, and social equality of the genders. Before the 1970s, she notes, scholars contended that women's equality followed an upward trajectory that paralleled industrialization and economic modernization (Boserup 1970). Feminist historians in the United States and Europe called that notion into question as they probed, in the 1970s, the development of separate gendered spheres, the decreasing involvement of (white, middle-class) women in the income-earning economy under industrialization, and the creation of a discourse that made the non-recognition of "ladies'" work the preferred norm (Welter 1966; Jones 1985). This erasure of all women's (not just ladies') contributions was what Mies called "housewifization." The shift in scholars' approaches to acknowledge that housewifization had not necessarily improved the lot of women occurred as women in the United States and Western Europe were increasingly employed in the paid economy and rejecting the housewife role as normative for adult women, a pattern Ochiai calls "de-housewifization." Antedating western scholars' linkage of modernity with housewifization, Indian economist J.N. Sinha (Sinha 1965) hypothesized a U-curve relationship (over time) between married women's labor force participation rates and economic development, with a drop in women's employment opportunities as the farming sector declined.

The chapters in this book indicate that the U-curve is not, however, universal. Despite its status as a "postmodern" economy with a fertility rate below replacement level, Japan does not display a U-curve of married women's employment rates over the last century. Married women's employment rates started out high and remained high – Ochiai notes that they remained above 40 percent throughout the twentieth century. The housewifization ideology was strongly pushed by the Japanese government in the late nineteenth and early twentieth centuries in the form of "good wife, wise mother" discourse (Uno 2005). Education was gendered by this discourse, with boys being trained for service to the nation in the public sphere and girls for service through wise motherhood. The media popularized socially constructed gender distinctions and made these available to the majority of Japanese who were not in the middle class. Although the "good wife, wise mother" discourse as well as feminists' linking of motherhood with women's rights in the 1910s (Molony 1993) could have led to a rapid decline in women's employment, many women remained in the workforce.

In recent years, Japan has continued to diverge from the U-curve model in another way; that is, despite sharing economic and demographic characteristics with Western Europe, Japan does not show a similar "de-housewifization." The chapters in this volume indicate that applying a supposedly universal model to the rest of East and Southeast Asia is even more problematic than it is in Japan. Indeed, a systemic pattern of housewifization followed by de-housewifization over a long historic period cannot be applied without modification to the societies studied in this volume. Taken together, the chapters show there is no single essentialized "Asian" family structure (some held strongly to Confucian values, others did not) and no single route to modernity (some societies were capitalist, some communist, some had greater degrees of planning than others).

That said, however, the studies in this volume that compare women's employment rates by age cohort in individual societies at discrete moments in time suggest that a particular type of housewifization is, in fact, emerging in societies with rapidly growing middle classes. This particular type of housewifization is not grounded in gendered employment differences between the husband and wife, the classic Miesian pattern, but rather in the increasing importance of the mother/child relationship. The data indicate a growing preference among some mothers to focus on their children – and in doing so, identify themselves as "housewives" – by leaving the work force during certain stages of their children's upbringing, but the chapters in this collection do not presuppose that mothers are the natural and traditional caregivers. Indeed, they discuss a remarkable variety of childcare practices and their evolution under differing economic, political, and demographic conditions. If most of the societies in this volume currently manifest some elements of housewifization with a maternalist orientation, the paths they took to get there were hardly identical. To borrow a useful paradigm from Park Keong-Suk in this volume – that of isomorphism, a concept taken from biology to suggest the convergence of forms among different species – similarities have emerged in divergent societies following different trajectories of development.

GLOBALIZATION AND MOTHERS

Mies also addresses the issue of globalization in her work, linking global capitalism and patriarchy, focusing on women's (housewives') necessary but unrecognized role in production for the global marketplace. Globalization is a key theme in this volume's chapters as well, but each author nuances its specific roles in the context of the society he or she analyzes. Several chapters – Ueno Kayako's chapter on foreign domestic workers in Singapore, Hashimoto Hiroko's discussion of foreign maids in Thailand, and Emiko Ochiai's chapter on new mothers in an era of globalization – analyze the movement of childcare labor across borders. The mothers of children in the labor-receiving countries often think in terms of preparing their children for the global professional world, while foreign domestic workers, frequently mothers themselves, hope to earn enough money to help their current or future families. What are the meanings of motherhood in those cases (Hochschild and Ehrenreich 2002)? Internal migration of childcare workers may not be global in the sense of border-crossing, but in some cases, particularly that of the People's Republic of China, migration may also occur over large distances.

Other mothers, also thinking in terms of preparing their children for the global professional world – such as those in Korea discussed in the chapters by Yamane Mari and Hong Sang Ook and by Park Keong-Suk – even take their children away from their natal societies to obtain a foreign education. These mothers are, of course, not working in Korea when they accompany their children overseas, but should they be considered housewifized during their long sojourns away from the household? The insertion of global considerations to further the education of children expands both the networks of childcare and meanings of housewifization.

As the chapters in this collection suggest, the middle classes in East and Southeast Asian societies appear to be trending toward increasingly gendered childcare patterns. While these patterns continue to differ enormously among the six societies studied in this volume, all seem to be making at least incipient steps towards viewing hands-on care by mothers or their surrogates – rather than the larger and very diverse childcare networks employed in the past – as important for children's upbringing in the postmodern global world. This is not, strictly speaking, a Miesian form of housewifization; rather the chapters in this volume offer a more sophisticated and culturally sensitive meta-version of housewifization.

This form of housewifization resembles Mies's in an important way, however; the idea that certain practices may be gendered. Although childcare networks in Thailand are not limited to care by the mother, a temporary trend towards mothers focusing on childcare (the M-curve of employment by age wherein women's employment drops off during the childrearing years) is described in the chapters by Kua Wongboonsin and Patcharawalai Wongboonsin and by Hashimoto Hiroko. Research by Ochiai and others in Chapters 2 and 8 indicates that it is not yet normative for childcare to be ascribed to mothers in China, but some data for middle-class families show trends in that direction. The research in these six societies does not indicate a similar housewifization of fathers. It was not always the case that gendering of childcare leaned towards the mothers' side. Confucian fatherhood in the past embraced childcare and education; for example, European observers in the late nineteenth century, accustomed to mothers caring for children, were astounded by the sight of Japanese fathers playing with their small children (Bacon 1891).

PATHS TO MODERNITY

In their chapter on modern population trends and the development of the "M-curve" pattern of women's labor-force participation in Thailand, Kua Wongboonsin and Patcharawalai Wongboonsin define modern societies as those characterized by individualism, decreasing percentages of intergenerational families, urbanization, labor-market tensions, and advances in science and technology. By that definition, the six societies are all either postmodern or beginning to experience modernity. All have a growing middle class, although there is a huge gap between the countries with the highest per capita Gross Domestic Product (Japan and Singapore) and the lowest (Thailand and China) in the percentage of their populations who are in the urban middle-class. Implicit in the interviews and surveys in the six societies is that middle-class status permits mothers to focus on childrearing if they are unemployed either by choice or by inability to find paid work or adequate child care. Their husbands' income is sufficient. Although not explicitly linked to economic class status in this volume, families' concerns for rearing children able to succeed in an increasingly competitive and globalized professional environment, a hallmark of middle-class attitudes, emerge in all the chapters in this volume. Some parents are exceptionally focused on their children's education, as the case of Korean mothers moving to Canada for their children's education indicates.

Korean women's employment patterns, like those in Japan, manifest an M-curve. But is this due to mothers' housewifization? Yamane and Hong suggest that it would be difficult to housewifize a society that had a historically low rate of female employment before industrialization. Park suggests that the M-curve dip in Korean women's employment rates has recently become more shallow, not because Korean women are all becoming more career-oriented (some are, but many are not), but because of social and demographic trends. The age of first marriages in Korea has been rising and the number of births per mother has been declining, making the M-curve shallower over time. At the same time, the percentage of women who never left employment has dropped because the percentage of farm workers has declined, and the percentage of women intending to return to work but not yet having done so due to late marriage and childbirth (a category Park calls "latent M-type") appears to have increased. All those factors contribute to a smoothing out of the M-curve. Yet neither Yamane and Hong nor Park assert that "de-housewifization" is occurring in Korea. Both chapters report survey and interview data that nuance what seems to be a simple observation that women are abandoning childcare. Indeed, their data show that mothers find greater self-fulfillment in childcare than in the poorly-compensated, dead-end jobs to which many women are limited. With almost complete control over questions concerning their children's education, many mothers feel empowered by childcare. Even though many use their own parents rather than their husbands' parents for (at times paid) assistance, a significant number of Korean women, like many Japanese women, leave employment for a childrearing phase during their life course. But Park worries that family-centered women may, in the end, be trapped in a gender-divided system despite their claims that their decision to leave the workplace to support their children's education is an active, conscious choice rather than passively following old-fashioned gender expectations.

Ochiai and others suggest the pitfalls of relying too much on mothers as children's sole caregivers. In particular, Japan's "three year myth" – a notion that children under the age of three are better off being taken care of by mothers – combined with demographic factors that have isolated mothers in small families, has created a worrisome condition called "childcare anxiety" that appears to be unique to Japan. The historical trajectory of ideas about childcare through war and a rapid postwar demographic shift gave rise to the conditions in which childcare anxiety could flourish. Maternalist discourses that underscored the centrality of mothers' responsibility for childcare had been growing in importance in Japan throughout the first half of the twentieth century, and the departure of men during World War II further enhanced mothers' roles (Miyake 1991). After the war, Japanese women were effectively housewifized, especially as mothers. With multiple siblings, many young mothers in the 1950s and 1960s had a comfortable network of childcare support. But birth rates plummeted in the postwar years, and by the 1980s, sibling networks had disappeared. Mothers created new networks among their neighbors, but these were a poor substitute and failed in their support role. Individual families were increasingly isolated. Mothers had been socialized to believe they were necessary caregivers to their young children, so with only their husbands and parents left in their support networks, many felt both cut off from adult society and unsuccessful at childcare. Sad statements like "Childcare is almost unendurable" are reported by Miyasaka Yasuko and Fujita Michiyo in Chapter 2.

By contrast, childcare anxiety is unheard of in the People's Republic of China, where grandparents on either the mother's or father's side are expected to care for small children and where parental care in guiding the education of older, school-age children is valued. In Chinese societies (China, Taiwan, and Singapore) as well as in Thailand, some young children move away from their mothers and fathers, to be raised by their grandparents, usually on the father's side, or other relatives such as aunts or uncles, until it is time for them to go to school. In Thailand, with a traditional bilateral family system (that is, one characterized neither by matilineality nor patrilineality), one father proudly told Ochiai that "I raised my two children all by myself, including changing diapers." Yet, as in Korea, parents stress the need to guide their older children's education. While the "three year myth" holds sway in Japan, a significant number of older children attend special tutoring programs, representing an outsourcing of education to professionals outside the family in Japan. The studies in this volume indicate that in Korea, Thailand, China, and Singapore, however, parents avoid outsourcing education. In Singapore, early childhood training and household chores like cooking that are ascribed to housewives in many other countries are outsourced to foreign domestic workers (FDWs), preferably those from Westernized, English-speaking countries like the Philippines. At the same time, some parents prefer to guide their children's education themselves. In China, grandparents are welcome caregivers – until the point when parents begin to worry that old-fashioned, undereducated grandparents may be inadequate to the task of helping with homework.

CHANGING CHILDCARE NETWORKS

The broader childcare networks of the past have increasingly been narrowed in a number of East and Southeast Asian societies, though the culprit is not always the discrediting of women's work as suggested by the model of Mies's housewifization. Indeed, in some cases, such as Singapore, government policy encourages the in-migration of foreign domestic workers to allow Singaporean women to continue to work, and its population of predominantly southern Chinese origin holds a positive attitude toward women's work. But a notion of the value of mothers contributing to their children's education has also begun to be increasingly normative in the region. This type of "housewifization" that is oriented towards maternalism is connected to a narrowing of childcare networks. For example, as urban housing has become expensive, young Thai families can no longer afford to live in the family compounds of contiguous houses that had lent themselves to a network of care in the past. Thus, the network of care has shrunk to the child's parents and his or her FDW caregivers. At the same time, Hashimoto's survey of Thai women suggests that only among university educated women did an M-shaped employment pattern persist after the end of the late 1990s recession. That is, the group most likely to be professionals appeared more likely to temporarily step out of the workforce. Kua and Patcharawalai Wongboonsin add demographic concerns to the interpretive mix, noting that by retreating from the workforce Thai women may diminish the benefits of the current and soon-to-be-ending demographic dividend – a period when the working population is high and the non-working population of children and the elderly is low.

The chapters in this collection view the rise of Asia's new mothers in a dynamic way. Change over time is implicit in the use of demographic data; today's working adult is tomorrow's dependent elderly person and today's elderly person is yesterday's child. History is also embedded in the graphs of employment rates by age cohort, and as the chapters in this volume show, those rates have changed over time. The interview data offer a compelling analysis of why those kinds of survey data express historical change not necessarily discernible in the raw numbers. In the end, these studies that focus explicitly on shifting childcare networks offer insights into the imbrication of globalization and modernity with gender, families, work, and demography. This is a development policymakers should not ignore.

Bibliography

Amarles, Bienvenida M. 1990. Female Migrant Labor: Domestic Helpers in Singapore. *Philippine Journal of Public Administration* XXXIV(4): 365–87.

Anderson, Bridget. 2000. *Doing the Dirty Work: The Global Politics of Domestic Labour*. London and New York: Zed Books.

Asian Development Bank (ADB). 1997. *Emerging Asia*. Manila.

Asis, Majuja M.B. 2002. From the Life Stories of Filipino Women: Personal and Family Agendas in Migration. *Asian and Pacific Migration Journal* 11(1): 67–93.

Bacon, Alice Mabel. 1891. *Japanese Girls and Women*. New York: Houghton Mifflin.

Beck, Ulrich, Anthony Giddens, and Scott Lash. 1994. *Reflexive Modernization*. London: Polity Press.

Becker, Gary. 1981. *A Treatise on the Family*. Cambridge, Massachusetts: Harvard University Press.

Benedict, Ruth. 1952. *Thai Culture and Behavior (An Unpublished War-Time Study Dated September, 1943)*. Ithaca, New York: Department of Far Eastern Studies, Cornell University, 1963.

Billari, F., T. Frejka, J.N. Hobcraft, M. Macura, and D.J. van de Kaa. 2004. Explanations of the Fertility Crisis in Modern Societies: A Search for Commonalities. (Discussion of Paper) *Population Studies* 58: 77–92.

Bloom, David E., David Canning, and Jaypee Sevilla. 2003. *The Demographic Dividend: A New Perspective on the Economic Consequence of Population Change*. Santa Monica: Rand.

Boserup, Ester. 1970. *Woman's Role in Economic Development*. London: Allen and Unwin.

Bott, Elizabeth. 1957. *Family and Social Network*. London: Tavistock.

Chae Jai-Seok. 2002. *Chogi Sahoehak gwa Gajok Yeongu* (Early sociology in Korea and studies on the family). Seoul: Iljisa.

Chan, Angelique. 2004. Singapore's Changing Age Structure: Issues and Policy Implications for the Family and State. In Kua and Guest, ed. 2005.

Chang, Grace. 2000. *Disposable Domestics: Immigrant Women Workers in the Global Economy*. Massachusetts: South End Press.

Chang Ji-Yun. 2001. Bijeonggyujik Nodong ui Hyeonsil gwa Jaengjeom (Realities and issues of non-regular labor, focusing on gender difference). *Gyeongje wa Sahoe* (Economy and Society) 51(fall): 68–96.

Chang Kyung-Sup. 1999. Compressed Modernity and Its Discontents: South Korean Society in Transition. *Economy and Society* 28(1): 30–55.

Cheng, Shu-du Ada. 1996. Migrant Women Domestic Workers in Hong Kong, Singapore and Taiwan: A Comparative Analysis. *Asian and Pacific Migration Journal* 5(1): 139–52.

Cho Cheung-Moon. 1997. Hanguk Sahoe Chinjok Gwangye ui Yanggyehwa Gyeonghyang ui gwanhan Yeongu (Studies on bi-linearity of intergenerational relationships in Korea). *Hanguk Yeoseonghak* (Korea Studies on Women) 13(1): 87–113.

Cho Nam-Hoon, Kim Seung-Kwon, Cho Aejeo, Chang Yeong-Sik, and Oh Yeong-Hee. 1997. *1997 nyeon Jeonguk Chulsannyeok mit Gajok Bogeon Siltae Josa Bogo* (1997 Survey on National Fertility and Family Health). KIHASA.

Chun Kwang-Hui. 2003. Chulsannyeok (Fertility). In *Hanguk ui Ingu* (Population of Korea), ed. Kim Doo-Sub, Park Sang-Tae, and Eun Ki-Soo: 81–114. KNSO.

Chung Hyun-Baik. 1991. *Nodong Undong gwa Nodongja Munhwa* (Labor Movement and Labor Culture). Seoul: Hangilsa.

Chung Young-Ai. 1996. Siganje Nodong gwa Seongbyeol Buneop: Siganje Nodong Nonui e gwanhan Yeoseonghakjeok Bipan (Part-time labor and sexual division of labor: A feminist critique of the discussions of part-time labor). *Hanguk Yeoseonghak* (Korea Studies on Women) 12(1): 75–111.

Cohen, Robin. 1987. *The New Helots: Migrants in the International Division of Labour.* Aldershot, UK: Avebury.

Constable, Nicole. 1997. *Maid to Order in Hong Kong: Stories of Filipina Workers.* New York: Cornell University Press.

Coontz, Stephanie. 2005. *Marriage, a History: How Love Conquered Marriage.* New York: Viking.

Demeney, Paul. 2004. Developing an Economic Support System for the Old-Age Population in Asia: Learning from the Mistakes of Western Welfare States. Paper Presented at International Conference on the Demographic Window and Healthy Ageing: Socioeconomic Challenges and Opportunities. Beijing, May 10–11.

Durand, John D. 1975. *The Labor Force in Economic Development: A Comparison of International Census Data 1946–1966.* New Jersey: Princeton University Press.

Ehrenreich, Barbara. 2003. Maid to Order. In Ehrenrich and Hochschild, ed. 2003: 85–103.

Ehrenrich, Barbara and Arlie Russell Hochschild, ed. 2003. *Global Woman: Nannies, Maids, and Sex Workers in the New Economy.* New York: Metropolitan Books.

Engardio, Peter. 2002. The Chance of a Lifetime: Poor Nations Get a "Demographic Dividend." *Business Week Online International*: Asian Cover Story, New York, March 25: 1.

England, K. and Bernadette Stiell. 1997. "They Think You're Stupid as Your English Is": Constructing Foreign Domestic Workers in Toronto. *Environment and Planning A* 29: 195–215.

Fauve-Chamoux, Antoinette ed. 2005. *Domestic Service and the Formation of European Identity: Understanding the Globalization of Domestic Work, 16th–21st Centuries.* Bern: Peter Lang.

Fei Xiaotong. 1947. *Xiangtu Zhongguo* (Homeland China). Beijing: Sanlian Shudian.

Fineman, Martha Albertson. 1995. *The Neutered Mother, The Sexual Family and Other Twentieth Century Tragedies*. New York: Routledge.

Fong, Pang Eng. 1981. Planning the Economy for a Surprise-free Future. In *Singapore Towards the Year 2000*, ed. Saw Swee-Hock and R.S. Bhathal: 34–43. Singapore University Press for the Singapore Association for the Advancement of Science.

Fong, Pang Eng. 1992. Absorbing Temporary Foreign Workers: The Experience of Singapore. *Asian and Pacific Migration Journal*, 1(3–4): 495–509.

Friedan, Betty. 1963. *The Feminine Mystique*. NY: Norton.

Funatsu Tsuruyo and Kagotani Kazuhiro. 2002. Tai no chūkansō: Toshi gakureki erīto no seisei to shakai ishiki (The Thai urban middle class: the formation of an educated elite and their social awareness). In *Ajia chūkansō no seisei to tokushitsu* (The formation and qualities of the Asian middle class), ed. Hattori et al. Institute of Developing Economies (IDE). 201–34.

Gaw, Kenneth. 1988. *Superior Servants: The Legendary Cantonese Amahs of the Far East*. Singapore: Oxford University Press.

Giddens, Anthony. 1990. *The Consequences of Modernity*. London: Polity Press.

Giddens, Anthony. 1992. *The Transformation of Intimacy*. London: Polity Press.

Gilligan, Carol. 1982. *In a Different Voice: Psychological Theory and Women's Development*. Cambridge, MA: Harvard University Press.

Guan Wenna. 2005. *Nitchū shinzoku kōzō no hikaku kenkyū* (Comparative study of family structures in pre-modern Japan and China). Kyoto: Shibunkaku.

Han Joon and Chang Ji Yeun. 2000. Jeonggyu/Bijeonggyu Jeonhwan eul Jungsim euro bon Chwieomnyeok gwa Saengaegwajeong (Labor History and Life Course of Regular and Irregular Jobs). *Nodong Gyeongje Nonjip* (Journal of Labor and Economy) 23: 33–53.

Hanenberg, Robert and Kua Wongboonsin. 1991. Labour Force Shortages in Thailand and Surpluses in Neighboring Countries: Recent Trends and Implications for the Future. In *Population and Labour Force of the Southeast Asian Region*. IPS Publication No. 181/34. Bangkok: Chulalongkorn University.

Hareven, Tamara. 2000. *Families, History and Social Change*. Boulder: Westview Press.

Hashimoto (Seki) Hiroko. 2002a. Nijusseiki shotō Tai ni okeru tsuma no chii: hōritsu to hanreishū ni miru tsuma no zaisanken (The status of wives in early twentieth-century Thailand: wives' property rights under traditional law). *Shakaigaku zasshi* (Sociological Review of Kobe University) 19: 73–91.

Hashimoto (Seki) Hiroko. 2002b. Tai toshi chūkansō ni okeru kazoku: Bankoku-to kōgai no jirei ni (Urban middle class families of Thailand: cases in the outskirts of Bangkok). *Shikoku Gakuin ronshū* (Shikoku Gakuin treatises) 109: 19–47. Zentsū-ji: Literary Society of Shikoku Gakuin.

Hashimoto (Seki) Hiroko. 2003a. Tomobataraki shakai ni okeru josei no "sengyō shufuka" o megutte (Why do Thai urban middle-class women quit their jobs to become housewives: on the increase of "housewives" in Asian working couple society). *Shikoku Gakuin ronshū* 111/112: 53–78.

Hashimoto (Seki) Hiroko. 2003b. Tai toshi chūkansō ni okeru kazoku bunka no jizoku to henyō (Continuity and change in family culture in Thailand's urban middle class). Paper presented at the 54th Annual Conference of the Kansai Sociological Association. Tokyo: Ottemon Gakuin University, May 24.

Hashimoto (Seki) Hiroko. 2004a. Tai toshi chūkan sō ni okeru kazoku bunka no jizoku to henyō (Continuity and change in family culture in Thailand's urban middle class). In Miyasaka, ed. 2004: 208–217.

Hashimoto (Seki) Hiroko. 2004b. Tōnan Ajia no "tomobataraki shakai" ni manabu – Tai toshi chūkan kazoku ni okeru ikuji to shigoto no ryōritsu (Learning from Southeast Asia's working-couple societies – balancing work and childcare in Thailand's urban middle-class families). *Shikoku Gakuin Ronshū* (Shikoku Gakuin Treatises) 116: 139–67.

Hashimoto (Seki) Hiroko. 2004c. Nijusseiki shotō Tai ni okeru danjo kihan o meguru ideorogii no saihensei (Redefinition of the ideology on gender and family norms in early 20th-century Thailand). *Shakaigaku Kenkyūka Kiyō* (Shikoku Gakuin Review of Sociology) 4: 1–18.

Hashimoto (Seki) Hiroko. 2005. Kindai kokka keiseiki Tai ni okeru danjo kihan kazoku kihan no henyō to jizoku: Rāma roku seiki saikō saibanrei o moto ni (Change and continuity in gender and family norms during Thailand's modern nation-building period: Based on the Supreme Court precedents in the period of Lama VI). In *Higashi Ajia no kazoku, chiiki, esunishitī* (Family, region, and ethnicity in East Asia), ed. Kitahara Atsushi: 126–41. Tōshindō.

Hashimoto (Seki) Hiroko. 2006. *Ajia kazoku no henyō to "dentō no sōzō" ni kansuru hikaku kenkyū.* (Comparative research on changes in the family and the "invention of tradition"). Final report, Grant-in-Aid Scientific Research B1, 2003–2005. Japan Society for the Promotion of Science.

Hattori Tamio, Funatsu Tsuruyo and Torii Takashi, eds. 2002. *Ajia chūkansō no seisei to tokushitsu* (Development and characteristics of Asian middle classes). The Institute of Developing Economies.

Hattori Tamio, Funatsu Tsuruyo and Torii Takashi. 2002. Ajia ni okeru chūkansō no seisei to sono tokushitsu (The middle class in Asia and its characteristics). In Hattori et al. ed. 2002: 3–29.

Hermalin, A.I. 1997. Drawing Policy Lessons for Asia from Research on Ageing. *Asia-Pacific Population Journal* 12 (4): 89–102.

Hirota Teruyuki. 1999. *Nihonjin no shitsuke wa suitai shitaka* (Has the discipline of children declined in Japan?). Kōdansha.

Hochschild, Arlie Russell. 2003. Love and Gold. In Ehrenrich and Hochschild, ed. 2003: 85–103.

Honda Yuki. 2000. Kyōiku mama no sonritsu jijō (The social background of the "education mama"). In *Oya to Ko* (Parent and Child), ed. Fujisaki Hiroko: 159–82. Kyoto: Mineruva Shobō.

Hsiao, Hsin-huang Michael, ed. 1999. *East Asian Middle Classes in Comparative Perspective.* Taipei: Institute of Ethnology, Academia Sinica.

Huang, Shirlena and Brenda S.A. Yeoh. 2003. The Difference Gender Makes: State Policy and Contract Migrant Workers in Singapore. *Asian and Pacific Migration Journal* 12(1–2): 75–97.

Hui, Weng-Tat. 1998. The Regional Economic Crisis and Singapore: Implications for Labor Migration. *Asian and Pacific Migration Journal* 7(2–3): 187–218.

Human Rights Watch. 2005. *Maid to Order: Ending Abuses Against Migrant Domestic Workers in Singapore* 17(10): 1–124. (http://hrw.org/reports/2005/singapore1205)

Im In-Suk. 2003. Hanguk gieoubui gajokchinhwajeok jedoui hanggye–Chwieop yeoseongeul wihan yuga jiwon jedoreul jungsimeuro (Limits of family-oriented institutions in Korean corporations: Focusing on childcare support institutions). *Gajok gwa Munhwa* (Family and culture) 15:63-86.

International Labour Organization. 1976. *Employment, Growth and Basic Needs: A One-World Problem.* Geneva: ILO.

Iwai Hachirō. 2002. Raifukōsu ron kara no apurōchi (A life-course theory approach). In *Kazoku to shokugyō* (Family and career), ed. Ishihara Kunio. Mineruva Shobō.

Jones, Gavin W. 2005. The Utility of Education in Thailand and Indonesia. In Kua and Guest, ed. 2005.

Jones, Jacqueline. 1985. *Labor of Love, Labor of Sorrow: Black Women, Work, and the Family from Slavery to the Present.* New York: Vintage Books.

Kail, Andree. 1980. Housewives. In *Chinese Women in Southeast Asia*, ed. Joyce Lebra and Joy Paulson. Singapore: Times Books International.

Kang Seyoung. 1995. Sa-eopche Seongbyeol Jikjong Bulli Yoin ui Bunseok (Analysis on Occupational Dissimilarity by Sex). *Hanguk Inguhak* (Korea Journal of Population Studies). 18(1): 46–61.

Kang Yee-Su. 2001. Byeonhwa haneun Nodong Sijang gwa Yeoseong Nodongja (Changing labor market and female workers). *Gyeongje wa Sahoe* (Economy and Society) 51(fall): 10–37.

Kaufman Sharon, 1986, *The Ageless Self: Sources of Meaning in Late Life*, Madison: the University of Wisconsin Press.

Kerber, Linda K. 1980. *Women of the Republic: Intellect and Ideology in Revolutionary America.* Chapel Hill, NC: University of North Carolina Press.

Khlong Samwa District Department for Social Development, ed. 2001. *Khomun chumchon* (Basic Data on the Communities). Bangkok.

Kim Byeong-Jo and Kim Sun-Yeong. 1996. Hanguk ui Yeoseong Siganje Nodongja, Geudeul eun Nuguinga? (Korean part-time female workers, who are they?) *Gyeongje wa Sahoe* (Economy and Society) 31(fall): 159–78.

Kim Hyun Mee. 2000. Hanguk ui Geundaeseong gwa Yeoseong ui Nodonggwon (Modernity and women's labor rights in Korea). *Hanguk Yeoseonghak* (Korean Studies on Women) 16(1): 37–64.

Kim Seong-Kwon, Joe Yai-Jo, Lee Sam-Sik, Kim Yoo-Kyung, and Song In-Joo. 2000. *2000 nyeon Jeonguk Chulsannyeok mit Gajok Bogeon Siltae Josa* (2000 Survey on national fertility and family health). Korea Institute for Health and Social Affairs.

Kim Tai-Hong. 2000. Yeoseong Gyeongje Hwaldong Chamga ui Gyeoljeong Yoin gwa Teukjing (Determinants of women's economic participation). *Yeoseong Yeongu* (Studies on Women) 59(winter): 93–114.

Kitahara Atsushi, ed. 2000. *Nikkan sonraku kōzō no hikaku kenkyū* (A Comparative Study on Village Structure in Japan and Korea). Final report, Grant-in- Aid Scientific Research, 1997–1999. Japan Society for the Promotion of Science.

Kitahara Atsushi, ed. 2005. *Higashi Ajia no kazoku, chiiki, esunishitī* (Family, locality and ethnicity in East Asia). Tōshindō.

Kiwaki Nachiko. 1998. Kosodate nettowāku ni kansuru saikō: kosodate sākuru no ruikei to konnichiteki kadai (A reconsideration of childcare networks: categories of childcare circles and current challenges). *Kazoku kankeigaku* (Family relation studies) 17: 13–22.

Kiwaki Nachiko, ed. 2003. *Ikuji o meguru jendā kankei to nettowāku ni kansuru jisshō kenkyū* (Investigative research on gender relations and networks related to childcare). Final report, Grant-in-Aid Scientific Research C1, 2001–2003. Japan Society for the Promotion of Science.

Kiwaki Nachiko. 2007. Shingapōru no kosodate to kosodate shien (Childcare and childcare support in Singapore). In Ochiai, Yamane and Miyasaka, ed. 2007.

Knodel, J. and Nibhon Debavalya. 1997. Living Arrangements and Support among the Elderly in Southeast Asia: An Introduction. *Asia-Pacific Population Journal* 12(4): 5–16.

Kobayashi Kazumi. 2004. Kankoku no kazoku to jendā o meguru gaikyō to chōsa no gaiyō (Overview of family and gender in Korea and investigation summary). In Miyasaka, ed. 2004 : 8–24.

Kobayashi Kazumi. 2007. Kankoku ni okeru shotō gakusei no sōki ryūgaku (Korean elementary school children studying abroad). In Sasaki Mamoru ed., *Ekkyō suru komyunitī no saikōsei* (Cross-border migration and reconstruction of community). Tōhō Shoten.

Kojima Hiroshi. 2005. Basic Skills, Thinking Skills, and Competencies of Skilled Workers: A Comparison of Thailand with East Asian and Other Southeast Asian Countries. In Kua and Guest, ed. 2005.

Korea National Statistical Office (KNSO). 2006. KOSIS, http://www.nso.go.kr/.

Kua Wongboonsin. See Wongboonsin, Kua.

Kurosu Satomi and Ochiai Emiko. 1995. Adoption as an heirship strategy under demographic constraints: A case from nineteenth-century Japan. *Journal of Family History* 20(3): 261–88.

Lan Pei-Chia. 2006. *Global Cinderellas: Migrant Domestics and Newly Rich Employers in Taiwan*. Durham, NC: Duke University Press.

Lee Hyo-Jae and Ji Eunhee. 1988. Hanguk Nodongja Gyegeup Gajok ui Saenghwal Siltae: Nodongnyeok Jaesaengsan Gwajeong eul Jungsimeuro (Family life of Korea's working class: focus on the reproduction process of labor). *Hanguk Sahoehak* (Korean Journal of Sociology) 22: 69–97.

Lee Jae-Kyung. 1999. The Glorification of "Scientific Motherhood" as an Ideological Construct in Modern Korea. *Asian Journal of Women's Studies* 15(4).

Lee Jae-Kyung. 2003. *Gajok ui Ireumeuro: Hanguk Geundae Gajok gwa Feminijeum* (In the name of family: The modern Korean family and feminism). Seoul: Tto Hana ui Munhwa.

Lee, Jean, Kathleen Campbell and Audrey Chia. 1999. *The 3 Paradoxes: Working Women in Singapore*. Singapore: Association of Women for Action and Research (AWARE).

Lee, Kuan Yew. 2000. *From Third World to First: The Singapore Story: 1965–2000*. Singapore: Singapore Press Holdings.

Lesthaeghe, Ton. 1991.The Second Demographic Transition in Western Countries. An Interpretation. IPD- Working Paper. Interuniversity Programme in Demography.

Lin, Chin-Ju. 1999. *Filipina Domestic Workers in Taiwan: Structural Constraints and Personal Resistance*. Master's thesis. University of Essex.

Litwak, Eugene. 1965. Extended Kin Relations in an Industrial Democratic Society. In *Social Structure and Family: Generational Relations*, ed. Ethel Shanas and Gordon Streib. New Jersey: Prentice-Hall.

Lu Xueyi, ed. 2004. *Dangdai Zhongguo shehui liudong* (Contemporary Chinese social trends). Beijing: Shehui kexue wenxian chubanshe (Social Science Writing Publishers).

Makino Katsuko. 1981. Ikuji ni okeru fuan ni tsuite (On anxiety in parenting). *Katei kyōiku kenkyūjo kiyō* (Journal of the Family Education Research Center) 2: 41–51.

Makino Katsuko. 1988. Ikuji fuan gainen to sono eikyō yōin ni tsuite no sai kentō (Parenting anxiety and factors influencing it). *Katei kyōiku kenkyūjo kiyō* (Journal of the Family Education Research Center) 10: 23–31.

Mason, Andrew. 2002. Population and Human Resource Trends and Challenges. *Key Indicators of Developing Asian and Pacific Countries*. Manila, Philippines: Asian Development Bank.

Masuda Kōkichi. 1960. Tekkin apāto kyojū kazoku no neighboring ("Neighboring" for families residing in steel apartment buildings). *Kōnan daigaku bungakukai ronshū* (Bulletin of Kōnan University Literary Society) 11.

Mies, Maria. 1982. *The Lace Makers of Narsapur: Indian Women Produce for the World Market*. London and New York: Zed Press.

Mies, Maria. 1986. *Patriarchy and Accumulation on a World Scale: Women in the International Division of Labour*. London and New York: Zed Books.

Mies, Maria, Veronika Benholdt-Thomsen and Claudia von Werlhof. 1988. *Women: the Last Colony*. London and New York: Zed Books.

Mies, Maria. 1997. *Kokusai bungyō to josei* (Japanese version of *Patriarchy and Accumulation on a World Scale*, 1986). Trans. Okuda Akiko. Nihon Keizai Hyōronsha.

Min Kyung-Hee. 2003. Nodongnyeok (Labor force). In *Hanguk ui Ingu* (Population of Korea), ed. Kim Doo-Sub, Park Sang-Tae, and Eun Ki-Soo: 393–428. KNSO.

Ministry of Information, Communications and the Arts. 2006. *Singapore Yearbook 2006*. Singapore: Landmark Books.

Ministry of the Interior Statistics Bureau. 2001. The analysis of the growth of women's social participation (in Chinese). <http://www.moi.gov.tw/W3/stat/topic/politic4.htm>. (Taiwan)

Miyake, Yoshiko. 1991. Doubling Expectations: Motherhood and Women's Factory Work under State Management in Japan in the 1930s and 1940s. In *Recreating Japanese Women, 1600–1945*, ed. Gail Lee Bernstein. Berkeley: University of California Press.

Miyamoto Tsuneichi. 1967. *Kakyo no Kun* (The way village people learned life). Iwanami Shoten.

Miyasaka Yasuko, ed. 2004. *Ajia shoshakai ni okeru jendā no hikaku kenkyū* (Comparative research on gender in Asian societies). Final report, Grant-in-Aid Scientific Research A1, 2001–2003. Japan Society for the Promotion of Science.

Miyasaka Yasuko. 2007. Chūgoku no Ikuji (Childcare in China). Ochiai, Yamane and Miyasaka, ed. 2007.

Miyasaka Yasuko and Fujita Michiyo. 2004. Chūgoku Kōso-shō Mushaku-shi ni okeru ikuji to jendā to shinzoku nettowāku (Childcare, gender, and kin networks in Wuxi City, Jiansu Province, China). In Miyasaka, ed. 2004: 135–49.

Mizuno Kōichi. 1981. *Tai nōson no shakai soshiki* (Social Organization in Farming Communities in Thailand). Sōbunsha.

Molony, Barbara. 1993. Equality versus Difference: The Japanese Debate over "Motherhood Protection." In *Japanese Women Working*, ed. Janet Hunter. London: Routledge.

Momsen, Janet Henshall, ed. 1999. *Gender, Migration and Domestic Service*. London: Routledge.

Morioka Kiyomi et al. 1968. Tokyo kinkō danchi kazoku no seikatsu-shi to shakai sanka (Life history and social participation of families in a housing complex in a suburban area of Tokyo). *Shakai kagaku jānaru* (Social Science Journal) 7: 199–275. International Christian University (ICU).

Nahm Choon-Ho. 2001. Seongbyeol Jikjong Gyeongni e daehan Saeroun Jeopgeun; Nujeok Buriik Mohyeong dae Hoejeonmun Gaseol (A new approach to occupational sex segregation: Cumulated disadvantages versus revolving doors). *Saneop Yeongu* (Studies on Industry and Labor) 7(1): 11–156.

National Economic and Social Development Board. 2005. *Population Projections for Thailand, 2005–2025*. NESDB, Bangkok.

National Institute of Population and Social Security Research. 2003. *Jinkō no dōkō: Nihon to sekai 2003* (Demographic trends in Japan and the world 2003). Kōsei Tōkei Kyōkai (Health and welfare statistics association).

National Statistical Office (NSO), Office of the Prime Minister. 2002. *Time Use Survey 2001*. (Thailand)

National Statistical Office. 2003. *Hanguk ui sahoe jipyo 2003* (Social indicators in Korea 2003). Seoul: National Statistical Office.

Norton, Mary Beth. 1980. *Liberty's Daughters: The Revolutionary Experience of American Women, 1750–1800*. Boston: Little, Brown.

Nyberg, Anita. 1994. The Social Construction of Married Women's Labour-force Participation. *Continuity and Change* 9(1): 145–56.

Ochiai Emiko. 1988. Gendaika rosen to "*funü huijia*" ronsō no yukue (The path to modernization and the debate over "women returning home"). *Bessatsu Takarajima* 85 Feminizumu nyūmon (Introduction to feminism): 210–21. JICC Shuppankyoku.

Ochiai Emiko. 1989a. Ikuji enjo to ikuji nettowāku (Childcare support and childcare networks). *Kazoku kenkyū* (Family studies) 1: 109–33.

Ochiai Emiko. 1989b. *Kindai kazoku to feminizumu* (The Modern Family and Feminism). Keisō Shobō.

Ochiai Emiko. 1993. Kazoku no shakaiteki nettowāku to jinkōgakuteki sedai (The social networks of the family and demographic generations). In *Nijusseiki Nihon no neokomyunitii* (Japan's neo-communities in the 21st century), ed. Hasumi Otohiko and Okuda Michihiro: 101–30. University of Tokyo Press.

Ochiai Emiko. 1997. *The Japanese Family System in Transition: A Sociological Analysis of Family Change in Postwar Japan*. Tokyo: LCTB International Library Foundation.

Ochiai Emiko. 2000. *Kindaikazoku no magarikado* (The modern family at the crossroads). Kadokawa Shoten.

Ochiai Emiko. 2003a. Tai toshi chūkansō no keisei to kazoku no kōfuku (The making of the urban middle class in Thailand and the happiness of the family). In *Ajia Shin-seiki 4 Kōfuku* (Asia's New Century 4: Happiness), ed. Aoki Tamotsu et al.: 211–33. Iwanami Shoten.

Ochiai Emiko. 2003b. Ajia no tomobataraki shakai ni okeru kosodate o sasaeru mono: Chūgoku, Tai, Shingapōru no baai (Childcare support in the doubleincome societies of Asia: A look at China, Thailand and Singapore). *Gendai no espuri (L'ésprit d'aujourd'hui)* 429: 93–107. Shibundō.

Ochiai Emiko. 2004. Chūgoku, Tai, Shingapōru ni okeru ikuji enjo patān to sono henyō: Ajia no tomobataraki shakai ni shufu wa tanjō suru ka (Patterns and changes in childcare support in China, Thailand and Singapore: the emergence of full-time housewives in Asian dual-income societies?). In Miyasaka, ed. 2004: 331–43.

Ochiai Emiko. 2005a. Gendai Ajia ni okeru shufu no tanjō: gurōbaruka to kindai kazoku (Birth of the housewife in contemporary Asia: globalization and the modern family). *Nihon Gakuhō* 24: 3–28 (Osaka University School of Letters, Department of Japanese Studies).

Ochiai Emiko. 2005b. The Postwar Japanese Family System in Global Perspective: Familism, Low Fertility, and Gender Roles. *U.S.-Japan Women's Journal* 29: 3–36.

Ochiai Emiko. 2006. Tai toshi chūkanso no kazoku (Urban middle class families in Thailand). In *Tai no jūmin jichi seido no hatten to shimin shakai keisei no kanōsei* (The development of autonomy of local community and the possibility of the formation of a civil society), ed. Hashimoto Takashi. Final report, 15402017, Grant-in-Aid Scientific Research B1, 2003–2005. Japan Society for the Promotion of Science.

Ochiai Emiko. 2007. Gurōbaruka suru kazoku: Taiwan no gaikokujin kaji rōdōsha to gaikokujin-zuma (Globalized families: foreign domestic workers and foreign wives in Taiwan). In *Gurōbaruka jidai no jinbungaku* (Humanities in the era of globalization), ed. Kihira Eisaku: 93–126. Kyoto University Press.

Ochiai Emiko, Yamane Mari and Miyasaka Yasuko, eds. 2007. *Ajia no kazoku to jendā* (The family and gender in Asia). Keisō Shobō.

Ochiai Emiko, Yamane Mari, Miyasaka Yasuko, Zhou Weihong, Onode Setsuko, Kiwaki Nachiko, Fujita Michiyo, and Hong Sang Ook. 2004. Henyō suru Ajia shakai ni okeru ikuji nettowāku to jendā: Chūgoku, Tai, Shingapōru, Taiwan, Kankoku, Nihon (Childcare networks and gender in changing Asian society: China, Thailand, Singapore, Taiwan, South Korea, and Japan). *Kyōikugaku kenkyū* (Japanese journal of educational research) 71(4): 2–18.

Ohta Motoko.1994. *Edo no oyako* (Parents and children in the Edo period). Chūō Kōronsha.

Ogawa Naohiro, Kondō Makoto and Matsukura Rikiya. 2004. Japan's Transition from the Demographic Bonus to the Demographic Onus. Paper Presented at International Conference on the Demographic Window and Healthy Ageing: Socioeconomic Challenges and Opportunities. Beijing, May 10–11.

Ogaya, Chiho. 2004. Filipino Domestic Workers and the Creation of New Subjectivities. *Asian and Pacific Migration Journal* 13(3): 381–404.

Onode Setsuko. 2003a. Kaji, ikuji, shigoto to fūfu kankei (Housework, childcare, work, and the relationship between husband and wife). In Kiwaki, ed. 2003: 30–7.

Onode Setsuko. 2003b. Dansei no katei shikō to shigoto shikō: katei shikō no imi suru mono (Family-oriented men, work-oriented men: What family orientation means). In Kiwaki, ed. 2003: 38–47.

Onode Setsuko. 2003c. Bankoku-to chūkansō kazoku ni okeru kaji, ikuji to jendā mondai (Housework, childcare, and gender problems in Bangkok's middle class). *Kachō Tanki Daigaku kenkyū kiyō* (Bulletin of Kachō Junior College) 48: 18–35.

Onode Setsuko. 2007. Tai Bankoku-to ni okeru chūkan sō no kaji, ikuji, kaigo: saiseisan rōdō no shakaiteki wakugumi (Housework, childrearing and elderly care in Bangkok's middle class, Thailand: The social frameworks for reproductive labor). In Ochiai, Yamane and Miyasaka, ed. 2007: 168–86.

Ooi, Keat Gin. 1992. Domestic Servants Par Excellence: The Black and White Amahs of Malaya and Singapore with Special Reference to Penang. *Journal of the Malaysian Branch of the Royal Asiatic Society* 65(2): 69–84.

Ōsawa Machiko. 1993. *Keizai henka to joshi rodo* (Economic change and female labor). Nihon Keizai Hyōronsha.

Palma-Beltran, Mary Ruby. 1992. Filipino Women Domestic Workers Overseas: Profile and Implications for Policy. In *Filipino Women Overseas Contract Workers: At What Cost*, ed. Mary Ruby Palma-Beltran and Aurora Javate De Dios: 3–138. Manila: Goodwill Trading Co.

Park Keong-Suk. 2003. *Goryeonghwa Sahoe, Imi Jinhaeng doen Mirae* (Aging Society, Future Already Proceeded). Seoul: Uiam.

Park Keong-Suk. 2004. Kankoku josei no raifukōsu ruikei: tei shussan to M-jigata shūgyō kyokusen e no shisa (The life course of Korean women: possible explanations of low fertility and the M-shaped curve of employment). In Miyasaka, ed. 2004: 37–79.

Park Keong-Suk and Yamane Mari. 2007. Kankoku josei no raifukōsu to shigotokatei yakuwari no imi (Korean women's life course and the meaning of the work-family role). In Ochiai, Yamane and Miyasaka, ed. 2007: 51–69.

Park Mee-Hae. 1991. Patterns and Trends of Educational Mating in Korea. *Korea Journal of Population and Development* 20: 1–15.

Park Min-Ja. 1991. Jayeong Sosangin Gajok ui Saenggye Yuji Bangsik gwa Yeoseong (Strategy for life subsistence of small business families and women). *Studies on Women* 32: 45–75.

Park Sang-Tae. 1999. Ingu Jaengjeom e daehan Gachigwan ui Byeonhwa (Change in Population Approach). *Hanguk Inguhak* (Journal of Population Studies) 22(2): 5–45.

Park Soomi. 2002. Hanguk Yeoseongdeul ui Cheot Chwieop Jinip, Toejang e Michineun Saengae Sageon ui Yeokdongjeok Yeonghyang (Impacts of Korean Women's Life Dynamics on First Entrance to and Exit from Occupations). *Hanguk Sahoehak* (Korea Journal of Sociology) 36(2):145–74.

Parrenas, Rhacel Salazar. 2003. The Care Crisis in the Philippines: Children and Transnational Families in the New Global Economy. In Ehrenrich and Hochschild, ed. 2003: 39–54.

Ponnampalam, Lingam. 2000. Mirror or Mold: Newspaper Reportage on Unskilled Labor Migration in Singapore. *Asian Migrant* 13(3): 75–80.

Parsons, Talcott and Robert F. Bales. 1956. *Family: Socialization and Interaction Process*. London: Routledge and Kegan Paul.

Patcharawalai Wongboonsin. See Wongboonsin, Patcharawalai.

Pratt, Geraldine (in collaboration with the Philippine Women Center). 1999. Is This Canada: Domestic Workers' Experience in Vancouver, BC. In Momsen 1999: 23–42.

Reid, Anthony. 1993. *Southeast Asia in the Age of Commerce 1450–1680* (2 volumes). New Haven: Yale University Press.

Richiter, Kerry, Chai Podhisita, Kusol Soonthorndhada, and Aphichat Chamratrithirong. 1992. *Child Care in Urban Thailand: Choice and Constraint in a Changing Society.* Institute for Population and Social Research. Salaya: Mahidol University.

Rajkai Jombor. 2002. Kaku kazokuka to kodomo chūshin shugi saikō (Reconsidering nuclearization and the child-centered family). *Kyōto shakaigaku nenpō* (Kyoto Journal of Sociology) 10: 189–200.

Reid, Anthony. 1993. *Southeast Asia in the Age of Commerce, 1450–1680.* New Haven: Yale University Press.

Rofel, Lisa. 1994. Liberation Nostalgia and a Yearning for Modernity. In *Engendering Modern China*, Christina Gilmartin, et al. ed.: 226–249. Cambridge, MA: Harvard University Press.

Ryan, Mary P. 1981. *Cradle of the Middle Class: The Family in Oneida County, New York, 1790–1865.* New York: Cambridge University Press.

Sacks, Harvey. 1979. Hotrodder: A Revolutionary Category. In *Everyday Language: Studies in Ethnomethodology Racism*, ed. G. Psathas: 23–53. New York: Irvington Publishers.

Saitō Junichi, ed. 2003. *Shinmitsuken no poritikusu* (The politics of the intimate sphere). Kyoto: Nakanishiya Publishers.

Saitō Osamu. 1996. Gender, workload and agricultural progress: Japan's historical experience. In R. Leboutte ed., *Proto-Industrialization: Recent Research and New Perspectives.* Geneva: Librairie Droz.

Sakai Naoki. 1996. *Shizan sareru Nihongo/Nihonjin* (Aborted Japanese). Shinyōsha.

Saw, Swee-Hock. 1981. Too Little Land, Too Many People. In *Singapore Towards the Year 2000*, ed. Saw Swee-Hock and R.S. Bhathal: 15–33. Singapore University Press for the Singapore Association for the Advancement of Science.

Saw, Swee-Hock. 1984. *The Labour Force of Singapore.* Census Monograph No. 3. Department of Statistics, Singapore.

Sechiyama Kaku. 1996. *Higashi Ajia no kafuchō sei: jendā no hikaku shakaigaku* (Patriarchy in East Asia: the comparative sociology of gender). Keisō Shobō.

Sekii Tomoko, Matsuda Tomoko, Onode Setsuko and Yamane Mari. 1991. Hataraku hahaoya no seibetsu yakuwari bungyōkan to ikuji enjo nettowāku (Views on sexual division of labor in working mothers and childcare support networks). *Kazoku shakaigaku kenkyū* (Japanese Journal of Family Sociology) 3: 72–84.

Shin Kyung-A. 2001. Nodong Sijang gwa Moseong, Gajok ui Munje; Namseong Jungsimjeok Nodongja Model eul Neomeoseo (Labor Market and Motherhood: Beyond the Male Worker's Perspective). *Economy and Society* 51(fall): 97–122.

Shinozaki Masami. 1999. Higashi Ajia no kōreika to iwayuru "oya kōkō hō" (Aging society in East Asia and the "filial piety" laws). In Tamura and Shinozaki 1999.

Shutō Toshikazu. 2003. *Chūgoku no jinchi shakai* (China or a society ruled by the people). Nihon Keizai Hyōronsha.

Singapore Department of Statistics. 2001. *Census of Population 2000 Statistical Release 5: Households and Housing.* Singapore Department of Statistics.

Singapore Department of Statistics. 2006a. *General Household Survey 2005, Statistical Release 2: Transport, Overseas Travel, Households and Housing Characteristics.* Release date, June 28, 2006. Singapore Department of Statistics, Ministry of Trade and Industry.

Singapore Department of Statistics. 2006b. *Population Trends 2006.* Singapore Department of Statistics.

Sinha, J.N. 1965. Dynamics of Female Participation in Economic Activity in a Developing Economy. United Nations World Population Conference, Document WPC/285.

Stiell, Bernadette and Kim England. 1999. Jamaican Domestics, Filipina Housekeepers and English Nannies: Representations of Toronto's Foreign Domestic Workers. In Momsen 1999: 43–61.

Sugano Noriko. 1999. *Edo jidai no kōkōmono: Kōgiroku no sekai* (The devoted family members of the Edo period: the world of *Kōgiroku*). Yoshikawa Kōbunkan.

Sussman, Marvin B. and Lee G. Burchinal. 1962. Kin Family Network: Unheralded Structure in Current Conceptualizations of Family Functioning. *Marriage and Family Living,* 24: 3: 231–40.

Tam, Vicky C.W. 1999. Foreign Domestic Helpers in Hong Kong and Their Role in Childcare Provision. In Momsen, ed. 1999: 263–76.

Tamura Keiko. 1999a. *Mareeshia to Shingapōru ni okeru josei to seiji: nashonarizumu, kokka kensetsu, jendā* (Women and politics in Malaysia and Singapore: Nationalism, nation building and gender). Kitakyushu: Ajia Josei Kōryū Kenkyū Fōramu (Kitakyushu forum on Asian women).

Tamura Keiko. 1999b. Tsukurareru "kazoku no shōzō" – "Ajiateki kachi" to Shingapōru no josei (The construction of a "portrait of a family" – "Asian values" and women in Singapore). In Tamura and Shinozaki 1999.

Tamura Keiko and Shinozaki Masami, ed. 1999. *Ajia no shakai hendō to jendā* (Social change and gender in Asia). Akashi Shoten.

Teng, Yap Mui. 2000. Labor Migration in Singapore: Policy and the Role of the Media. *Asian Migrant* 13(3): 68–74.

Tsubouchi Yoshihiro and Maeda Narifumi. 1977. *Kakukazoku Saikō* (Reconsidering the nuclear family). Kōbundō.

Tyner, James A. 1994. The Social Construction of Gendered Migration from the Philippines. *Asian and Pacific Migration Journal* 3(4): 589–617.

Umemura Mataji ed. 1988. *Chōki keizai tōkei 2: rōdōryoku* (Long-term economic statistics 2: labor force). Tōyō Keizai Shinpōsha.

United Nations Development Programme (UNDP). 1992. *Human Development Report 1992.* New York: Oxford University Press.

United Nations Development Programme (UNDP). 2003. *Human Development Report 2003.* New York: Oxford University Press.

Uno, Kathleen. 2005. Womanhood, War, and Empire: Transmutations of "Good Wife, Wise Mother" before 1931. In *Gendering Modern Japanese History*, ed. Barbara Molony and Kathleen Uno. Cambridge, MA: Harvard University Asia Center.

Van de Kaa, Dick J. 1987. Europe's Second Demographic Transition. *Population Bulletin* 42–1. Population Reference Bureau.

Wakita Haruko, ed. 1985. *Bosei wo tou* (Inquiring about motherhood). Jinbun shoin.

Welter, Barbara. 1966. The Cult of True Womanhood: 1820-1860. *American Quarterly* 18(2): 151–74.

Wong, Diana. 1996. Foreign Domestic Workers in Singapore. *Asian and Pacific Migration Journal* 5(1): 117–38.

Wong, Diana. 1997. Transience and Settlement: Singapore's Foreign Labor Policy. *Asian and Pacific Migration Journal* 6(2): 135–67.

Wongboonsin, Kua. 2002. *Prachakornsat: Sara phua kantatsinjai choeng thurakit* (Sociology for business decision-making). Bangkok: Chulalongkorn University Press.

Wongboonsin, Kua. 2004a. The Demographic Dividend and M-Curve Labor Force Participation in Thailand. In Miyasaka, ed. 2004: 182–207.

Wongboonsin, Kua. 2004b. The Demographic Dividend and M-Curve Labor Force Participation in Thailand. *Applied Population and Policy* 1(2): 115–22.

Wongboonsin, Kua, Philip Guest and Viphan Prachuabmoh. 2004. Demographic Change and the Demographic Dividend in Thailand. Paper Presented at International Conference on the Demographic Window and Healthy Ageing: Socioeconomic Challenges and Opportunities. Beijing, May 10–11.

Wongboonsin, Kua and Philip Guest, ed. 2005. *The Demographic Dividend: Policy Options for Asia*. Bangkok: College of Population Studies, Chulalongkorn University, Asian Development Research Forum and Thailand Research Fund.

Wongboonsin, Patcharawalai. 2003. Kan punpon tang prajakorn: kwam ta tai ASEAN nai satawat ti 21(Demographic dividend: window of opportunity and challenges for ASEAN in the 21st century). In *Karn triam pan rub chuang pajubun lae chuang lung kong okad karn rub karn punpon tang prajakorn* (Policy preparation for demographic-dividend and post demographic-divided periods), ed. Wongboonsin, Kua. Proceedings of National Conference on Six Remaining Golden Years for International Competitiveness: Impacts of Demographic Transition. Bangkok: Chulalongkorn University Printing House.

Wongboonsin, Patcharawalai. 2004. Asian Labour Migration: Challenge and Regional Arrangement. Paper presented at *Workshop on Global Mobility Regimes*, organized by the Institute for Future Studies, the Centre for History and Economics, Kings College, Cambridge University and the Global Equity Initiative of Harvard University, Stockholm, June 11–12.

Wongboonsin, Patcharawalai and Joannis Kinnas. 2005. Maximizing the Demographic Dividend Via Regional Cooperation in Human Resource Development. In Kua and Guest, ed. 2005.

World Bank. 1994. *Averting the Old Age Crisis: Policies to Protect the Old and Promote Growth*. Oxford University Press.

Yalom, Marilyn. 2002. *A History of the Wife*. New York: Harper Collins.

Yamane Mari. 2000. Ikuji fuan to kazoku kiki (Childcare anxiety and family crisis). In *Kazoku mondai* (Family issues), ed. Shimizu Shinji. Mineruva Shobō.

Yamane, Mari. 2004. Gendai Kankoku josei no raifukōsu to jendā (Women's life course and childcare in today's Korea). In Miyasaka, ed. 2004: 25–36.

Yamane Mari. 2005. Kankoku no kazoku to jendā: Josei no raifukōsu to ikujienjo wo chushin ni (Family and gender in South Korea : focusing on women's life course and childcare networks). In *Higashi Ajia no kazoku, chiiki, esunishitī* (Family, locality and ethnicity in East Asia), ed. Kitahara Atsushi. Tōshindō.

Yamane Mari and Hong Sang Ook. 2007. Kankoku no bosei to ikuji nettowāku (Motherhood and childcare networks in Korea). In Ochiai, Yamane and Miyasaka, ed. 2007: 33–50.

Yamato Reiko. 2000. Shakai kaisō to shakaiteki nettowāku saikō: "kōsai no nettowāku" to "kea no nettowāku" no hikaku kara (Social class and social networks: a comparison of social interaction networks and care networks). *Shakaigaku hyōron* (Japanese Sociological Review) 51(2): 235–50.

Yamato Reiko. 2003. Ikuji nettowāku to sei bungyō ishiki (Childcare networks and consciousness of gender-based division of labor). In Kiwaki, ed. 2003: 8–29.

Yamato Reiko. 2004. Kaigo nettowāku, jendā, shakai kaisō. In *Gendai kazoku no kōzō to henyō: zenkoku kazoku chōsa* [NFRJ98] *ni yoru keiryō bunseki* (Structure and change in the contemporary family: quantitative analysis of findings of the National Family Research of Japan [NFRJ98]), ed. Watanabe Hideki, Inaba Akihide, and Shimazaki Naoko. University of Tokyo Press.

Yang Shanhua and Shen Chonglin. 2004. Changes in Family Income Patterns in Urban China since the Reform. Paper presented at the 36th World Congress of International Institute of Sociology, Beijing, July 7–11.

Yap Mui Teng. 2000. Labor Migration in Singapore: Policy and the Role of the Media. *Asian Migrant* 13(3): 68–74.

Yazawa Sumiko, Kunihiro Yōko and Tendō Mutsuko. 2003. *Toshi kankyo to kosodate: Shōshika, jendā, shitizunshippu* (Urban environment and childrearing: fertility decline, gender and citizenship). Keisō Shobō.

Yee Jaeyeol. 1996. Yeoseong ui Saengsan Nodong gwa Jae-saengsan Nodong ui Sangho Yeongwanseong i Chwieop e Michineun Yeonghyang e gwanhan Gyeongheomjeok Yeongu (A dynamic analysis of the women's labor market transition with a focus on the relationship between productive and reproductive labor). *Hanguk Inguhak* (Korea Journal of Population) 19(1): 1–45.

Yeoh, Brenda S.A. and Katie Willis. 1999. "Heart" and "Wing", "Nation" and "Diaspora": Gendered Discourses in Singapore's Regionalisation Process. *Gender, Place and Culture* 6(4): 355–372.

Yeoh, Brenda S.A. and Shirlena Huang. 2000. "Home" and "Away": Foreign Domestic Workers and Negotiations of Diasporic Identity in Singapore. *Women's Studies International Forum* 23(4): 413–29.

Yeoh, Brenda S.A. and Shirlena Huang. 2004. Transnational Domestic Workers and State Policy in Singapore. *Migrant Domestic/Care Workers and the Reconfiguration of Gender in Asia*. Workshop Proceedings, Ochanomizu University Frontier of Gender Studies: 6–27.

Yeoh, Brenda S.A., Shirlena Huang and Joaquin Gonzales III. 1999. Migrant Female Domestic Workers: Debating the Economic, Social and Political Impacts in Singapore. *International Migration Review* 33(1):114-136.

Yin Fengxian. 2004. Chūgoku no "Onna wa uchi ni kaere" (*funü huijia*) kyanpēn no rekishi to genzai (The history and present of the "women, return home" campaign in China). *F-GENS Journal* 2.

Yoo HeeJung. 1998. *Janyeo yangyuk seobiseu ui jiljeok seobiseu sujun e gwanhan yeongu* (A study on the level of qualitative improvement of childcare services). Hanguk Yeoseong Gaebalwon (Korean Women's Development Institute).

Yoo HeeJung. 1999. Suyoja gwanjeomeseo bon boyuk jeongchaek ui pyeonga (Evaluation of nursery policy from a demander's point of view). Hanguk Yeoseong Gaebalwon (Korean Women's Development Institute).

Yuan Xin. 2004. Elderly Support in Single-Child Families in China: Whether the Demographic Window Exists From Micro-Analysis. Paper Presented at International Conference on the Demographic Window and Healthy Ageing: Socioeconomic Challenges and Opportunities. Beijing, May 10–11.

Zarembka, Joy M. 2003. America's Dirty work: Migrant Maids and Modern-Day Slavery. In Ehrenrich and Hochschild, ed. 2003: 142–53.

Zheng Yang. 2003. Chūgoku toshibu no kazoku nettowāku to kokka seisaku (The networks of urban families in China and governmental policy). *Kazoku shakaigaku kenkyū* (Japanese Journal of Family Sociology) 14(2): 88–98.

Index